Walls and Bridges

SUNY series in Public Policy

Anne Schneider and Helen Ingram, editors

WALLS AND BRIDGES

Social Justice and Public Policy

ANTHONY J. CORTESE

STATE UNIVERSITY OF NEW YORK PRESS

Published by
STATE UNIVERSITY OF NEW YORK PRESS
ALBANY

Printed in the United States of America

For information, address
State University of New York Press,
90 State Street, Suite 700, Albany, NY 12207

Production, Laurie Searl
Marketing, Michael Campochiaro

Library of Congress Catalogining-in Publication Data

Cortese, Anthony Joseph Paul.
Walls and bridges : social justice and public policy / Anthony J. Cortese
p. cm.—(SUNY series in public policy)
Includes bibliographical references and index.
ISBN 0-7914-5907-1 (alk. paper)—ISBN 0-7914-5908-X (pbk. : alk.paper)
1. Social justice. 2. Social policy—Moral and ethical aspects. 3. Social ethics. I. Title. II. Series
HM671.C67 2004
303.3'72—dc22

2003059083

10 9 8 7 6 5 4 3 2 1

CONTENTS

PREFACE

Throughout history, people have been building walls and bridges—for different reasons. The Great Wall of China, for example, was built centuries ago to protect folk from invading hordes. Thus, walls serve as a barrier—to separate. Now it appears this great wall only keeps people in. The Berlin Wall, also known as the "Iron Curtain," was secretly constructed in 1961 and joyously torn down in 1989. It was a wall of separation, mistrust, and hatred. The walls of the federal penitentiary at Leavenworth, Kansas, are twenty feet high and four feet thick; they are meant to punish, isolate, and deter escape. The national Vietnam Memorial in Washington, D.C., is a wall of healing. I watched as a veteran, without speaking, painstakingly dragged his fingers over inscribed names of dead comrades on the stone wall.

Bridges bring people together, providing a route for transportation and, sometimes, notoriety (e.g., the London Bridge and the San Francisco Golden Gate Bridge). Laws, social policies, displays of power, and social justice are also walls or bridges in the sense that they too keep people out or bring them together. It is basically an issue of inclusion or exclusion.

If we examine recent major trends and events within this country, as well as globally, there is a pattern of intensified economic and social inequality (see chapter 1). Media reflect this inequality. Investment commercials (for people who have more money than they know what to do with but want more) precede fast-food firms advertising burgers for ninety-nine cents. Walls of privatism—the attitude that one should be uncommitted to or avoiding involvement in anything beyond one's immediate interests—spring up. Of course, the events of September 11, 2001, have forced us to reexamine and, at least temporarily, abandon this wall of isolationism. Bridges of community prosperity crumble. Political motives sometimes outweigh social responsibility. Nationalistic and multicultural ideologies clash. Distributive justice—the equitable sharing of social and economic resources—is not evident.

Our cultural values tell us that we are responsible for our own success or failure since equal opportunity ensures an even playing field. (We even have affirmative action, which critics suggest results in reverse discrimination, primarily against white males.) There is hegemony to privatize business and industries. Transportation, utilities, health-care delivery, security and law enforcement, incarceration, education, and housing are transforming from public to private control and ownership.

We expect people to take care of their families, but we take away their jobs and send business abroad. We expect people to be responsible for their own health, but we build toxic waste disposals in their neighborhoods. We expect independence, yet we impose institutional barriers and claim to be compassionate. We expect families to be responsible for mentally or chronically physically ill, aged, and handicapped members, but do not realize that for many families, human and financial resources are already stretched to the limit. They do not have the financial means or competency to adequately care for those family members. Even if we defer to the notion of self-sufficiency, should we not try, at least, to stop a cycle that has

- perpetuated psychological oppression over generations of families;
- provided a sense of alienation from society;
- produced a crisis in society where economic strain and moral decay have flooded society with crime, affecting us directly or indirectly?

Consequently, is it not in the best interest of society to lessen crime, poverty, and homelessness and improve health care and education? Should we not help the children—those who, through no fault of their own, are born into a hopeless and destitute condition? I present these social problems, in part, as ethical crises facing us. *Social problems* are conditions that adversely affect significant numbers of individuals (part or sometimes all of a population) in a similar way (e.g., property crime and family breakup). They often generate public controversy.

In the spirit of tearing down walls and building bridges, this book uses contemporary social theories, current social research, and a social justice approach to examine and provide policy implications for these problems. *Social* or *public policy* is a formal strategy to shape some dimension of social life

(Maciones, 2002). Racial and ethnic themes are woven throughout this book in each chapter; there is focus on resolving intergroup conflict.

I hope to trigger dialogue, research, and theory at the scholarly level. At a more pragmatic level, I hope to contribute to the development of social policy that alleviates social inequality and institutional discrimination. This book suggests how justice, law, and power could be synthesized; as it now stands, they are often in conflict with one another.

Social problems are especially adaptable for "hands-on" pedagogy. For this reason, I have included student exercises and activities in the *What You Can Do* section at the end of each chapter. This feature actively engages students in applying sociological understanding to social problems. When students apply what they learn, they become enthusiastic scholars and often determined activists.

ONE

A SOCIAL ETHICS APPROACH TO SOCIAL PROBLEMS

There are many who would sacrifice much for their children, fewer for their grandchildren.

—Robert Heilbroner, *Twenty-first Century Capitalism*

I HOPE THIS TEXTBOOK will guide students to acquire:

1. a sociological understanding of contemporary social problems and accurate information about them;
2. awareness of their social origins, collective definition, and how they might be effectively treated;
3. discernment on the importance of sociological theory, methods, and multilevel analyses;
4. a social ethics approach to public policy addressing social problems;
5. social activism—a commitment to positive change in society and in the larger global community.

This is, perhaps, the age of moral ambiguity. More and more, isolated individuals, disconnected from external moral reference points, have come to view themselves as the sole judge of moral decisions. In fact, 93 percent of all

Americans report that they alone determine what is moral in their lives. What has happened to what has classically been referred to as society's "collective conscience" or "moral consensus" (what Durkheim, [1893] 1964, called "mechanical solidarity")? Accordingly, morality is collectively constructed, not individual, in nature. What holds society together are the emotional bonds that foster a sense of obligation or duty to social good. Ideally, these bonds prevail over purely selfish, private, egotistic motives (Cortese & Mestrovic, 1990; Cortese, 1990; Durkheim [1912] 1965: 482). Émile Durkheim ([1897] 1951) discovered that individuals with low social integration are linked to high rates of suicide.

As a consequence of this lack of collective aspect of moral support, Americans are increasingly coming to view the key moral issues of the day as "gray"—without a clear right and wrong. More than one-third of Americans believe there is no clear right or wrong position when it comes to the following issues: affirmative action (54 percent); creationism in schools (52 percent); the right to die (44 percent); school busing (44 percent); homosexuality (43 percent); flag burning (38 percent); pornography (38 percent); and capital punishment (37 percent).

SOCIAL PROBLEMS: A HISTORICAL APPROACH

During the late nineteenth century, the United States (as well as Western Europe) was undergoing rapid and basic social change. Such changes resulted in a variety of social problems. Flourishing industrial cities in the Northeast and North Central states produced a regular flow of migration and rural inhabitants who were tugged by the prospect of decent employment. Surges of immigrants from other countries also gushed into the United States for basically similar reasons.

The hopes of these newcomers were dashed by the stark contrast between expectations and the actual conditions they encountered in the cities. Their poor economic situation forced them to reside in crowded crime-infested ethnic ghettos. They labored in dangerous conditions and faced an often-antagonistic social climate. There was also cultural conflict and economic competition among the different new residents of the cities. The new discipline of sociology, with its scientific method to social interaction, human groups, and society, was perfectly geared to examining the urgent social problems of the time. Sociologists began to study how social and physical environments affect individuals and groups.

Some of these original social problems are still with us today: Poverty, crime, unemployment, inadequate health care, homelessness, racial and ethnic conflict, education, and gender inequality. Today, there are still many people who arrive in the United States crossing international boundaries and aspiring to a better life. However, because of scant education and employment skills, language obstacles, and ethnic stereotypes, immigrants soon become stuck in destitute poverty. Undocumented workers cross the border between the United States and Mexico only to struggle with life circumstances similar to those who emigrated from Mexico nearly one hundred years ago.

Certainly, this pervasive pattern is not universal for immigrants. *Ethnic enclave theory* is based on the notion that immigrant workers may be part of a special type of economy that provides unusual routes of upward mobility (Portes, 1981; Wilson & Martin, 1982; Butler & Wilson, 1988). It is rooted in community solidarity, a reserve of disadvantaged ethnic laborers, and vertical and horizontal integration. An ethnic enclave is a grouping of immigrants who organize a variety of business enterprises (Portes & Bach, 1985: 203).

At the top of the stratification system are those who have jobs within the enclave that are parallel to those in the mainstream economy (Butler, 1991: 30). Examples of ethnic enclave economies include the ones developed by the Cubans in Miami and Los Angeles, the Japanese in Honolulu and Los Angeles (Logan, Alba, & McNulty, 1994: 717), and the Jewish experience (Portes & Bach, 1985: 203).

The contemporary structures of racial, ethnic, and gender inequality are rooted in previous societal processes and cultural patterns. These social problems must be understood within their particular historical and cultural context. The fact that working black men and women today earn significantly less than white males is based, in part, on historical institutional discrimination against blacks and women. Connections between past social problems and present ones are not unusual.

Intervention to alleviate social problems can have damaging unintended consequences resulting in new and startling problems. For example, in the 1920s moral entrepreneurs who viewed alcohol use as immoral successfully lobbied against the manufacture, sale, and consumption of alcohol. Instead of stopping people from drinking, the new legislation boosted organized criminals who profited tremendously from the illegal manufacturing, distribution, and sale of alcohol. Moreover, during Prohibition many people died from drinking tainted alcohol. Although the intent of banning alcohol was moral regeneration, it resulted in expanded criminal activity and lawlessness.

Some present-day social problems are unlike previous problems. The identical industrial economy in the United States that produced millions of new jobs and a modernized lifestyle for much of the population also grievously polluted our natural environment—arguably the most critical social problem in contemporary society as well as a central political issue.

Some relatively recent social problems, on the other hand, have emerged from conditions that have existed for quite a while. It is fruitful to examine a variety of social problems not only sociohistorically but also in a cross-cultural perspective, for various reasons. Foremost, intervention in social problems in one society can have a further effect on social dynamics and problems in another. When American firms ship low-wage, low-skill, and dangerous jobs to developing countries, they are essentially responding to domestic problems (economic recession, pollution, and hazardous work environments) by shifting them to other nations. A cross-cultural examination of social problems is also consequential because many of the problems we now encounter are global, affecting many, if not most, human societies.

Thinking Sociologically

Sociology is based on the assumption that individuals belong to groups. These groups influence our attitudes and behavior. This includes the groups to which we belong as well as those to which we aspire to belong. Groups take on characteristics independent of its members. Consequently, the group is greater than the sum of its individual members. Sociologists focus on the behavior patterns of groups. We are particularly interested in different patterns based on ethnicity, race, gender, age, social class, and religion.

Sociologists use various theories and methods to scientifically study social problems. The sociological perspective is very different than intuitive, commonsense, and media approaches to social problems. *Research methods* are techniques for systematically collecting and analyzing information; they include data-gathering techniques such as surveys, observation, and experiments. Research methods also include statistical techniques that allow sociologists to classify and interpret patterns in the data gathered.

A *sociological theory* is a systematic explanation of social relationships, processes, and arrangements that can be examined using research methods. Using these tools, sociologists are able to dig beneath the exterior and investigate social problems systematically and in-depth, pushing well beyond often misleading, inaccurate, and incomplete commonsense understanding.

Sociologists can employ theory and methods to better understand social problems on two different levels: micro and macro. A *micro-level* approach to social problems includes taking a close-up look at social relationships and social structure, focusing on details. Micro-level approaches study small-group behavior. Thus, the sociologist places social problems and human individuals affected by them under a figurative microscope for close examination.

Macro-level analyses, in contrast, are big-picture approaches. They focus on the totality of society. Macro-level approaches are like using a wide-angle lens to view social problems, including the context of the problem within the frame. Both micro-level and macro-level approaches are needed to provide distinct insights and thoroughly understand social problems. Consequently, I fuse together both approaches in the chapters in this book.

From a micro-level perspective, the problem of poverty would be inspected by assessing how individual traits and characteristics of the poor contribute to their poverty, as well as how individuals and families are affected by poverty. Correspondingly, a macro-level approach would analyze the problem of poverty by assessing the impact of poverty on a larger social system and the social institutions that comprise it. *Institutions* are collections of norms, roles, and values fitted into a patterned organized way of living. Major social institutions include the economy, politics, education, family, religion, and the military.

Sociological theories can be classified according to their theoretical perspectives. Sociological perspectives are classifications of theory that furnish comprehensive beginning points about society, social processes, and social interaction. Sociological theory can be classified as structural-functional, social conflict, or symbolic interaction. The structural-functionalist and social-conflict paradigms are macro-level oriented, while the symbolic interaction paradigm involves micro-level analyses.

Structural-functionalist theory views society as a complex system of interdependent parts that work together (Maciones, 2002). Structural-functionalists view society as a relatively stable system. The major parts of this system are institutions—major spheres of social life, or societal subsystems, organized to meet a basic human need (Maciones, 2002). The functions of social structures that are intended and widely recognized are called "manifest functions." Those which are unintended and less well-known are called "latent functions." The negative functions of social patterns are called "dysfunctions."

Early functionalism viewed society as a living organism, giving rise to a social pathology model. Accordingly, social problems are occasional disturbances or disruptions in society's normal operation—just as a medical illness disrupts the normal operation of a human being. Social problems are analyzed in terms of their impact on the whole of society. The structural-functional model investigates social problems as bad or dysfunctional for the entire society, not just for the individuals who suffer from them.

The structural-functional view, fascinatingly, justifies the continuation of some social problems by maintaining that they, in fact, contribute to the stability of society. Although these negative conditions harm individuals or segments of society such as the family, the economy, or ethnic groups, the structural-functional model observes them as supplying society with something positive, albeit often indirectly.

A structural-functionalist approach to poverty, for example, concedes the negative results of poverty on individuals. However, it simultaneously emphasizes some important purposes or functions for society as a whole. This may involve provoking the majority of society's members to work hard or at least find a route to escape from poverty. Keeping part of the population poor also guarantees a reserve of desperate, destitute people unable to acquire more than low-wage, dislikable, and dangerous jobs. Poverty also provides an outlet for philanthropists.

The *social-conflict model* views society as divided by inequality and conflict (Maciones, 2002). Poverty, according to social conflict theory, is an outcome of competition for scarce and valuable resources such as wealth, power, and status. For that reason, poverty results from social divisions between the haves and the have-nots. Poor people are badly losing the battle for society's rewards. One cannot view the nonsuccess of people living in poverty without recognizing the link to their handicapped position relative to those of others within the larger society. The social-conflict perspective suggests that the fundamental arrangements and cultural characteristics of the social system produce advantages for some people while others are disadvantaged; this is a macro-level approach.

The social-conflict model sees poverty as a condition brought about by dominant groups bent on self-promotion who accumulate a lopsided portion of scarce and valuable resources. Social problems such as environmental pollution are harmful to the greater social system and are a consequence of the decisions and conduct of controlling groups who chase after their own financial success. Persisting social problems can be interpreted from this perspective by observing that the behavior that results in them are advantageous to dominant groups in society. Pollution, for instance, has become a persisting social problem because the expenses to advantaged groups of eliminating it are perceived as too costly.

Social conflict chiefly occurs along class, ethnic, racial, and gender lines. Karl Marx's theory of class struggle is an example of social problems based on socioeconomic conflict. How else could a society so affluent have so many who are so destitute? Capitalism is an economic mode of production in which companies are privately owned by people who manage them for profit. The business owners making up the capitalist class are able to produce enough food and material goods for everyone and, thus, end poverty and other types of social misery. However, greed and profit come before the basic needs of the working class; this generates and maintains poverty and other social problems such as homelessness, poor education, poor health care, and, for some, the need to turn to criminal activity for basic needs. Class social-conflict theorists support a drastic restructuring of society as the best means to address social ills.

Conflict can also be based on skin color and culture. Multiculturalists view social problems in terms of ethnic and racial inequality. Historically, racial and ethnic minorities have been, and currently remain, disadvantaged—at higher risk of poverty, poor health, street violence, homelessness, poor education, as well as other social problems. The structures of racial and ethnic inequality bestow high status on some people, particularly white Anglo-Saxon Protestants, while failing to recognize others (particularly people of color). The persistence of racial and ethnic prejudice suggests that some people view the very presence of minorities in their communities as a social problem.

The structure of gender inequality is also pervasive. Women—especially single women and their children—suffer more from poverty and many other social problems because society historically gave, and continues to give, men economic, political, and social advantages over women. This amounts to affirmative action for men, especially white men.

Feminists (those who favor social equality for women and men) view social problems as men's domination over and oppression of women. Even though the social, economic, and political standing of women and men has begun to approach equality during the twentieth century, women working full time still earn just 73 percent as much as men do (Maciones, 2002). In addition to higher rates of poverty than men, females—from childhood to old age—also are often subject to violence at the hands of men.

The social-conflict paradigm currently overshadows other approaches in the examination of social problems. Yet perhaps the significance of social divisions is given too much weight. After all, technological advances have resulted in a noticeable increase in the standard of living for society's members.

Ethnic minorities and women have had greater opportunities than in the past. The recent rise of a black and Latino middle class in the past thirty-five years demonstrates economic and social upward mobility for ethnic minorities.

Social-conflict theory surrenders scientific objectivity for political activism. Nevertheless, structural-functionalism is also political in the sense that it supports the status quo. Both structural-functionalism and social-conflict theory depend on imprecise sweeping statements far removed from how individuals actually come into contact with their world. This apprehension has led to the growth of a third major approach: symbolic-interactionism.

The third important theoretical paradigm in sociology, *symbolic interaction*, sees society as the product of individuals interacting with one another (Maciones, 2002). It seeks to make sense of how people understand their own lives. Symbolic-interactionism has a sharply distinct view of social problems, suggesting that social problems are subjective. They are constructed through the negotiations of social interaction.

Learning theory suggests that people learn attitudes and behaviors within specific cultural or subcultural environments. Symbolic-interactionism also examines how people socially construct reality. Labeling theory proposes that the reality of any particular situation depends on how people define it. People often label others based simply on who they are.

Symbolic-interactionists also analyze why some actions are labeled deviant while others are not. The labeling theory of social deviance addresses why particular forms of crime, while less expensive and menacing to society, are seen as more serious than other varieties of crime that may be limited or have less of an effect on human beings. People are much more worried about property crimes such as theft than the white-collar crimes such as embezzlement. The public's labeling of and direct response to negative conditions are what results in the collective definition of social problems.

Symbolic-interactionism contributes a micro, "street-level" dimension to the study of social problems. Nevertheless, by emphasizing the tremendous variability in every day, this approach ignores or fails to recognize how the structure of class, ethnicity, race, and gender molds and controls individual lives. In other words, labeling and the construction of reality occur within a particular social structure.

In summary, the structural-functional and social-conflict paradigms operate at the macro level, while symbolic-interactionism operates at the micro level. According to structural-functionalism, society is a system of interrelated parts, all of which contribute to its overall operation. It proposes that society is basically good and views problems as the result of deficient people, too-rapid social change, or dysfunctional consequences.

Social-conflict theory views society as a system of social inequality, whereby some benefit at the expense of others. It claims that problems stem from inequality in terms of class, ethnicity, race, and gender. Symbolic-interactionism conceptualizes society as arising from the ongoing interaction of individuals. People's perceptions of reality are alterable and shifting. It stresses how people learn attitudes and behaviors and how people may or may not define situations as problems.

Each of the three sociological paradigms offer unique advantages for examining social problems, including why they persevere and how we can eliminate or, at least, lessen them. The chapters in this book are representative of various sociological theories. I use multiple levels of analysis and composite theoretical perspectives to analyze social issues that have been labeled "social problems."

THE PROBLEM WITH "UNIVERSAL" ETHICS

Superior morality is always the morality of the superior.

—Zygmunt Bauman, *Globalization*

Much of modern ethical thought is based on universality. Accordingly, there are ethical prescriptions that compel every person to internalize them as right and, consequently, to accept them as obligatory. For lawmakers, universality means a blanket application of a set of rules or laws in the territory over which their authority stretches.

Since its inception, the Frankfurt School set about to evaluate the classic works of the Enlightenment tradition as well as social theorists such as Friedrich Engels, Karl Marx, and Sigmund Freud. This included borrowing from these references, yet at the same time, remaining critical of them and of modern society—thus, the name *critical theory*. Critical theorists, such as Max Horkheimer, Herbert Marcuse, and Theodor Adorno, exposed the deceptions of modern culture by which the vision of a universal ethics based on Western ideals imposes itself and thus restricts human freedom.

Jürgen Habermas, arguably the most important critical theorist today, like his predecessors, is critical of the Enlightenment tradition with its menacing enticement to reduce humanity into a unidimensional whole devoid of real differences. Despite his critical stance, Habermas has a deep, abiding respect for the liberating and community-building potential of human beings. This position is called "radical modernism" because it attempts to find the liberating potential in modern culture.

I use social ethics to offer a case for doubting Habermas. Does the modern world still realistically offer what, for so long, it has promised? The gloomy realities of the modern world, at the beginning of the present millennium are difficult to overlook.

- The terrorist threat of weapons of mass destruction.
- Personal income, around the globe, is declining nearly at the same rate as economic productivity and cumulative wealth are growing.
- Continuous working employment—jobs productive of personal income and benefits sufficient to support family life are disappearing for the majority.
- Social and economic inequalities are growing worse, not better—most dramatically in the United States, which the modern world had always looked up to as the land of opportunity.
- Food supplies are declining to their lowest levels in decades with world grain reserves dropping to just forty-eight days' worth at current consumption levels.
- Social conflict—from violence against women and children to ethnic, class, and racial conflict—is pandemic.

The modern world guarantees human rights, individual freedom, economic and moral progress, and social equality. In the lack of which, individuals now correctly marvel why they encounter so much inequality, hunger and disease, poverty, oppression, and civil disharmony. The modernist views the glass as half full. The postmodernist views the glass as half empty. I view the glass, simply, as too large.

I concur with the postmodern challenge to the myth of social and moral progress. Zygmunt Bauman (1998) proposes a postmodern ethics that embraces social diversity and cultural pluralism. According to *cultural pluralism*, ethnic subcultures are maintained and celebrated; at the same time, various ethnic groups share societal resources and institutional arrangements, as well as a general culture. This articulated vision, of course, does not square with the preponderance of genocide, terrorism, and urban violence in our world today.

Postmodern ethics is accommodating, to a fault. It is excessively relativistic and eclectic, receiving many voices and perspectives. Postmodern ethicists stress tolerance but, ironically, are critical of a "privileged" point of view. Postmodern ethics can be liberating and minority-friendly. But postmodern ethics is not satisfying. It is not able to evaluate what course of action should be taken when confronted with competing stances, for example, on key social issues such as health-care delivery, poverty, affirmative action, and education.

Postmodernists believe, sincerely but naively, that dialogue itself will resolve the obstacle. This does little to help the victims of social policy who appear to require immediate assistance and response. Consequently, postmodern ethics is irresponsible and incapable. The goal of this project is to provide a critical way out of this ambiguous, regretful predicament in contemporary social theory as well as implications for social policy based on a social ethics of distributive justice, equity, and fairness.

THE PROBLEM WITH RELATIVISTIC ETHICS

The basic problem with relying on a relativistic ethics is that we are left with shifting bases of decision rules or principles by which to judge whether we or whether society is acting "ethically." There is a basic consensus among different ethnic and religious ethics—that is to say, consensus among the ethical principles of Christians, Muslims, Jews, and Hindus. Moreover, the U.N.'s charter and other articles support human rights as well as some implicit universalistic principles for solving social problems around the world. From this opportunity, I derive a common set of principles of social ethics for public policy. Most ethnic and religious cultures have overlapping prescriptions and proscriptions (moral codes approximating the Ten Commandments). Ethical principles condemning killing, stealing, or coveting thy neighbor's goods or wife can also be used as principles for determining whether a particular social policy is ethical.

The give-and-take model of conflict resolution always leaves opponents as part-winners and part-losers. A new model is needed. I propose the principles of equity, distributive justice and fairness for a social ethics approach to public policy. This new collaborative model is a win–win strategy based on human and civil rights.

A SOCIAL ETHICS APPROACH TO PUBLIC POLICY

Justice is an essential theme in social life. To be sure, the notion of justice as fairness underscores the claims of legitimacy by a society's social and political institutions (Greenberg & Cohen, 1982). When such claims start to lose their legitimacy, social change usually occurs. At the same time, the issue of social justice in everyday life is pervasive. However, the definition of justice and its guidelines for rules of ethical conduct may vary considerably between subcultural groups. This raises the important issue: Is a universal justice possible? Is there a "fair-treatment" policy for subculturally diverse people? Is there "fair play" in decision making involving ethnic minorities?

Minority groups have a culture of their own—a *subculture*, with a distinct set of values (Meyers, 1984). Each ethnic minority group has its own unique *ethical ideology*—systematic belief systems about what one ought to do or who one ought to be. The negation of subcultural values and related ethical ideology places *majority groups* in the elitist position of asserting that they know what is good for a people even though those in question may not want it (Henshel, 1990). *Cultural relativism* (see Herskovits, 1972) observes the validity and equality of all cultures and, therefore, the right to cultural self-determination. The problem with cultural relativism is that it implies nonintervention or a laissez-faire approach to social problems. If all values are relative, there are no objective criteria in moral reasoning or in the definition of social problems.

Any discussion of human rights implies *universalistic ethics*—applicable to all people regardless of ethnicity, culture, social class, or gender. If one assumes a position of cultural relativism, nevertheless, ethical criteria become intuitive and insufficient. Thus, a tension emerges from the attempt to reconcile universal ethics or human rights with *pluralistic ethics* or moral relativism.

It is clear that just, good, or acceptable behavior varies tremendously across cultures (even between and within subcultures within a more general culture) and time. Happiness is achieved in exceedingly diverse ways that are fluid and subjective. Yet, a considerable degree of consensus or accord exists among the ways subcultures characterize extreme misery, torment, or suffering. This type of discourse allows one to move beyond cultural relativism by focusing on conditions of extreme misery, conditions on which there is substantial agreement. Such analyses can be gainfully applied to ethical issues in a subculturally diverse society.

SOCIAL ETHICS AND DISTRIBUTIVE JUSTICE

No victory over inhumanity seems to have made the world safer for humanity.

—Zygmunt Bauman, *Globalization*

There is a great deal of social inequality throughout the world, including within the United States. Distributive justice is a major ethical issue in a subculturally diverse society. On what basis do we distribute society's resources to people? What is the fairest way to assess need?—First-come, first-served?

The problem of distributive justice also emerges at a more basic level: How should society distribute resources that develop particular types of new procedures at the expense of others or that acquire new knowledge in some areas while ignoring others? We must consider that the resources used to fight terrorism are also needed to reduce gender and ethnic discrimination, urban decay, environmental pollution, and poverty and to improve the quality of education and accessibility to health care.

I propose an applied social ethics to use as a basis for law, social policy, and solving social problems. Social ethics is "a methodology of applying moral principles to social issues. The purpose is to clarify the moral principles and social goals inherent in social issues and public initiatives. It asserts that the relative strength of various moral claims can only be compared within the context of a particular social issue" (Winfrey, 1998: 2).

I apply distributive justice and social ethics to each social issue. In addition, I examine gender and ethnic issues for each topic. I favor a model that shuns dogmatic moral rules, respects ethical principles but not blind obedience to them, and carefully considers the fabric of realistic "trade-offs" in law and policy decisions without succumbing to the trap of relativism. We are left with a social ethics based on distributive justice, equity, and fairness.

THE GROWTH OF ETHNIC MINORITIES

The face and color of America's cities have greatly changed in the past sixty years, owing to the vast movement of blacks from the South to the North after World War II, a sharp increase in immigrants from Mexico and Latin America, and a constant flow of Asian newcomers, especially South Koreans and Filipinos. In 2000, Latinos became this country's largest ethnic minority (35,305,818; U.S. Census Bureau, 2001; see table 1.1). This represents 12.5 percent of the total U.S. population. Data on Latinos are conservative because they do not include undocumented immigrants who cross the border illegally. There are estimates that 46.2 percent of all Latinos who immigrate to the United States do so without legal documentation.

African Americans (34,658,190) are the second largest ethnic minority category in the United States, with 12.3 percent of the total population (U.S. Census Bureau, 2001). Both the black and Latino populations are younger than the white population. Latinos and Asians are the fastest-growing minorities. Since 2000, half of all elementary school children in the United States are

TABLE 1.1

Social Standing of Ethnic and Racial Categories in the United States, 2000

Race/Ethnicity	*Median Family Income*	*Percent in Poverty*	*Percent with 4 Years of College*	*Percent of Population*	*Actual #*
Latino	$31,663	25.6	10.9	12.5	35,305,818
Mexican American	$31,000	27.1	7.1	8.3	23,337,000
Puerto Rican	$24,600	30.9	11.1	1.1	3,178,000
Cuban American	$42,800	13.6	24.8	0.5	1,412,000
African American	$31,778	23.6	15.4	12.3	34,658,190
Native American	$30,784	25.9	9.3	0.9	2,475,956
Asian/Pacific Islander	$56,316	10.7	36.0	3.6	10,242,998
Chinese American	$55,000	10.7	38.9	0.9	2,433,000
Filipino	—	—	—	0.7	2,000,000
Japanese American	$69,000	5.4	32.9	0.2	797,000
Asian Indian	—	—	—	0.6	1,679,000
Korean	$45,000	10.5	32.9	0.4	1,077,000
White (non-Latino)		8.0		75.1	211,460,626
Multiracial				2.4	6,826,228
Total	$48,950	11.8	25.2	100	281,422,000

Note: Percentages do not total 100 percent, and subcategories do not add up to the figures in the main categories, because of overlap between groups. Therefore, numbers and percentages should be considered approximations.

Source: U.S Census Bureau, 2000a, 2000b, 2000c, 2001.

now ethnic minorities; nearly half (44 percent) of all residents in the United States under the age of twenty are nonwhite (U.S. Census Bureau, 2001).

The United States has undergone racial change throughout its history, but never at the rate and mode happening now. Within the next fifty years, whites as a share of the total population will decline from 75 percent (U.S. Census Bureau, 2001) to just over 50 percent. The black population will increase in size but will remain at about 12 percent of the total population. Asians may increase from their present 3.6 percent (U.S. Census Bureau, 2001) to 8 percent.

By 2050, Latinos will comprise about one-quarter of the U.S. population and blacks; less than one-sixth. Latinos are also the least educated ethnic group (U.S. Census Bureau, 2000a; see table 1.1). Only 7.1 percent of all Mexican Americans have four or more years of college, compared with 15.4 percent of blacks, 9.3 percent of Native Americans (Maciones, 2002), 36 percent of Asians, and 25.2 percent of the entire population (U.S. Census Bureau, 2000a; table 1.1). Social responsibility requires us to examine how an increase of culturally diverse people directly or residually affects the larger society. Issues include poverty, housing, education, health care, crime, jurisprudence, prison, racism, sexism, and affirmative action.

ETHNIC ETHICS

Human social and cognitive development is largely an outcome of the child-rearing practices of the cultural subgroups that compose a modern complex society (Havighurst, 1976: 56). *Ethnic groups* are people who have a common history and generally share ways of life, including language, religion, country of origin, and social identity. They affect individuals through family activity, peer group, linguistic concepts, common literature, work in formal associations, in-group marriage, and residential and work segregation. *Social classes,* too, are pervasive and powerful in their influence on individuals (Maciones, 1996; Gordon, 1964: 52; Havighurst, 1976: 56). Ethnic groups, however, are also effective, more so at the lower- and working-class levels than at the middle- and upper-middle-class levels.

Sociologists use the term *subculture* to refer to the cultural patterns of any type of subgroup within the national society (Gordon, 1964: 38–39). Each ethnic group is a subculture with its own set of behaviors and attitudes (Havighurst, 1976: 56). Subcultures, nevertheless, do not exist in isolation. They affect and are affected by the general culture as well as other subcultures. One may speak of the subculture of a neighborhood, a factory, a hospital, a university campus, or even a gang. Cohen's study (1955) of the cultural patterns of a delinquent gang uses this notion of subculture.

My (Cortese, 1990) critical approach to cognitive development theory addresses the humanizing effects of the ethnic and cultural sources of moral values. Morality is socially constructed, not based on rational principles of individuals (Cortese, 1989c). This alternative theory conflicts with the "universal" theories of morality and societal development as formulated by Immanuel Kant (1949), Jean Piaget ([1932] 1965), Lawrence Kohlberg (1969, 1981, 1984), John Rawls (1971), Jürgen Habermas (1984), and J. C. Harsanyi (1982).

Critiquing the cognitive-developmental model, I (Cortese, 1980, 1982a, 1982b, 1984a, 1989b, 1989c) examine social class, gender, and ethnic differences in moral judgment. This argument (Cortese, 1990) is situated in relation to both Kolbergian theory and the feminist critique of this theory (Gilligan, 1982).

The major thesis is that "moral judgment reflects the structure of social relations, not the structure of human cognition" (Cortese 1990: 4). The agenda is to

- explore the impact of ethnicity, culture, and language on moral development (Cortese & Mestrovic, 1990);
- elucidate conceptual problems linked to justice and objectivistic-subjectivistic tensions (Cortese & Mestrovic, 1990);
- identify methodological problems in the study of moral judgment (Cortese, 1984a, 1987, 1989a);
- clarify the relationship between Kohlberg's (1984) approach and sociological theory (Cortese, 1985).

This critique of Kohlberg (Cortese, 1986a) also challenges the moral theory of Habermas (1984): "Moral reasoning and behavior are determined largely by social factors—role demands, class interests, national policies, and ethnic antagonisms. One cannot be moral in an immoral social role, whatever one's childhood socialization, psychological predispositions, or commitment to abstract rational principles" (Cortese 1990: 2).

Social forces and individual cognition interact to shape moral judgment (Cortese, 1985). A pure structural framework cannot totally account for the wide range in moral reasoning among people in similar social roles. Yet it is important to focus on the ethnic origins of moral reasoning. Latinos and African Americans typically base their moral judgments on principles of responsibility, fidelity, and caring, vis-à-vis abstract principles of justice (Cortese, 1984b).

Kohlberg's work borrows from Piaget's ([1932] 1965) theory of cognitive moral development, Kant's (1949, 1950, 1963) philosophy of science, Rawls's (1971) theory of justice, and Durkheim's (1961) concept of morality. I (Cortese, 1990) adopt Mannheim's (1971) sociology of knowledge to criticize Kohlberg. Habermas makes extensive use of Kohlberg's ideas in his theory of communicative ethics. Habermas recognized that the implicit social evolutionary model in Kohlberg's stage theory fit nicely with his own developmental theory of communicative ethics and instrumental rationality.

The pivotal issue is the alleged universal generalizability Kohlberg attached to his six-stage developmental model. He presumed that as individuals mature they move from simplistic forms of moral reasoning to the use of more complex moral principles, although most never achieve the higher stages. Kohlberg's theory has spawned considerable research and controversy (Cortese, 1986b; Gilligan, 1982; Simpson, 1974).

Kohlberg's theory is, at best, a heuristic model and, at worst, false, because it ignores the fact that ethnic and cultural factors shape the moral development of individuals in ways that would make any universalized model of moral development fail when comparative testing was used (Cortese, 1990). While Kohlberg's hypothetical moral dilemmas were designed to test the ability to comprehend and implement more highly complicated forms of "justice," real-life decisions are complex and go beyond abstract questions of justice.

Kohlberg's moral dilemmas are unrealistic and depict situations as having rigid either/or choices and consequences (Cortese, 1984a). In particular, Latino and African American responses to moral questions reflect moral orientations often different from those of whites. Moreover, women's responses differ from those of men, indicating gender-specific socialization regarding moral reasoning (Gilligan, 1982). In the well-known Heinz Dilemma, a destitute man is faced with the choice of stealing a life-saving drug for his wife from a pharmacy or allowing her to die. I (Cortese, 1990) document how women focused on Heinz's care, responsibility, and love for his wife, not justice or rights, the intended focus of the question.

American ethnic minorities and those raised in non-Western cultures sometimes give responses that indicate alternative forms of moral reasoning. Labeling these alternate forms of reasoning morally inferior is ethnocentric. The Standard Issue Scoring system tends to favor complex reasoning and abstract dialogue; thus, alternate types of solutions are typically scored at the lower stages (Cortese, 1989a).

Kohlberg's (1984) presumption that individuals mature from lower, less sophisticated stages to higher, more complex ones exposes his theory to the criticisms of various forms of evolutionary frameworks. He created ideal types of discreet forms of moral reasoning and presumed an inevitable sequence of development, much as nineteenth-century anthropologists presumed that they had uncovered the inevitable sequence of social change that led from savagery to civilization. Habermas (1984) transformed Kohlberg's individual stages of moral growth into stages of increasingly rational societal communication.

CONCLUSION

It is urgent that social theorists, social ethicists, and policy makers address the types of social questions that have begun to emerge in postmodernity. I focus on economic inequality, cultural diversity, gender and ethnic discrimination, individual health and community welfare, and social policy. I hope to contribute to social ethics, public discourse, scholarly dialogue, humanistic understanding, law, and public policy.

A basic goal is to show how social structure and social processes affect individual attitudes and behavior. I provide an interpretation of social issues within a principled social ethics based on distributive justice, equity, and fairness. I apply sociological methods to hurdle misconceptions and ideological barriers and debunk cultural myths. Practical solutions to alleviate economic inequality and social conflict are offered.

WHAT YOU CAN DO

The discipline of sociology does not furnish ultimate conclusions about pressing social questions. Accordingly, a major goal of this text is to assist you in thinking critically about the topics presented. My objective is not to inform you what to think. There are no simple or "correct" solutions to these social problems.

Once one is able to use a sociological imagination (Mills, 1959), there are numerous potential paths for reacting to social arrangements, processes, and problems. Some of these will be specific with particular ramifications for social policy. Others appear unpractical, apparently separated from the physical and social milieux. My expectation is that the reader will choose a perspective and, perhaps, a course of action that fits one's own strengths and interests. The objective of this book is to enhance your capacity to reflect critically on contemporary social problems.

Use sociological understanding to view yourself, analyzing your beliefs and values in terms of the particular social position you occupy. Following is a sample from one of my students:

My experiences in life and social class persuade me to view the world as just, honest, and peaceful. Social class is determined by economic indices such as occupation, education, and income. Further, our society also stratifies by skin color. Although I do not have my own income, I can relate my opportunities to my father's fortunes. I am a white female whose father's income is above average. I have received the best possible education all my life and assume to have a successful occupation in the future.

Although money or social class can't buy happiness, it has brought me a lot of opportunities to influence me to view the world as just. For example, my neighborhood consists of middle class, white families. Everyone in the area is a good role model and there is little rebellion, crime, anger, or revenge. I was not exposed to the neighborhood like the inmates [at the New Mexico State penitentiary (class field trip)] where I had to protect myself or my property. Therefore, I see the world as peaceful. Furthermore, since public schools are divided by districts, I went to a school with all of those motivated, positive people. Our school had plenty of funding (a fair share of taxes came to us) and we had excessive alumni and parental support.

In the school district across town, where most of the lower-class students attended, there was very little funding and support. Their lack of education led to other factors like crime, unemployment, and poor income while my school educated me and prepared me for the future. I haven't had to struggle to find jobs or internships and this influences my view of a just world.

Finally, my father's income allows me to have material items, as well as, opportunities. I have never had to struggle or save to buy something and I have never known a bill that wasn't paid. This security kept peace within my family. There was never struggles or arguments over who left the light on, who made a long-distance call, or who spent more on shopping or gambling. Financial issues cause domestic violence, abuse, and divorce. I have never faced these confrontations.

I know I have lived in a bubble, but at my level, you become naïve to what is happening in the rest of the world. I have never struggled financially. I have never experienced racism. I have never been involved in excessive violence. My parents are Mr. and Mrs. Brady and I am happy. Although others are struggling, my social class and experiences lead me to believe that this is a just world. Maybe I need a reality check!

TWO

THE CRISIS AND DENIAL OF ACCESS IN EDUCATION

Our nation is at risk. Our once unchallenged preeminence in commerce, industry, science, and technological innovation is being overtaken by competitors throughout the world.

—U.S. National Commission on Excellence in Education, *A Nation at Risk*

ACCESSIBILITY TO QUALITY education is a basic problem for many in the United States. Although it is widely available, it is evolving into a double-tiered system of public and private education. The current policy of providing vouchers for private schools to students who could not otherwise afford to attend such schools has been highly controversial and has polarized this issue even further. At the time of this writing, the U.S. Supreme Court has ruled that school vouchers are constitutional. More recently, however, the Florida State Supreme Court has ruled that school vouchers violate the state's exhaustive constitution that specifically states that public funds cannot be used for religious organizations and private schools despite good-will intentions. Since education is the major basis of social mobility for individuals, educational stratification results in a wider gap between the haves and the have-nots.

Schools have both academic and social consequences on students. Educational participation and academic achievement are critical for students as a foundation for occupational attainment and parity in political decision-making processes. A low quality of high school education leaves students poorly prepared for college. Without a college education, chances for a good job are greatly reduced.

Increasing the quality of education is generally viewed as necessary for increasing employment and productivity while cutting crime, poverty, and the need for welfare. Yet if we examine the relative performance on basic subjects such as math, students in the United States are near the bottom. Consequently, education has been socially constructed as a crisis, a major social problem. Now critics are challenging the philosophy, objectives, and methods of education.

There is also strong evidence that socioeconomic, cultural, and family background is connected to academic achievement in individuals. This chapter reviews evidence of the effects of these variables and provides implications for social policy based on distributive justice. Educational problems focus on the low rates of participation and academic achievement for the disadvantaged, ethnic minorities, and members of lower social classes, as poor students. This chapter presents data on enrollment, persistence, and achievement as an indication of the extent of underrepresentation of ethnic minorities and the economically disadvantaged. The sociolegal background of tracking in education is sketched.

THE CRISIS IN AMERICAN SCHOOLS

I got no prospects, no education.
I was lucky getting a job at this gas station.

—Sting, *Fill Her Up*

A great deal of effort was directed at improving the quality of education during the 1960s and 1970s, especially for disadvantaged ethnic minority students. Despite all this work, there was little gain. The U.S. National Commission on Excellence in Education published a booklet, *A Nation at Risk*, which painted a very grim picture (Gardner, 1983: 8–9). Not only had there been little academic progress among the children of the disadvantaged, the test scores of the children of affluent parents had declined.

Although a larger portion of the U.S. population earns a college degree than in any other nation (Organization for Economic Cooperation and Development [OECD], 2000), on science, math, and language skills, young

Americans bring up the rear in comparisons with a dozen other First World countries. A recognized measure of academic performance brings to light the cause for concern. The Scholastic Assessment Test (SAT) measures verbal and mathematical performance; the average scores for both sections of the test declined after 1967 for both young men and young women, and verbal scores remain significantly below the 1967 levels today (College Board, 2000a). Three-fourths of university faculty feels that students are seriously underprepared for college (Mooney, 1989). The average tested achievement of students graduating from college is also lower.

If the average performance of American students raises anxiety, the achievement of socially disadvantaged students is even more alarming. Blacks score about 200 points below the average of white students on the SAT; Latinos trail whites by 130 points, and Native Americans trail by 95 points (College Board, 2000b). Latinos and Native Americans are the least likely ethnic group to graduate from college (less than 10 percent; OECD, 2000). Asian Americans score at about the same level as whites. Why? Blacks are more likely to live in single-parent families and have to contend with racial stereotypes that undercut their academic ability. Many Latinos do not speak English well; it is often their second language. Many Native Americans view school as a symbol of foreign culture and a misguided tool to acculturate them.

The common factor among these ethnic groups is poverty. The child poverty rate for Latinos (30 percent), blacks (33 percent), and Native Americans (40 percent) is far greater than that for whites (14 percent) (U.S. Census Bureau, 2000c). In addition, schools with affluent students have much greater funding per student. Some of the poorest public school districts spend approximately $2,000 per year to educate each student, while the wealthiest spend nearly $17,500 (Macionis, 2002). This raises students' performance on achievement tests. In recent years, students from families with incomes of $100,000 or higher per year scored more than 250 points better on the SAT than students from families who earn below $20,000 per year (Bowles & Gintis, 1976; U.S. Census Bureau, 1999; Zernike, 2000).

Eleven percent of the U.S. population aged sixteen to twenty-four (3.7 million people) dropped out of school before earning a high school diploma (U.S. National Center for Education Statistics, 1999). The dropout rate is merely 7 percent for whites, but 13 percent for blacks, 29 percent for Latinos, and 33 percent for Native Americans. Just as in academic performance, dropout rates are significantly correlated to income. The dropout rate for students from families with incomes in the top 20 percent (approximately

$88,000 and higher) is just 3 percent. For students from families with incomes in the bottom 20 percent (approximately $23,000 and lower), the dropout rate is 24 percent (U.S. National Center for Education Statistics, 1999).

The major reasons for dropping out for all students include the necessity to earn an income, pregnancy, a lack of ability to speak English, and boredom. Some misguided explanations use the personal traits of individuals rather than membership in a socially disadvantaged category of people (e.g., ethnic minorities, the poor, and those whose parents had little or no education). Dropping out also increases the risk of future obstacles such as unemployment, alcohol and other drug abuse, and poverty as adults (U.S. National Center for Education Statistics, 1999). In conclusion, education continues a multigenerational cycle where affluent parents pass "achievement and success" on to their children, while poor parents pass along "disappointment and failure" to theirs. Besides the decline in test scores, fewer students are taking foreign language courses, especially females. Moreover, fewer students are enrolling in the natural sciences.

Had test scores not begun to decline in 1967, but continued to increase as they had in the past, the quality of the labor force would be much higher. Certainly, a more highly educated workforce would result in lower rates of unemployment and higher rates of productivity. The United States has been unable to fill many job openings in the natural sciences and engineering fields. It is not surprising that foreign-educated professionals have filled the demand. Even so, U.S. corporations have gone overseas to find a skilled workforce. This is likely to increase. Finally, the decline in test scores by whites has increased competition for jobs with minorities, whose test scores have been steadily increasing. This could have contributed to maintaining higher rates of unemployment among nonwhites in inner cities.

Explanations for the decline in test scores have included:

1. Decreases in student motivation to learn, including increases in alcohol and drug use, declines in hours of homework done, and increases in the hours of watching noneducational television;
2. Changes in family background, including the sharp increase in single-parent families; the increase in the number of working mothers; changes in family size; and increases in the number of children from lower-status families taking the tests;
3. Changes in student body characteristics, including the consequences of desegregation;
4. Changes in teacher characteristics, including decline in teacher test scores; changes in teacher educational attainment; and changes in teacher attitudes toward education;

5. Changes in school quality, including changes in graduation requirements; watering down of curriculum; changes in textbook difficulty; and grade inflation;
6. Increases in violence in school and changes in teacher roles, emphasizing more student behavior monitoring and punishing and less time spent in actual teaching.

Desegregation cannot explain the drop in white student test scores because it is not correlated with their achievement. Most whites attend suburban public and private schools that have not been affected by integration.

With respect to teacher characteristics, there has been a decline in test scores of elementary and high school teachers. However, teacher differences in educational attainment are only slightly related to student achievement (Koretz, 1987). In addition, the decline in teacher test scores occurred well after the decline in student test scores began.

Regarding changes in school quality, increasingly lenient graduation requirements by school districts contributed to the decline; the return to more rigorous graduation ended the decline. Specifically, increases in school graduation requirements occurred in at least forty-one states by 1974 (Koretz, 1987). However, student test scores continued to decline for several years; when the decline ended, no additional graduation requirements had been introduced nationwide.

If family background is a key predictor of student achievement, what changes in family background characteristics would contribute to lower student achievement in whites? The increase of female-headed households was not relevant because most of the white students with lower SAT and American College Test (ACT) scores live in two-parent families.

If family background were a critical factor, one would expect that kindergartners would have come to school less prepared to learn. In fact, the opposite occurred. Elementary test scores actually increased. White test scores began to decline in the fifth or sixth grades. One possible explanation is a change in student attitudes. Students' lack of discipline to study, the desire to learn, and the motivation to achieve comprise one of several possible dimensions affecting academic performance.

Another related factor is a remnant from the counterculture in the 1960s: recreational drug use. During the late 1960s and early 1970s, college students became disillusioned by the Vietnam War, political corruption (i.e., Watergate), and glaring racial inequality. Student activism, however, waned by the mid-1970s, long before the decline in student test scores decreased. One aspect of the counterculture that did not wane but, in fact, increased and spread to high school and even elementary and junior high school students was illegal drug use. We are remiss if we do not recognize the role that drug use has played in the decline of academic achievement.

Child developmentalists acknowledge that the effect of family background on student achievement declines after elementary school, a period in which peer group influence clearly increases. Adolescent subculture takes over at the time when parents are no longer capable of devoting the time or possess the skills necessary for preparing children for future adult roles. Schools also serve as dating markets. Though male and females form platonic friendships as adolescents, such relationships are more difficult to maintain than same-sex friendships because they are generally based on traditional gender roles that are equated with romance, sex, and marriage.

The media also affect the aspirations of high school students, often in a way that deemphasizes academic achievement. It is not surprising that teenage girls want to be a model more than a nurse, schoolteacher, or artist. Males aspire to be athletic heroes more than brilliant students, while females aspire to be the most popular or the most brilliant student. Most teenagers prefer to date someone considered the "best looking" and/or the "most popular" rather than the "smartest." Students who belong to a peer group in which high grades are expected for popularity and dating tend to place greater emphasis on the value of academic success.

SEXUAL ACTIVITY AND ACADEMIC ACHIEVEMENT

Another factor that perhaps relates to changes in academic achievement is adolescents' sexual attitudes and behavior. Early dating and nonmarital sex have long been associated with lower levels of academic achievement (Coles & Stokes, 1985; Furstenberg et al., 1987; Urdry & Billy, 1987). This is partially due to student differences in family background; lower classes become sexually active earlier than upper classes.

Today, half of all boys have sexual intercourse by their sixteenth birthday, and half of all girls do so by age seventeen (Stodghill, 1998). Social class, early dating, frequent dating, and nonmarital sex is correlated with lower educational attainment. Why? Changes in student motivation (owing to dating and sexual behavior) are the most likely factors. The more time one spends dating or having sex, the less time one has for studying and schoolwork. A second factor is the instability of dating and sexual relationships. Conflicts in these relationships and breaking up can result in depression, anger, or rage. Problems associated with repeatedly breaking up can make studying and concentrating difficult, even for students with high achievement motivation.

The sexual revolution reduced the disparity in nonmarital sexual intercourse between blacks and whites. Increases in sexual activity by whites were linked to a sharp decline in average reading and math test scores for those attending suburban schools (Byrd, 1991). Increases in female-headed households are also associated with a decline in test scores, presumably because it is more difficult for a female single parent to monitor the dating behavior of her children. As sexual activity increases, expectedly pregnancy rates also rise despite the technological development of contraceptive devices. The younger a girl becomes a mother, the less chance she has for educational attainment. Moreover, the younger a girl becomes a mother, the more likely she will blame her pregnancy for causing her to have to quit school.

A latent function of education is that schools are dating markets as well as centers of learning. Nevertheless, sex education is very controversial. Right-wing religious organizations have forcefully argued that teaching about sex will only encourage it and, in fact, seem to provide at least implicit acceptance. Family planning groups counter that information about sex is necessary in order to reduce unwanted pregnancies and sexually transmitted diseases such as AIDS. Studies find no consistent results to show that sex education courses either increase or reduce sexual activity. Some studies did show that sex education courses positively correlated with an increase in the use of contraceptives by females.

There is scant evidence to show that sex education courses actually reduce pregnancy. Most sex education courses are limited to ten hours (or fewer) of formal and impersonal instruction. Perhaps peer pressure and media influences outweigh any effect of sex education in the classroom. On one side is a teacher with technical scientific material on human reproduction. On the other side is the media-drenched, oversexed world in which teens actually live—shaped by television, film, music lyrics, video games, encouraging peer groups, their own developing hormones, and sometimes not the most responsible adult role models.

School-based health clinics are promising alternatives or complements to sex education. Such programs offer more personal and interactive counseling about sexuality, family planning, birth control, and pregnancy testing. Conservative religious groups have challenged these types of clinics and family planning agencies. Some states have passed laws requiring parental consent for teenage abortions. This does not solve the problem, however, since pregnant teenagers will then cross state lines for abortions.

SOCIOHISTORICAL BACKGROUND OF PUBLIC SCHOOL DESEGREGATION

The case for or against desegregation should not be in terms of academic achievement. If we want a segregated society, we should have segregated schools.

—Christopher Jencks, *Inequality*

Ever since the founding of this country, there has a been stratified system of social inequality, including education, for its residents. Whites were citizens with all the rights and privileges afforded them under the Constitution. The nation's earliest minorities, blacks and Native Americans, and later, Mexicans and Chinese, had little or no rights. For example, black slaves, reduced to chattel, could not own property, testify in court, congregate with other blacks except at church, carry firearms, strike a white person in self-defense, or learn to read or write. Consequently, in the eighteenth and the early part of the nineteenth centuries, very few blacks attended school.

After the end of slavery and the Civil War (1865), black education was still restricted. There were few schools for black children. In 1876, following the election of President Rutherford B. Hayes, federal troops were removed from the South. This was nothing more than a political payoff for southern support during the election. This removal signaled a return to white supremacy and a reduction of black rights temporarily afforded by the presence of federal militia.

This regression to antebellum conditions and a series of Supreme Court decisions had a chilling effect on black rights. Black school enrollment, already low, declined further. Although the Civil Rights cases of 1883 outlawed state discrimination based on the Fourteenth Amendment (i.e., equal protection under the law), individuals and organizations were free to follow a vendetta against blacks. In 1896, the Supreme Court, in *Plessy v. Ferguson*, ruled that racial segregation was legal as long as separate facilities for blacks and whites were roughly equal. In 1899, in *Cummings v. County Board of Education*, the Court validated laws establishing separate schools for whites and blacks.

School segregation continued under the rhetoric of "separate but equal." In reality, however, black and white schools were highly unequal. White students attended schools in contemporary buildings, with well-trained instructors and current textbooks. Black students, however, attended run-down schools with many poorly trained teachers and old, worn textbooks. In short, public schools for black children were far inferior to white schools.

Segregation can either be the result of state law (de jure) or the result of housing patterns (de facto). Although segregation was de jure in southern states, northern states were just as segregated. Most schools in the North were segregated not by law but by the fact that almost all blacks were forced to live in all-black neighborhoods with underfunded schools (de facto segregation) (Morgan, 1995).

In a landmark decision in 1954, the Supreme Court ruled in *Brown v. Board of Education, Topeka, Kansas*, that racially segregated schools are inherently unequal. This reversed *Plessy v. Ferguson*. Even if per pupil expenditures were equal (which, in fact, they were not), de jure segregation by race was considered to violate a citizen's right to equal protection under the law. Outraged, southern legislatures in Georgia, Alabama, and Virginia, as well as other states, banned school desegregation even under court order. Southern resistance to school desegregation ranged from litigation to paralyze integration efforts for decades in court to "white flight," as white families fled to suburbs to avoid sending their children to schools with blacks.

White flight has resulted in the resegregation of inner-city schools. For example, in Boston there were 96,000 students in the 60 percent white school system prior to desegregation. At that time, most whites went to white schools, blacks to black schools, and Latinos to Latino schools. However, by 1988, there were 59,000 students in the school system and only 24 percent of them were white (Associated Press, 1988).

Some metropolitan areas have attempted to remedy this through cross-district busing (between cities and suburbs). However, the majority of U.S. residents (between 65 and 85 percent), including all races, are opposed to forced busing (Farley, 2000). Given the general opposition to busing, local governments (such as the city of Dallas) have begun to build low-income housing in suburban areas (Coleman, 1990). Of course, there is also opposition to this based on fears of an increase in crime and property devaluation.

School desegregation and intervention programs such as Head Start increase academic achievement in minority students. But, perhaps more important, they have important social effects. School desegregation is linked to desegregation in other areas of social life. Blacks who have attended integrated elementary and high schools are more likely to attend integrated colleges and universities, have white friends and social contacts, live in integrated neighborhoods, and work in integrated companies.

Such apparent benefits of educational desegregation must be mitigated by two circumstances: First, black enrollment at all-black colleges and universities is on the increase. This is related to the backlash of affirmative action and the increase of hate crimes, racial prejudice, and discrimination at predominantly white institutions of higher education. Students at black colleges report a greater sense of acceptance and satisfaction with campus life. Moreover, there is little evidence to suggest that black colleges provide "inferior" education.

Spurred on by *Brown v. Board of Education* and the 1964 Civil Rights Act, the goal of education became increasing the academic achievement of disadvantaged children. Public education was designed to compensate for the consequences of deprived backgrounds; desegregation was implemented to offset the deleterious effects of racial discrimination. However, by the early 1980s, low academic achievement was no longer restricted to poor minority students. Instead, the standardized test scores of middle- and upper-class white students had virtually collapsed since the passage of the Civil Rights Act, while the test scores of the poor were slowly increasing. Critics blamed this on desegregation. However, the decline in test scores of middle- and upper-class white students was occurring among those who attended all-white public and private high school. This could not be blamed on desegregation.

THE DISPUTE OVER MAINSTREAMING OR INTEGRATING SCHOOLS

The social demographics of a student body affect educational achievement. For example, isolating the lower classes from the middle classes tended to reduce the former classes test scores. Integration was one solution, either through forced busing or changes in residential patterns. The racial integration of schools has been only partly successful because residential patterns have become even more racially and ethnically segregated. However, those who maintain segregation may produce better academic results have also attacked integration or mainstreaming.

Before the 1964 Civil Rights Act, it was common to segregate those with handicaps from the general population. The Civil Rights Act, banning discrimination by race, color, religion, and national origin, became a benchmark for those who wanted to end discrimination against the handicapped. Why should persons bound to wheelchairs or the hearing and visually impaired be excluded from public schools when schools, with minor changes, could easily accommodate them?

Since 1965, efforts to integrate the handicapped in their local school districts have probably been more successful than integrating whites and ethnic minorities. Given the unique status of the hearing-impaired, they can be better educated in a segregated school. The issue of role models again becomes germane. There is more likely to be hearing impaired teachers and other staff at state schools for the hearing impaired. Additionally, there is more likely to be courses in deaf heritage covering the achievements that hearing-impaired Americans have made. Communication is more likely to be in American Sign Language, the "natural" language of the hearing impaired in the United States.

Busing and Racial Segregation

De jure segregation meant that even where black and white children lived in the same neighborhood, they were bused to separate schools. The *Brown* decision mandated that public schools must desegregate with all deliberate speed. Southern states, however, forcefully resisted desegregation. In the decade following the decision, only 2 percent of black children attended schools with white children in the South.

The passage of the Civil Rights Act of 1964 enhanced the process of school desegregation by putting enforcement in the hands of the Justice Department of the federal government. Nevertheless, in the North and the West, racial segregation in schools persisted; segregation was ruled to be constitutional because it was considered to be de facto. Generally, the situation was that minority children attended inner-city schools, while whites attended schools in the suburbs. However, if there were evidence of intent to discriminate by schools boards (e.g., Boston), court busing was ordered (O'Brien, 1991).

Unlike southern cities where racial segregation was de jure, in Boston the case had to be established by studying patterns of segregation. After review, the case was compelling. The Boston school boards had gerrymandered school district lines to fit changing neighborhood patterns, built new schools in the center of racially segregated neighborhoods, and concocted other methods to assign students to schools based on race.

As mentioned above, the *Brown* decision increased white flight from inner cities to suburbs or to private schools. Clearly, those in the higher socioeconomic levels were most likely to move since they had the greatest financial resources. Naturally, if the area to be desegregated included both the city and surrounding suburbs, there was less movement by whites because there was no place to move.

When desegregation was mandatory and offered no choices in where parents could send their children to school, there was more likely to be white flight. Whites were more likely to move if their children were to be bused to black neighborhoods rather than vice versa. Not surprisingly, negative media coverage of desegregation plans was found to increase white movement. Nevertheless, interracial contact in public schools did increase for many cities.

Minorities have done better in integrated schools than segregated ones. Academic achievement for whites was not related to the racial composition of the schools since family background was the most important predictor of success in schools. Minority students, however, benefit academically by attending schools where the majority of students are white upper-middle class. This advantage is not so much due to additional resources but to a change in the learning milieu of the school.

One explanation is that middle-class white students bring a more positive attitude toward learning to the classroom that rubs off on minority students. Accordingly, minority students work harder and learn more than they might otherwise have, if only to be socially accepted. However, this position incorrectly assumes that black students in integrated classroom settings must have white student role models. In fact, blacks gain from desegregation whether they have white friends or not.

Thus, it is more likely that teacher expectations increase, propelling harder work and higher academic achievement by students. Teachers and administrators in schools where students are mostly upper-middle class tend to maintain high academic standards for all students. Those from schools whose students are mostly lower-class tend to label students as "slow learners." This perpetuates a self-fulfilling prophecy (see Rosenthal & Jacobson, 1968).

Labeling theory may be gainfully applied to the dangers of tracking students based on an initial measure of "cognitive ability." Those students who are labeled "slow" can unintentionally play that role, conforming to teacher expectations. The concentration of children from disadvantaged homes in one school may produce a social transmission of problems that reduces academic achievement and graduation rates.

PARENTAL CHOICE AND PUBLIC VERSUS PRIVATE EDUCATION

Traditionally, private schools have been much more effective in producing high academic performance in their students as well as preparing them for college than their public counterparts, especially with blacks and Latinos. The larger public schools that are not effective in teaching have principals and faculty who are tightly controlled by school boards that do not give them the freedom to impose discipline or require high academic standards. Discipline is a greater problem in public schools where students are more likely to be reported for disciplinary problems and placed on probation than students at private schools. Private school administrators tend to be more intolerant of deviance and have greater authority to stop it from escalating. Consequently, private schools have a climate that is more conducive to learning.

One solution to this unequal educational quality is to give parents the choice between sending their child to a neighborhood public school, a more effective public school not in the neighborhood nor perhaps even in the district, or (given financial assistance) a private school. Transferring students between public schools costs little but may result in greater academic achievement. This position has a great deal of public support. Americans favor parental choice of schools by a two to one margin (Eskey, 1990). Competition between schools for students would force the losing students to be more effective or the school would be closed. This position, thus, uses market dynamics for increasing academic learning.

This approach assumes that parents have the knowledge to decide what schools provide effective learning environments and the responsibility to act in their child's best interest. It is not certain, however, that parents would make their choice based on their perceptions of the school's effectiveness. In one study (Henig, 1990), white parents based their decision on race, not on effectiveness measures such as student–teacher ratio, type of curriculum, or crowding. Parents preferred the school with the smallest proportion ethnic minority—typically the neighborhood school.

Sometimes students and even overzealous parents would favor a school with a stellar reputation in sports. In addition, students could manipulate their parents into sending them to a school best known for partying or dating or sexual activity. Plus even if parents are sincere, there is still no guarantee that their perceptions of school effectiveness are correct.

Nearly half of all Catholic high schools are single gender; approximately 60 percent of Catholic high school students attend single gender schools (Riordan, 1990). Previous studies comparing private and public schools have failed to take this key intervening variable into account in concluding that Catholic schools are more effective than public schools, especially for minority students. A major factor in academic achievement is gender segregation. Students who attend single-gender Catholic schools show the greatest gains between their sophomore and senior years compared to those who attend coed Catholic schools (Riordan, 1990). This difference was greater for females and ethnic minority males (Riordan, 1990).

In two years, females in single-gender schools learned one-third of a grade equivalent more than females in mixed-gender schools as measured by tests in science, math, writing, and civics. In science alone, girls in single-gender schools learned nearly a year more (0.9) (Riordan, 1990). If we consider all four years of high school instruction, we could expect these already impressive gains to double. Females do better because the social climate of the learning environment changes when girls and boys are educated separately: Girls are more likely to conform to traditional feminine roles in coed schools. This includes nonparticipation, obsession with physical appearance, submissive behavior toward male classmates, and low academic performance.

While Catholic schools have fewer disciplinary problems than public schools, single-gender Catholic schools have the least. As expected, boys get into trouble more often than girls. However, boys and girls in single-gender schools get into trouble less often then in coed schools. Perhaps in single-gender schools males and females do not have to simultaneously compete for grades and for dates. With girls absent, teenage boys might have less motivation to show off or act tough to demonstrate their masculinity. While minority males benefit from single-gender schools, whether their white counterparts benefit is less evident.

In summary, the alleged distinction in educational effectiveness between private and public schools is spurious. The issue has less to do with school resources or administrative autonomy than with the gender composition of the school.

ACADEMIC EFFECTS OF GENDER SEGREGATION

Historically, only boys received a formal education in the United States. After state governments began supporting mass education, boys and girls were taught in a "common school." Today, single-gender schools are only available in the private sector, usually for religious reasons.

Yet coeducation does not necessarily mean "equal" education. In 1832, Oberlin became the first college to admit women. Nevertheless, they were not allowed to speak during assemblies and were required to serve meals, clean rooms, and do laundry not only for themselves but for the male students as well. Moreover, female students at Oberlin were expected to become nurses and teachers, while the males were expected to enter business, law, and medicine.

Today, although no institution of higher learning would try to impose such rigid gender roles on its student body, certain aspects of coeducation discriminate against women. Institutional discrimination is to blame when women who attend school with men learn less and graduate with lower levels of achievement motivation than women who attend school with only other women. Women who attended all women's colleges were 55 percent more likely to appear in *Who's Who among College Students in American Colleges and Universities* than women who attended coeducational colleges (Rice & Hemmings, 1988). There is a similar pattern for female Catholic high school students (Riordan, 1990).

Why do females do better academically in gender-segregated school settings? One potential answer is role models. In all-female schools, many of the teachers, counselors, and administrators are women. This can provide female students with additional sources of aspiration and motivation that coeducational schools typically do not furnish.

In the United States, boys generally score higher than girls in math and the natural sciences. These are disciplines that, historically, have been male dominated. In Thailand however, girls generally score higher than boys in the physical sciences. Perhaps this can be attributed to the fact that in Thailand, most science teachers are female (Riordon, 1990).

Teachers can unintentionally favor male students by validating their comments or calling on them more often than females (Fiske, 1990). Based on these types of discriminatory behaviors by teachers, students can come to the conclusion that females have less to offer to classroom discussion than males. Even academic counselors may unintentionally track women into stereotypical roles.

A second possible explanation is role conflict. At coed schools, girls must not only compete with other girls and boys for grades but they must compete with other girls for popularity and dates. Female students who are among the academic elite of a coeducational school can find themselves near the bottom of the social pecking order of a particular adolescent subculture.

Another type of role conflict involves gender differences in dating norms. Generally, boys and girls of the same age compete for grades in high school and college. However, first-year and sophomore females are much more likely to be dating than their male counterparts since females are more likely to be dating upperclassmen (Riordan, 1990). This puts females at an academic disadvantage. First-year sorority women are the most likely to lose their achievement motivation during the first semester in college.

Although the "Coleman Report" (Coleman et al., 1966) found that family background is an important predictor of academic success, background and academic ability are much better predictors of the academic success and occupational attainment of college males than females. Role conflicts and other disadvantages of coeducational instruction could differentially affect women's academic success and occupational attainment.

Perhaps a decline in single-gender schools can be linked to the unexplained decline in the test scores of college graduates. In 1960, 25 percent of all institutions of higher education in the United States were single gender. By the 1980s, this had declined to 7 percent (Riordan, 1990). If single-gender education produces superior academic attainment, especially for females, then this could partially explain why students from the United States perform so poorly on standardized tests compared to other Western nations. In other Western countries over one-third (34 percent) of all schools are single gender. In the United States, only 7 percent of all secondary schools are single gender.

If we compare the math scores of eighth grade students across the globe, students from the United States are ranked near the bottom. Students from The Netherlands and Belgium rank near the top. They are also nations where the majority of schools are single gender (73 percent and 59 percent, respectively). Swedish students performed even more poorly than U.S. students on this test; Sweden has no single-gender schools. In conclusion, both national and international data provide evidence that single-gender schooling needs to be considered in any future attempts at educational reform.

SOCIAL EFFECTS OF SCHOOL-GENDER COMPOSITION

Gender segregation in schools has economic and social consequences as well as academic ones. Educating boys and girls separately is more expensive than educating them together. This is especially true in rural areas since population density is low. Some argue that coeducation settings guarantee equal educational opportunity and equal funding for boys and girls. Others argue that boys and girls should be educated together for social reasons—a "natural setting." It follows that gender integration reduces gender prejudice and stereotypical thinking, just as in the case of racial integration. Coeducation also prepares males and females for marriage and working in mixed-gender work environments. Yet there is no difference in the levels of self-esteem and marital happiness between females who graduated from all women's colleges and those who graduated from coeducational institutions (Riordan, 1990).

When females do drop out, it is usually in the first or second year and it is usually for social reasons (pregnancy, marriage, or family exigencies). This is the period where gender differences in dating are at their greatest. Males drop out of college somewhat later, but their reason is often boredom.

Given the feminization of poverty in the United States and given that single-gender schooling is especially beneficial to females, the continuation of coeducation may unintentionally contribute to the cycle of poverty. Since mothers play a vital role in the socialization of children, increasing their level of education also increases the level of education of their children.

HOMESCHOOLING

Some parents refuse to send their children to school, preferring to educate them at home. There are two reasons for this. First, parents sometimes want to give their children a religious education that the public schools cannot provide. However, parents could always enroll their children in religious education programs after regular school or on weekends. Or parents can instruct their children in religious matters and still send them to public schools.

Second, many parents want to buffer their children from the debilitating aspects of adolescent subculture at school. However, to be effective at this, parents would have to shield their children from other adolescents all the time, not just by removing them from public school. Homeschooling is not widely practiced because it requires having a parent with a high level of competence and the time to instruct their children. Another problem with homeschooling is that the ability of parents to instruct their children tends to decline as their children progress to junior and senior high school.

Adolescent subculture also has a positive impact on students. Belonging to an adolescent subculture involves the student's conscious choice to establish his/her own identity. In other words, this separation from parents and connection to peers (usually through school) is highly important for identity formation independent of parents.

PROBLEMS WITH MEASURES OF ACHIEVEMENT: STANDARDIZED TEST SCORES

Test scores are based on answers to multiple-choice questions that are standardized—they indicate how well you did compared to others taking the test. These scores are used as an indicator of student achievement and school effectiveness. However, other measures are also available, including essay exams and high school grades. The latter are better at predicting a student's chances of success in college than are standardized achievement tests.

High school grades are better predictors of success in college than standardized achievement tests because the latter measure one's abilities only on one day—the day the student takes the test. Anyone can have a bad day and, consequently, do poorly on a standardized test. High school grades, however, measure one's ability to perform on various types of tests, homework, reports, and so on for an entire term. This would also include organizational skills such as note taking and the motivation to attend class on a regular basis.

Standardized exams are advantageous because they allow national comparisons. In the United States, the administration of essay exams is not efficacious because of high costs and the problems of grading such as inter-rater reliability and grader bias. Yet Japan does this and the Japanese dominate national comparisons on standardized tests. Additionally, comparisons of high school grades are not always valid or reliable since they are not based on the same curriculum, course content, and grading standards (Koretz, 1987).

Multiple-choice tests often contain cultural bias. The meaning of standardized test questions may not be the same for various subcultures (e.g., black, Latino, and Native American) (Farley, 1988). Nevertheless, cultural bias is minimized when scores are used to evaluate how members of particular subcultures perform over time.

GOAL OF EDUCATION

"To get ahead in society, all you need is an education." This well-known statement is a myth. Education is necessary, but not always enough for getting ahead. Though upward mobility does occur, most people either remain in or do not move very far from the social class of their parents. Success depends significantly on one's social class origins; the formal education of one's parent or parents; and one's race, ethnicity, and gender (Anderson & Taylor, 2002).

There has been quite a bit of dispute, in recent times, about the objectives and consequences, often unforeseen, of education. Campus shootings and other violence have added a sense of urgency to resolving a wide array of problems at schools. On the one hand, the goal of education is to stimulate a passion for investigation and promote problem solving, critical thinking, creativity, and self-reliance. Accordingly, education institutions should create environments where the interests and talents are developed and channeled into productive occupations. In short, the purpose of education is personal development. Success, however, varies by individual; there are no universal norms for evaluating success.

On the other hand, the goal of education is socialization—the process of preparing individuals to become members of society. Schools teach children how to behave and interact in small groups. Thus, schools should train students to function effectively in the real world (Tepperman & Blain, 1999). This would include familiarizing students with stock answers, promoting obedience and orderliness, and teaching skills. Accordingly, the proper outcomes of education are high scores on standardized tests and credentials to those who earn them.

To be sure, schools are not the only institutions that socialize individuals; there are also families, clubs, associations, religions, and the media. Nonetheless, large investments of time, money, and faith are entrusted to schools with the expectation that individuals will receive positive benefits (Lemert, 1999). Schools also have their owns sets of expectations for students. Schools offer instruction, and eventually certification, with the expectation that students behave in ways that authority figures define as "proper and productive." Despite the prevalent images of rebellion and defiance, schools are generally able to force students to comply with rules when necessary. In short, schools teach obedience.

We all know that a great deal of misconduct occurs in schools, none of which has anything to do with the noble goals of formal instruction and critical thinking. But if schools are able to teach students how to successfully prepare for their integration into social life, society, as a whole, benefits through greater stability and proficiency. In the process, individuals could enjoy the benefits of knowing the social rules that could inform their activities and, possibly, reduce the potential anxiety of social isolation. It has become increasingly clear that these two notions of education diverge and are possibly incompatible. They represent two different conceptions of human nature. Moreover, they guide us to different strategies for attaining goals.

Critical theorists claim education functions to reinforce basic inequalities in society rather than to provide students with the tools to change their situation. Inequalities in low-grade test scores due to family background are highly correlated with inequalities in test scores in high school. Students from higher social class backgrounds generally do better on the SAT than those from lower-class backgrounds.

Critics complain that schools in lower-class communities emphasize obedience and discipline, while schools in middle- and upper-class communities stress achievement. Of course, upper-middle-class parents can avoid public education entirely by sending their children to private schools. Consequently, the way schools are organized and funded in the United States tends to perpetuate social and economic inequality.

TRACKING, LABELING, AND TEACHER EXPECTATIONS

Lamar Simmons is a bright eleven-year-old black boy. He is growing up with both his parents in Boston. His dad works fifty hours per week trying to make ends meet, but the family is still poor. Lamar's family showers him with considerable love, encouragement, and respect. Yet Lamar feels like he is a failure, labeling himself "worthless." The psychologist who worked with him for three years indicates conclusively that Lamar's self-doubt can be linked directly to his school, not his family or friends. In Lamar's case, the feeling of worthlessness was significantly created by the system of *tracking*, the ranking, or stratifying, of students within the educational system.

In his own words:

> The only thing that matters in my life is school, and there they think I am dumb and always will be. I'm starting to thing [*sic*] they are right. . . . Every word those teachers tell me, even the ones I like most, I can hear in their voice that what they're really saying is, "All right you dumb kids. I'll make it as easy as I can, and if you don't get it then, then you'll never get it." Upper tracks? Man, when you think I see those kids? I never see them. . . . If I ever walked into one of their rooms, they'd throw me out before the teacher ever came in. They'd say I'd only be holding them back from their learning. (in Persell, 1990:82)

This type of illustration is not rare. Lamar's story raises the issue of tracking. Should children be grouped by ability, permitting them to learn at their most comfortable pace, or should they be grouped simply by age? The latter could slow the progress of fast learners and be too fast for slow learners.

Does the tracking of unequally talented children reduce inequality, providing them with quality education, or does it perpetuate social inequality? Is segregating the so-called better students from the worst ones the best way to educate our youth? On the one hand, proponents of tracking maintain that when students are carefully selected for classes each receives instruction at the level that he or she needs. Opponents of tracking, conversely, argue that grouping by ability perpetuates inequality by disadvantaging a majority of students, especially those from poor and/or ethnic minority groups, by the provision of different materials and by labeling students according to their instructional group.

Teachers, administrators, and even students themselves label both high- and low-track students. Once a student is put into a particular track and is thereby labeled, the label tends to stick, irrespective of its accuracy. Once a student is labeled, others react according to the label, not the individual. Students labeled "slow" and "low ability" receive negative reactions and low expectations for academic achievement. Conversely, students labeled "gifted" and "high ability" receive encouragement and support.

Even when a student is promoted from a lower track to a higher one (because of a high test score), the stigma of the lower track still carries forward. Teachers, other students, and even the student may view her/himself in light of the previously established low-track identity.

Who gets put in which track? Students are not assigned to groups entirely on academic ability. Students with the same test scores often get put into different tracks because of their social class and ethnic background, albeit not necessarily deliberately (Anderson & Taylor, 2002). Given identical test scores, higher social class students consistently get assigned to higher tracks than lower-class students. Asians and whites are more likely to be assigned to higher tracks than their Latino, black, and Native American counterparts who score just as high as they do on cognitive measures.

Let us examine both sides of the issue. First, I will assume the position that tracking is good for everyone involved. Tracking, rather than perpetuating inequality, actually reduces it by providing students with instruction that is designed for their particular abilities, hence, allowing them to attain their maximum potential.

One of the greatest criticisms of tracking has been that it is highly correlated with social class and ethnic background. This can be avoided with a standardized curriculum and provided remedial education to level the playing field. Eventually, even with a standardized curriculum, students develop differences in interest, skill, and ability. It makes sense then that they should have access to a system that will allow them to develop their individual talents to the fullest extent possible (Tepperman & Blain, 1999).

Through academic testing, we know that children are not the same when it comes to ability and performance. If all children have the same curriculum and the same teacher, learning will suffer. In such classes, bright children become bored with the slow pace of instruction and progress of the class. Thus, quick learners may become alienated from their studies, classmates, and teachers.

Slower learners are more likely to fall behind, often irretrievably, in a mixed-ability setting. Discouragement and alienation is likely to occur for them as well. Average learners may receive less attention from teachers who are spending time with children requiring special attention, or with troublemakers, who are bored or discouraged. Without tracking, instruction is tenuous at best.

With tracking, instructors provide students with materials that are best suited for keeping their interests. Bright students do better in ability-segregated classes than in mixed-ability classes, controlling for intelligence (Tepperman & Blain, 1999). The tracking debate is not new. In fact, publications on the pros and cons of tracking have been around since at least 1931 (Slavin, 1990). Advantages include:

- Tracking allows students to progress commensurate with their ability.
- It makes possible an adaptation of pedagogy to group needs.
- It reduces failures.
- It helps to retain student interest and incentive because bright students are not bored with a slower pace required for slower learners.
- Slower learners participate more when not competing with brighter students.
- It makes teaching easier and less problematic.
- It permits more individualized attention in small slower groups.

Some instructors feel that teaching a classroom of mixed-ability students is an ordeal that should be avoided at all costs. Bright children from all ethnic backgrounds and social classes deserve to be pushed with materials that will broaden their horizons and extend their aptitude. This generally cannot occur in mixed-ability classrooms. In conclusion, tracking will actively reduce inequality not perpetuate it.

Now we will consider the opposite position: Tracking does, in fact, perpetuate inequality. Disadvantages include:

- Slow learners need the presence of brighter students to stimulate them and encourage them. Jean Piaget's ([1932] 1965) cognitive-developmental framework for children and Lawrence Kohlberg's (1969) model of moral reasoning as well as feminist frameworks (e.g., Gilligan, 1982) that are sensitive to gender and cultural differences have been well documented. What propels individuals to progress developmentally through these cognitive stages is exposure to ideas slightly above their own capacity. When this occurs, the individual is able to perceive a conflict between their own thinking and that of a slightly higher level. This conflict produces an imbalance or disequilibrium in the individual's thinking. One accommodates to the higher level to regain cognitive harmony and progress developmentally through the stages. Without this type of stimulus, fixation at a lower stage is likely to occur.

- A stigma is attached to low sections or classes, operating to discourage children. Teacher expectations affect how much students learn (independent of cognitive ability). In a classic study (Rosenthal & Jacobson, 1968), elementary teachers were told that some of their students were gifted while others were slow. Actually, both groups were of the same cognitive ability and assignments were random. At the end of the school year, all students had shown some improvement. However, students who had been labeled "gifted" improved more than their negatively labeled counterparts. Replications of this study have established the reliability of the findings.

Negative teacher expectations convert into poor student performance. Merely applying a label has the effect of justifying it (Cardenas, 1996; Darley & Fazio, 1980). This is known as the "self-fulfilling prophecy." If a student is labeled "slow," she/he performs poorly. The process occurs in steps. First, a teacher is told that a student is "slow." This label may come from administrators or from the scoring key of a standardized test. The label then affects the teacher's perception of the student. A student labeled "slow" may be discouraged, neglected, or emotionally abused. The student then responds to largely negative teacher verbal or nonverbal behavioral cues.

Generally, a student who is expected to perform poorly does, in fact, perform poorly. And one who is consistently discouraged from excelling does not excel. Thus, the original prophecy is fulfilled: The teacher observes the behavior of the student, notes a decrease in performance, and concludes that the label "slow" is deserving since the "slow" students perform poorly on standardized indices. Further discouragement and punishment follow. Teachers unaware of the total effect will not realize that the label itself produces "slow" learners.

These research findings have had a major impact on educational policy and the practice of tracking (Anderson & Taylor, 2002). Although tracking propels "gifted" students, it also hurts ones labeled "slow." Teachers expect less of lower-track students, lowering their standards and offering no encouragement. Ongoing research corroborates that teacher expectancies affect how teachers treat their students (Anderson & Taylor, 2002). When teachers have high expectations of students, they engage them more frequently, encourage and compliment them more often, and call on them for ideas and information more often.

Latino, black, and Native American students, as well as lower social class students of all ethnic backgrounds, are more likely than white middle- to upper-class students to be tracked. Such research (Rendon & Hope, 1996; Cardenas, 1996; Hallinan, 1994; Gamoran, 1972, 1993) has spawned educational reform, specifically a thrust toward detracking.

At the national level, the dropout rate for tenth through twelfth grade Latinos is more than double that of their non-Latino counterparts, even blacks (U.S. Department of Education, 1994, see fig. 1). Why? Lower parental education, poverty, placement in disadvantaged schools, higher proportion of foreign-born students, limited English proficiency, and increasing ethnic isolation. Since even second-generation Mexican American students have relatively high dropout rates, the media's exclusive attention on immigration status and language is misleading.

American students, in general, score below their grade level in math. This is a serious problem because computer use requires students and workers to use more sophisticated types of knowledge. There is a stereotype that minorities cannot perform as well as others on standardized tests.

Teacher competency is a key issue. There are still problems after higher pay, broader competency testing, and tougher certification standards. There are often teacher shortages in large school districts (e.g., the Dallas Independent School District, 1999–2000 academic year).

Programs such as Head Start can help to improve education. They are designed for poor preschool children, focusing on self-esteem, social skills, and basic lessons to get them ready for school. There is also a program called Even Start where illiterate parents actually go to school with their child to take their own classes. To effectively address the problems of minority education, social services should be brought into the schools (e.g., health care and family counseling).

There is a popular misconception that multicultural curricula in education are harmful rather than helpful. There is mixed evidence on whether young black males do best in racially and gender-segregated classrooms. All-male schools in Baltimore seem to be working, while Detroit has abandoned plans for all-male schools (Keisha Vandekot KRLD-All News 1080AM). Milwaukee has had similar problems.

PUBLIC EDUCATION IN TEXAS

In 1998, the state of Texas issued a glowing report of its record in public education. But the report is misleading because it focuses on overall improvement at the expense of a widening gap between white and minority students. Minority gains are only marginal. If we look closely, the report tells us that there is a serious problem with public education. Texas is not providing ethnic minorities equal educational opportunities. Yet it is not surprising; traditional patterns show that white students score significantly higher than minorities. Among minorities, Mexican Americans and Native Americans score the lowest and have the highest dropout rates.

The report sends an urgent signal to reform education policy. Texas schools are not meeting the academic needs of minority students. There are three factors that prevent Texas public education from providing equal opportunity for all students: educational costs, testing and tracking policies, and curriculum content.

There are social factors and cultural elements within the traditional community that may act as barriers to educational achievement. Yet not all potential cultural barriers should be eliminated. For example, a cooperative orientation in Mexican American students is well documented. This is more suitable to decision making in multicultural or international settings than the individualistic, competitive modes that characterize the traditional model. The negative psychological effects of poor schooling on Mexican American students are devastating.

FAMILY BACKGROUND AND ACADEMIC DEVELOPMENT

The "Coleman Report" (Coleman et al., 1966) was an extensive investigation of the factors of educational attainment in the United States. Mandated by the Civil Rights Act of 1964, one of its goals was to determine if ethnic minorities (blacks, Latinos, and Native Americans) were being given equal educational opportunity. The Civil Rights movement revealed the underfunding of minority schools and blamed underfunding for the low educational achievement of minority groups. The "Coleman Report" found that school quality and race of the student had little effect on academic achievement. Instead, family background prior to schooling and its effect on the student's self-concept and motivation to learn were the key determinants for academic success.

Family background affects later achievement in three ways: finance capital (family income), human capital (parents' education and educational aspirations for their children), and social capital (intact versus single-parent family) (Coleman, 1988). Finance capital is important because parents with high incomes are better able to send their children to school well nourished, sufficiently clothed, and reasonably healthy. Children who come to school malnourished and hungry, on the other hand, are more likely to be fatigued, irritable, sick, and miss twice as much school as other children (Fersh, 1991).

Concerning social capital, children raised by one parent are more likely to drop out of high school than those raised with both parents present. Moreover, dropouts are likely to have a large number of siblings. It follows that smaller, intact families are better able to care for, protect, discipline, and academically encourage their children. Conceptualize parents as teachers and their children as their students. Students will learn more if there are two teachers present, as the teacher–student ratio is lower. Moreover, children who have lived through marital conflict and divorce are more likely to experience academic problems. Boys tend to express aggressiveness and have disciplinary problems; girls tend to withdraw and become depressed (Brody, 1991).

Children from smaller, intact families with parents who expect them to attend college are much more likely to graduate from high school than children from larger, one-parent families whose mother, or father, does not expect them to attend college. High-income families are less likely to live in houses and communities that expose their children to environmental hazards such as lead-based paint and lead-based water pipes. High levels of lead in the body have been found to cause a sixfold increase in reading difficulties and a sevenfold increase in school dropout rates. Low-income families and those that live in the Northeast are at the greatest risk of lead pollution. Minority families, especially blacks and Puerto Ricans, heavily populate the Northeast (Associated Press, 1990; Koretz, 1987). In short, children in large, poor, one-parent families with little parental encouragement are severely disadvantaged academically. Educational intervention in disadvantaged families includes federal programs such as Head Start.

Students whose parents are highly educated are better able to compensate for inferior schooling than are the parents of disadvantaged students. In other words, the effects of school funding on educational achievement vary by race and social class. For whites, school effects accounted for only 7.4 percent of the variation in test scores, while the comparable effect for poorer minority students (blacks, Latinos, and Native Americans) were two to three times as great (Riordan, 1990).

Children from advantaged homes have access to the Internet, cable television, encyclopedias, dictionaries, maps, museums, and other facilities that can be used to enhance or stimulate academic development. It follows that children who come from homes lacking such facilities are disadvantaged unless such items are available at school. In short, not only are schools inequitably funded, but those students who would benefit most from equal funding (i.e., poor ethnic and racial minorities) do not receive it.

Approximately 45 percent of school funding in the United States is attained through local tax revenues. This means that residential segregation of the affluent from the relatively disadvantaged is a key factor of the disparity in how much money is spent on schooling each child. Even though disadvantaged communities may have higher property tax rates, they still are not able to raise as much money to support education and other public services. For example, in Texas, the most affluent one hundred communities spend 2.4 times more money per student than do the most disadvantaged communities. In Illinois, the wealthiest community spent six times as much on education per student than the poorest one (Carroll, 1990). In Alabama, the comparable ratio is fifteen to one (Staed, 1990).

In the United States, individual states have a great deal of control in establishing per pupil funding levels, educational standards, and curriculum requirements. In other countries, however, education is centralized and national standards are set. In Japan, for example, the federal government not only establishes the curriculum but attempts to correct funding disparities between schools. A poor community may receive 40 percent of its education budget from the national government, while a wealthier community receives only 15 percent of its budget for schooling from the government.

This difference explains why per pupil expenditures are much more egalitarian in Japan than in the United States (Vogel, 1979). Japan does a good job of ensuring that funding for poor communities is comparable to that of affluent communities. It is not surprising then that Japanese students do better in school than their U.S. counterparts.

Tax equalization efforts have been tried in a few states such as Texas, California, New Jersey, and Kentucky. Such reforms place greater responsibility for equitable funding for education at the state level. Though these efforts may reduce disparities in public educational funding, there are still potential problems of inequity. Because communities are stratified by wealth, there is opportunity to fund local public schools through means other than local property taxes, resulting in the persistence of unequal schooling. For example, some communities have established private foundations to provide money for teacher aides or the latest in computer hardware and software (Carroll, 1990). In Omaha, billionaire investor Warren Buffet announced he was sending his children to a publicly funded school; he did not mention that he paid for a new swimming pool for the school's campus. In addition to school funding reform efforts, two-thirds of U.S. residents favor a uniform national curriculum (Eskey, 1991).

INTERVENTION AND ACADEMIC ACHIEVEMENT

Head Start began in 1965 as part of the War on Poverty efforts by the federal government. In addition to increasing academic potential of disadvantaged preschool children, Head Start aims to improve their social skills, "to bring about . . . social competence [and] everyday effectiveness in dealing with both present environment and later responsibilities in school and life" (McKey et al., 1985: 2). The program provides needy children with access to health and dental care as well as meals that furnish up to half of the nutrients recommended for their age. In short, children in the program come to school better fed, with fewer health problems, and with fewer cavities.

These programs produce immediate academic gains in children, albeit short-lived ones. This is because other low-income children tend to catch up to them in about two years. Improvements in self-esteem, achievement motivation, and social behavior are also found among preschool children in such programs; these differences also tend to disappear after several years. In addition to these short-term gains, there are also long-term benefits: the children are less likely to fail a grade; be placed in a special education track; and are less likely to become delinquent, drop out of school, or be unemployed.

INTERVENTION AND SOCIAL RELATIONSHIPS

Ostensibly, it does not make much sense that advances in academic achievement from intervention programs can be apparently short-lived and yet increase rates of high school graduation and employment (long-term issues). Perhaps academic success alone does not guarantee that a student will stay in school. A significant factor is the social relationships that students develop that bond them to each other and to the school. Students are less likely to drop out if they have made friends with other students or have acquired a close connection with a faculty member or adviser. In conclusion, students not only have varying needs for achievement but needs for meaningful connection with others as well. Thus, intervention programs accomplish a social as well as an academic need for preschool children who participate.

Intervention programs share information and resources with local school systems. Moreover, parents of children in intervention programs often participate in their children's schooling as teacher aides or cafeteria help. Hence, one indirect consequence of such programs is to stimulate the social bonding of parents to both the child and the school. The values that are responsible for keeping these children in school may be exactly what prospective employers seek in their workers, resulting in higher rates of employment. Although intervention programs have proven track records, they are seriously underfunded.

EDUCATIONAL ACHIEVEMENT AND YEAR-ROUND SCHOOLING

In 1851, at the time of the industrial exhibition at the Crystal Palace in London, Great Britain was the dominant world power. The United States was number two in industry but was closing in fast. Muskets, reapers, and tools manufactured in the United States marveled the British businessmen at the show. U.S. manufacturing was based on the first true mass production. A delegation of worried British industrialists set sail for the United States to investigate. They found that U.S. prowess in the global economy was based on an educated workforce. The Yankees had an astonishingly high literacy rate of 90 percent among its population (excluding slaves); in contrast, just two-thirds of the people in Britain were literate.

By the 1980s, the United States was the dominant world power, and Japan was number two but catching up fast. By 1988, Japan's functional literacy rate was better than 95 percent. In the United States it was down to about 80 percent (Nussbaum, 1988: 100–101). Examining relative performance on standardized math tests, students from the United States are near the bottom, while students from Japan are at the top.

Students in the United States attend school fewer days per year compared to the other major industrialized nations: Japan, Germany, Great Britain, Canada, France, and Italy. In Japan, for example, high school students spend eight hours per day for 240 days per year. In Great Britain and Canada, students attend school 196 days per year. U.S. students spend only six hours per day in class for 180 days per year. It seems rather obvious that increasing quality class time should increase educational attainment. In fact, most U.S. residents favor extending the school year by six weeks (Eskey, 1991).

There are good reasons to do this. The gap in academic achievement between children from advantaged and disadvantaged homes widens when school is not in session (during summer). Children from advantaged backgrounds either learned more during the summer or retained what they had learned in school than their disadvantaged counterparts. Perhaps the amount of time spent in school has less of an effect on the educational attainment of advantaged children than on disadvantaged children.

Even high school dropouts from advantaged backgrounds learn more than their disadvantaged counterparts. These findings are consistent with the "Coleman Report" (Coleman et al., 1966) which found that the effects of schooling on academic achievement are greater for disadvantaged students. What this means is that advantaged children are more likely than their disadvantaged counterparts to participate in activities that promote cognitive development (e.g., educational games, travel, reading) even when they are not in school.

As mentioned above, Japan has more equitable funding between advantaged and disadvantaged communities. They also have near year-round schooling. If one considers their overall high academic attainment, it is clear that Japan has been very successful in educating its lower classes. In the United States, the lion's share of educational funding goes to the upper classes, those who least need it or least benefit from it. This misallocation of financial resources is perhaps part of the reason why the median U.S. student is below average in global educational comparisons.

SUMMARY AND CONCLUSION

The "Coleman Report" (Coleman et al., 1966) indicated that family background is an important factor in the academic achievement of students, much more important than school facilities. Yet school facilities are more important to the educational attainment of the lower classes than they are to the middle and upper classes. Unfortunately, those who least need these school resources have the most. Cultural lag explains the problem of lengthening the school year that would increase educational achievement.

Labeling theory explains why the proportion of disadvantaged students in schools is related to overall academic achievement. Functional theory to show that schools have become not only places to learn (manifest function) but places where male and female students form relationships and date (latent functions). Value conflicts have been generated over issues such as ethnic and gender segregation, sex education, pregnancy counseling, and mainstreaming. Critical theory argues that education functions to reinforce basic inequalities in society rather than to provide students with the tools to change their situation.

Schools must meet high performance standards or lose federal funding. We cannot afford to allow our schools to continuously fail our students. Upon graduation, students should be prepared for work, further technical training, or a university education. Many of our high school students fall between the cracks. Those who do not attend college have little technical training to fall back on. Those who are tracked for college often have such poor academic skills that they require remedial education to begin basic introductory college classes in mathematics and English.

Our schools must provide equal opportunity for all students to guarantee an excellent education. They should be funded by a fair formula that does not reward wealthy property holders with more elaborate schools and resources, while penalizing poorer property holders. Now school-funding formulas are set at the local level; this, of course, results in highly unequal allocations per pupil. Schools, even neighborhood ones, often have significantly different amounts of resources such as computers, books, films, videos, athletic facilities, electives such as art or music, class sizes, and teacher salaries, simply because of the variation in the collection of property taxes. It is no wonder then that dropout rates and the need for remedial education are more pervasive in poorer schools.

Applying distributive justice, we should improve educational quality for the poor and minorities. Rather than trying to improve self-esteem, educators should instead compensate for the negative consequences of poverty. Positive changes include courses on multicultural history and teacher education programs that "unlearn" the stereotypical responses of Anglo educators. White teachers sometimes hold negative attitudes toward minority children. We know that teachers' expectations can affect student achievement.

Empowerment is also necessary. This means giving ethnic minority communities greater decision making and responsibility in the education of their children. Parents should encourage their children to have a positive attitude about school.

Financial problems continue to hurt educational quality, particularly those of minorities. But educational quality goes beyond financial matters.

The point is that public schools have a lot of independence in nonfinancial matters that have enormous significance for minorities: the content of academic programs, methods of instruction, procedures of grading and testing, and the hiring of teachers and staff. These are all factors that can be gainfully applied to increase academic achievement in students.

WHAT YOU CAN DO

- Contact a high school in your community. Find out whether students are tracked. If so, learn how it operates. Does the social class of students affect the type of courses they are required to study or choose to study?
- Does your college or university use race or ethnicity as a criterion in its admissions policies? Contact staff members at your admissions office. What are the admission policies concerning affirmative action? What is the philosophy or reasoning behind admission procedures? What is the difference between affirmative action and equal opportunity? Does your college or university have a "legacy" policy that favors applicants with parents who are alumni? Survey students on whether their parents are alumni.
- What are examples of gender differences at your college or university? What are examples of gender differences in your high school experience? How have gender stereotypes been displayed or otherwise communicated? Are there any other hidden curricula that you can identify in your educational experience?

THREE

WELFARE, POVERTY, AND THE LEGITIMIZATION OF SOCIAL INEQUALITY

We tried to provide more for the poor and produced more poor instead. We tried to remove the barriers to escape from poverty, and inadvertently built a trap.

—Charles Murray, *Losing Ground*

IN 1964, THE SOCIAL security administration developed a poverty index, creating a dichotomy for placing people above or below an official and ever-changing "poverty line." This index includes only money income and is equivalent to the level, set by the U.S. Department of Agriculture, necessary to purchase basic food and consumer goods. Using this formula, 32 million people—11.8 percent of the population—are poor (U.S. Census Bureau, 2000c). This represents a decrease from more than 38 million people, approximately 14.5 percent of the population who resided in poverty in 1994 (Daly, 1996). The average poor family receives approximately $6,700 less than the poverty line in annual income. This difference is referred to as the "poverty gap."

The poverty level for a family of four in 1999 was $17,029 (U.S. Census Bureau, 2000c). But can a family actually live on poverty-line income? Critics argue that the poverty line underestimates what a family actually needs to live on. Realistically, it would take an income at least 25 percent higher to provide a family with basic economic security (McQuiston, 1991; Schwarz, 1992). This forces us to confront the myth that welfare has gradually improved as we move into the new millennium. Nevertheless, keeping the poverty line low has political appeal, because it makes the social problem of poverty seem less important than it actually is.

Social-policy debate over poverty seems to be politically or ideologically driven. In an era of rugged individualism and laissez-faire capitalism, who is deserving of help in the form of public assistance? Some favor massive government intervention and a lot of money to reduce poverty. Others label the poor "undeserving" and attribute social problems to an "underclass of . . . poor people who chronically live off mainstream society (directly through welfare or indirectly through crime) without participating in it" (Murray, 1984: 5).

Popular ideology reflects this belief and rejects increased spending on social programs. Efforts to cut poverty are sometimes resented by those who consider the poor undeserving. Welfare critics have long argued that program recipients often acquire a learned dependence on financial assistance, thus displaying a *culture of poverty*—"cultural patterns that make poverty a way of life" (Macionis, 2002: 46). Increased funding is unlikely unless it is demonstrably cost effective in the long run, socially useful, and ideologically acceptable.

In explaining poverty, one can either blame the poor person, the social system, or a combination of the two. Blaming the victim stresses the behavior, attributes, deficits, and characteristics of poor people. It tends to confuse cause and effect; it presumes that the lifestyle of those discomfitted by particular social conditions is the cause of those conditions. These types of frameworks inadvertently deflect attention from key structural problems in the economy and social system.

This chapter addresses why some people are poor and/or often on welfare. It is important to note that one cannot understand and effectively attack poverty without understanding its inherent linkages to globalization, immigration, ethnic stratification, and employment opportunities. Global economic changes play a significant role in recent increases in poverty. I examine the structural roots of social inequality and poverty. This chapter builds solidly on existing research and analyses of life-course gradients of poverty. I support alternatives to welfare, such as education, health care, job training, and work incentives that do not stigmatize participants.

GLOBALIZATION, IMMIGRATION, AND POVERTY

> *The second half of the twentieth century may someday be recalled as the time that we became painfully aware of the social and ecological costs of industrialization. . . . We cannot rely on normal market forces nor on people's best intentions to save their environments and themselves. . . . In the 1960s and 1970s . . . the only thinkable solution to common dilemmas was government intervention. [Today] the same problems trigger discussion of another solution: privatization.*
>
> —Bonnie J. McCay and James M. Acheson, *The Question of the Commons*

Effective intervention to poverty includes a balanced approach with public and voluntary sector programs that are sensitive to actual needs, while simultaneously boosting an individual's capacity for self-help (Daly, 1996). In trying to significantly reduce poverty, we must first acknowledge our social reality: shrinking public mandates and fiscal restraint, changing notions of "community," and increasingly unchecked global economic forces.

Capital and global markets have led to free trade, deregulation, and obsessive privatization. The traditional sense of community has become lost. Globalization has meant that multinational firms and financial institutions dominate economically by controlling worldwide networks of production and the flow of labor, goods, services, and information (Castells, 1991: 307–347).

High rates of immigration also affect the economy, unemployment, and poverty. Immigrants are highly concentrated in certain areas and districts: More than 35 percent of New York City's population is foreign-born (Daly, 1996). One in four immigrants live in the city. New York City has the highest concentration of West Indians; along with Los Angeles, it has the highest concentration of Latinos. Along with San Francisco and Los Angeles, New York City has the nation's highest concentration of Asians.

Globalization has led to new kinds of ethnic tensions. Regions have often been divided into smaller, sometimes hostile units. Global conflict has resulted in ethnic cleansing (e.g., Kosovo, Bosnia–Herzegovina, Rwanda). "Economic and social strains inherent in rapid post-communistic social change have sometimes resulted in new surges of minority victimization and fanatical movements" (Cortese, 1999: ix). Ethnic cleansing should be regarded within a global framework; what happens in one region of the world has a true and immediate impact on other regions around the globe (Ahmed, 1997).

Immigrants are arriving in near record numbers in the United States (Portes, 1996). Most of these immigrants are from Mexico, Latin America, South America, Southeast Asia, and western Africa; this type of immigration has been referred to as the "browning of America" (McLemore et al., 2001). The migration of ethnic minorities into new communities greatly affects the economy (especially employment opportunities) and social relations, including kinship and friendship networks and education.

The Los Angeles riots in 1992 broke a delicate social order in which new patterns of international migration exasperated conventional ethnic stratification. The Miami riots in the 1980s are another example of how immigration and racial oppression have ignited ethnic conflict and violence. Occasional outbreaks of racial violence appeared to be oddly disharmonious with the evolution of modern urbanization in the United States.

Even while black workers assisted the transformation of a once lethargic Miami economy into a burgeoning tourist industry, rigid southern segregationist norms still endured. The riots symbolized a prevalent rage in black Miami over its loss to keep up economically, politically, and socially with other ethnic groups. Black Miami is ethnically diverse, including non-Latino native-born African Americans and Caribbean immigrants, especially Cubans and Haitians (Cortese, 1999).

Global cities (e.g., Miami, New York, San Francisco, Toronto, Dallas, and Los Angeles) are spatially stratified. Inner-city neighborhoods are segregated along ethnic, color, and socioeconomic lines. "The enclaves where new arrivals live and work appear on the city's topographical map as pockets of poverty in close proximity to gentrified districts adopted by well-paid professionals" (Daly, 1996: 5–6). *Gentrification* refers to the immigration of middle-class people into a deteriorating or recently renewed city area.

Ethnicity, social class, gender, and race are closely linked to quality of life, particularly in these stratified urban areas. The economic survival of immigrants and ethnic minorities is often dependent on the future success of the city. They also find that their labor may no longer be needed. Many are unable to find jobs except marginal, unprotected, part-time, or temporary service sector positions, and they are locked into inner-city ghettos by market and exclusionary forces (Cross, 1992: 16). Such dynamics create greater cleavages between the haves and the have-nots, escalating chances for intergroup hostility, displacement, and poverty for those left behind by labor market changes. For some, results are even more drastic, homelessness occurs (see chapter 4).

Frustration and indignity by underclass victims of economic restructuring typically is not directed at economic elites who cause their downfall. Instead, other poor, ethnic minority or immigrant groups conveniently serve as scapegoats (e.g., Koreans in the Los Angeles riots). Occupational divisions are obvious—between ethnic groups, new immigrants and citizens, men and women, and legal and illegal immigrants. Ethnic minorities move into particular niches based on their contacts, resources, and job skills.

Many have adjusted by depending on an informal economy that is external to city building codes and land-use regulations, health and safety requirements, minimum-wage laws, and the workers' compensation law. Others are forced to participate in the underground economy, engaging in illegal activities such as prostitution and drug trafficking and sales. Many immigrants and ethnic minorities become replacement labor, taking jobs previously held by whites. Whites returning to the central city have generated other jobs for immigrants. Gentrification results in a market for domestic labor and personal services. These jobs are typically poor paying and often temporary; workers lack health and other benefits and are not protected by labor legislation.

For the poorest of the poor, the benefits of economic growth do not trickle down, heightening income inequality. Despite prosperity for the middle classes and above, nearly one-fourth of the population of global cities live in poverty (Daly, 1996). Poverty crisscrosses ethnicity, gender, age, and race, disproportionately affecting ethnic minorities, single mothers, and children. We have tended to turn our backs on these categories of people.

The conservative nature of the federal government in the 1980s and 1990s responded to global economic changes by deregulating and privatizing public sector activities. Social services, especially, were marked for reduction and contracting out to the private sector. When the federal government opted out of these areas, for-profit private firms filled the void, often paying minimum wages and offering little security to an already marginalized and alienated workforce of ethnic minorities and immigrants, many of whom were women who had young children.

The presence of these groups in urban centers has intensified ethnic polarization and new types of spatial disparity as the upper-middle class isolates itself within gated communities in the suburbs. The areas they leave behind, marked by poverty and a concentration of ethnic minorities, are seen as peripheral, and problems associated only with the inner city, like homelessness, are ignored.

In racially polarized American cities, the abandonment of the collective is indisputable as the middle class leaves the center, choosing instead to move to protected communities on a city's fringe. This exodus may be seen as a social parallel to the political and economic movements of privatization and deregulation. Because they heighten disparities between income groups and are predicated on a reconstruction of Social Darwinism, these processes yield a relatively narrow range of perceived solutions to the issues of poverty.

POVERTY BECOMES A SOCIAL PROBLEM: A HISTORICAL FRAMEWORK

We have hundreds of varieties of breakfast cereal but no help for the hungry.

—Barbara Ehrenreich, "Our Health Care Disgrace"

What we consider social problems today were not always viewed as social problems. Social problems are social in origin. The idea that poverty is a social problem is a relatively recent development in the history of Western societies. What we call poverty today was viewed from fatalistic, religious, or military perspectives. Poverty was not seen as a problem that could be treated. When no possibility of a solution exists, a negative condition is just a fact, not a problem. Poverty only becomes a social problem when there are resources available that could be used to reduce it. A society must become prosperous before it recognizes the problem of poverty.

Religious explanations of poverty focus on God's will or punishment for transgressions. Similarly, "poverty was considered part of the natural social order, and was not necessarily taken as a defect of the social structure" (Secombe, 1999: 26). Driven by Social Darwinism, the competitive struggle to secure one's economic status allowed the "fittest" to win out over the "weakest." Conservatives argued that government should stay out of these matters.

It is important to look at the history of poverty. In medieval times, the poor were entitled to assistance even though poverty was blamed on individual sins or faults rather than on social factors. In the 1500s, following prevalent looting, vagrancy, and crime including dramatic food riots, public opinion and official treatment of the poor changed. Harsh treatment of the poor followed. Beggars and others relying on charity were treated as criminals. For example, in 1532, beggars were arrested in Paris and chained together in the sewers to work. War devastated the French economy; 30 percent of the population were beggars (Henshel, 1990).

In the 1820s and 1830s, there was reform. "Our history of rugged individualism, a spirit of Calvinism, and the idea that hard work will reap results set the backdrop for the development of our social welfare system in this country" (Secombe, 1999: 26). The poor were placed in almshouses. This removed the poor from the community. Since it was believed that the poor were responsible for their own poverty, the goal was "moral treatment": teach the poor discipline, work, and morality, in hope of rehabilitation.

Based on English law, the United States distinguished early on between the "worthy poor" (orphans and the aged and handicapped without family) and the "unworthy poor" (the able-bodied). While the worthy poor deserved help, the unworthy poor were deemed to be undeserving. Those who did not work were considered lazy. There was no awareness or recognition of how social factors affect unemployment.

Welfare emerged from and continues to reflect this dual notion of the poor. While generous toward the worthy poor, public opinion ranged from reluctant to callous disregard for others (Jansson, 1988). Current welfare debates focus on who is deserving and how much should we help.

The treatment of the poor was related to the current economic situation and ideology. The threat of overpopulation adversely influenced the treatment of the poor. The Poor Law provided money for families based on the number of children. Conservatives argued that welfare encouraged the poor to reproduce dramatically. Helping the poor was said to encourage laziness.

Although the government created workhouses to help the poor, they were designed to be as unpleasant as possible to discourage charity. In the modern welfare state, only if the economy is very bad and there are large numbers of vocal persons unemployed does help begin to be satisfactory.

In the late nineteenth and early twentieth centuries, stressful adaptation to industrialization and urbanization produced radical changes in social structure and lifestyle. City slums developed. The working class was exposed to long workdays; filthy and often hazardous work conditions; poor nutrition, health, and housing; and great poverty. This led to unprecedented urban revolts and the rise of a large middle class. How else did the poor cope? Alcohol. Mental illness. Sexual promiscuity. Brutality—even within the family. In short, there were large numbers of people working and living in miserable conditions and small cramped spaces.

David Ricardo's "iron law of wages" (Sraffa, 1951) is based on classical economics. Accordingly, wages of workers could not remain far above the subsistence level. If wages rose higher than bare subsistence, then more workers would live longer, and through their reproductive ages; larger families would result; and because of better conditions, more children would survive. An excessive number of workers (supply) for available jobs (demand) would result in a return to lower wages. Alternately, if wages dropped too low, dropping below the subsistence level, more workers would die before producing children, and fewer children that were born would survive to working age, thereby creating a shortage of workers. This would cause wages to rise. Thus, wages overall would stay at subsistence level.

The twentieth century saw growing humanitarianism, middle-class reformers, and democratic trends (the fall of communism in the former Soviet Union, Eastern Europe, and parts of Africa). Besides problems of survival and physical pain, psychological pain became recognized as a social problem. Modernism ushered in an era of faith in progress, science and technology, democracy, legal equality, and common rationality in humans. Improvement in the life of the common citizen was now possible. Suffering was not inevitable and unavoidable. Social order was criticized by rationality. People no longer viewed social order as dictated by God and thus unchangeable. This represented a more optimistic and active view of humanity. Science could be used for the good of society.

Modernism meant the use of science to treat social problems. Middle-class reformers labeled "negative conditions" as social problems without the victim's perspective. Between 1920 and 1950, American sociology abandoned social problems (except criminology) and gave it to social workers. Sociology viewed social workers as do-gooders without academic objectivity. Conversely, social workers viewed sociologists as pseudoscientists in ivory towers isolated from social reality. Sociologists began to study society scientifically to discover social patterns and laws. In 1952, the Society for the Study of Social Problems was formed, signaling a return to the study of social problems.

AID TO DEPENDENT CHILDREN

Aid to Dependent Children (ADC) emerged to assist women and their children who were viewed as more vulnerable to conditions of poverty than men, and consequently worthy of aid. Mother's Pension, the predecessor of Aid to Families with Dependent Children (AFDC) and ADC, began in the Progressive Era (1896–1914), giving government greater responsibility in the care of poor women with children. White widows were almost the exclusive recipients of financial assistance because there was still a stigma for unwed births and divorced or abandoned women.

Three factors contributed to welfare policy:

- A sharp increase in delinquency among unsupervised children left at home (Abramovitz, 1996a, 1996b; Gordon, 1994; Mink, 1995);
- An increase in children living in orphanages because their mothers could not support them or care for them while they worked;
- Women in the workforce (5.3 million) were viewed as taking jobs away from men.

The public thought that the future of our country, and proper citizenship, depended on proper upbringing of children by mothers. Mother's Pension was created to provide payment for the responsibilities and duties of motherhood, hence giving it legitimacy, and trying to remove the stigma linked to social welfare. Yet low benefits and enforced patriarchal norms about gender roles, women's moral character, and sexuality did nothing to add legitimacy to motherhood and assistance. For example, women were monitored for relationships with men, improper child-rearing techniques, poor housekeeping, indications of alcohol abuse, and possible fraud (Secombe, 1999). Minorities and foreigners were pressured to assimilate and take on white, middle-class values. Policy makers typically viewed immigrants inferior to the native born (Abramovitz, 1996b).

Postmodern welfare is founded on long-standing notions of moral reform and assimilation. AFDC or "Welfare" was created in 1935 as Title IV of the Social Security Act, a critical piece of legislation produced during the New Deal when millions of families were suffering financial hardship (Secombe, 1999). It was "designed to release from the wage-earning role the person whose natural function is to give her children the physical and affectionate guardianship necessary not [only] to keep them from falling into social misfortune, but more affirmatively to make them citizens capable of contributing to society" (Committee on Economic Security, 1985: 5–6).

Welfare legislation, perceived as synonymous with prosperity, good health, and well-being, passed easily in Congress. Welfare was aimed at keeping mothers at home to raise their children. Mothers were not expected to care for their children and work at the same time (Abramovitz, 1996a). Unlike Mother's Pension, which served almost exclusively white widows, ADC served mothers who were abandoned, divorced, never married, or mothers whose husbands were unable to work (Secombe, 1999).

Individual states controlled eligibility and benefit levels. Southern congressmen opposed federal control and would support ADC only if each state were allowed to establish its own eligibility and benefits (Quadagno, 1988,

1994). Not surprisingly, dramatic statewide disparity in the amount of benefits resulted. For example, in 1939, ADC benefits ranged from an average of $2.46 per child per month in Arkansas to $24.53 in the state of New York (U.S. Social Security Board, 1940). Southern states claimed that black families needed less than did white families (Abramovitz, 1996b). This sharp disparity continues to this day. In 1996 a two-person family (usually mother and child) received $96 in Mississippi and $821 in Alaska (U.S. House of Representatives, Committee on Ways and Means, 1996: 439–441, table 8-13).

ADC did not originally include benefits for the mother or the caregiver for the child. It maintained the traditional practices associated with Mother's Pension, dispersing money to demand behavioral standards and cultural norms. There were home visits and occasional eligibility checks. Parenting skills, sexual behavior, and housekeeping were closely monitored. These policies distinguished between worthy and unworthy individuals, intimately preserving the basis of the Mother's Pension program (Secombe, 1999).

Institutional racism was a latent consequence of congressional revisions to ADC in 1939. The transfer of widows to Social Security's Old Age Insurance (OAI) program further stigmatized remaining program benefactors. Never-married, separated, or divorced women were considered undeserving of assistance. Ethnic minority widows, typically, were not eligible for OAI because their husbands did not qualify for Social Security benefits. Consequently, for these widows, ADC was the only option. Later, relatives were allowed to be included with a dependent child as recipients. Although the program increased in size, it did not reach the overwhelming majority of its intended targets. By 1950, only 25 percent of single mothers were on ADC (Secombe, 1999).

MODERNISM AND ATTITUDES ABOUT WELFARE

Postwar modernism was based on a sense of faith in inevitable progress and economic optimism. Consumers demanded major household goods unavailable during the war. Social mobility for some led to the myth that it was available to everyone. Within this social climate grew an attack on ADC. This hypocritical attitude failed to recognize that other, more popular federal programs were also welfare. OAI, the Mental Health Act, the Hill–Burton Hospital Act, the GI Bill, and the Veterans Administration are some of the programs that helped many middle-class citizens (Secombe, 1999).

Child poverty emerged as the greatest social problem in the 1950s, overshadowing concerns for the elderly. This was reflected in federal assistance programs. Poor mothers with children quickly and dramatically increased from one-half to nearly three-quarters of the total public assistance population between 1950 and 1960 (Secombe, 1999). The costs of ADC increased more than 90 percent to more than $1 billion during this period (Axin & Levine, 1975: 235).

Public sentiment about welfare weighed negatively, focusing on rising costs and the moral character of welfare mothers. Administrators adapted punitive policies to remove "unworthy" recipients. Media and politicians claimed that the sharp increase in poverty was due to the immoral behavior of poor women and access to assistance. Media images displayed welfare mothers as "lazy, unmotivated, immoral, and fraudulent, spending money on lavish cars, jewelry, and clothing" (Secombe, 1999: 30). Of course, the issue of race was primary. Taxpayers labeled the disproportionately high number of black and unmarried mothers on welfare as undeserving. Welfare mothers were required to demonstrate that they provided "suitable homes" for their children and that their moral character was high. Caseworkers threatened welfare applicants that negative evaluations might force them to remove children from the home, putting them in foster homes or institutions (Abramovitz, 1996a).

Divorce rates rose to unprecedented levels after World War II. Births outside of marriage tripled for white women and increased, somewhat less, for blacks (Secombe, 1999). Changes in family structure, clearly, were blamed for the "breakdown in family values"—a patriarchal term about the moral fitness of poor women. Single mothers were stigmatized. If they worked outside the home, single mothers were condemned for neglecting and abusing their children, contributing to juvenile delinquency and truancy. Caseworkers once again monitored the gender roles and sexual behavior of single mothers. Just as parolees were subject to surprise visits by their parole officers, welfare mothers were subjected to late-night raids and other demeaning intrusions on their lives. Moral entrepreneurs tried to catch women with overnight guests. Some states penalized women for having a relationship with a man that was not the father of her children (Abramovitz, 1996b).

If we examine poverty historically, we can observe a cycle in attitudes toward the poor and consequent social policy. The cycle includes both progressive treatment and charity versus regression with harsh treatment of the poor. What we consider unemployment today and perceive as a systemic problem of the economy was considered a problem of "idleness." For example, a study of the poor was titled *London Labor and the London Poor, An Encyclopaedia of the Condition and Earnings of Those That Will Work, Those That Cannot Work, and*

Those That Will Not Work (Mayhew, 1967). In short, the poor have often been blamed for their indigent condition.

This cycle of reform versus regression continued into the 1960s. Economic recessions coupled with high unemployment rates increased concern, compassion, and a "rediscovering" of poverty. The shift in the composition of welfare recipients continued; they were increasingly becoming synonymous with single and divorced mothers.

The culture of poverty perspective focuses on subcultural norms, beliefs, and values that allegedly develop among the poor, including an antiwork orientation and dependency focus. In fact, pervasive dependency on welfare is sometimes viewed as a type of slavery. A critical explanation suggests that people are poor because of macroeconomic factors as well as inadequate human capital (e.g., formal education, job skills, and experience in the labor market). Moreover, social services are necessary to compensate for these debilitating conditions.

In the early 1960s, the name of the program changed to Aid to Families with Dependent Children to emphasize an expanded family focus. The 1962 amendments to the Social Security Act increased federal funding for social services. President John F. Kennedy sought to shift welfare to "training for useful work instead of prolonged dependency . . . to maintain family life where it is adequate and to restore it where it is deficient" (cited in Bandler, 1975: 380).

After the assassination of President Kennedy in 1963, President Lyndon B. Johnson continued social programs on poverty. In his War on Poverty, Johnson pushed for a variety of legislation for poor children and adults designed to provide them with the tools, resources, and human capital to hoist themselves out of poverty. The essential supposition of the War on Poverty was that poverty is basically the consequence of poor education, job training, and marketable skills. With an emphasis on job training, policy makers began to expect single mothers to work outside the home. The War on Poverty was partially administered on the local level, a departure from previous policy.

The War on Poverty was relatively unsuccessful. Gains through the Civil Rights movement and affirmative action programs led to white backlash. Public opinion shifted against welfare; the media and politicians labeled the condition "out of control"—a crisis. By the late 1960s and early 1970s many Americans resented and resisted the ever-growing benefits extended to the poor. The number of families on welfare continued to rise due to expanding eligibility (permitting women on AFDC to work, allowing some two-parent families to be eligible for aid, and extending benefits to children between the ages of eighteen and twenty-one who were still in school) (Secombe, 1999).

An increasing number of women, many of them with children, were working out of economic necessity. By 1975, 52 percent of married women with children between the ages of six and seventeen and 37 percent of married women with children under age six were employed outside the home (U.S. Department of Labor, 1994). Working mothers came from all socioeconomic classes, ethnic groups, and age categories. The cultural ideology that a woman's place was in the home (with her children) was no longer dominant. If women are now working, then why are taxpayers paying single mothers to stay home and take care of their children? The worthiness of poor mothers was questioned. Welfare benefits became too attractive to single women, the argument continued.

Benefits increased faster than wages. The full range of AFDC benefits was greater than an entry-level job. Consequently, women chose to go on welfare rather than work in low-wage, dead-end jobs. This increased long-term dependence on welfare, thus, perpetuating poverty. President Richard M. Nixon held these views. The accumulative effect of federal services, the increased costs of welfare, the rising number of caseloads, and welfare fraud resulted in a focus on the motivations of recipients.

President Nixon's plan for intervention was the Family Assistance Plan (FAP). FAP allotted a meager $1,600 per year for unemployed families of four (Secombe, 1999). (This amount was $2,000 below the official poverty line at that time.) The working poor could receive benefits until they made $4,000 annually. Perhaps the most important policy change reflected a growing belief that single mothers should work. Women with children older than age three would be forced to work or placed in job training. Should single mothers with preschool children have to work? Could the economy accommodate the additional workers? FAP stalled in a Senate committee and never became law.

President Ronald Reagan's administration represented mistrust and regression in social welfare programs. Social conservatives (e.g., Mead, 1986; Murray, 1984; Gilder, 1981; Anderson, 1978) attacked welfare and proposed drastic cuts. Instead of ameliorating poverty, they suggested that welfare worsened it, discouraged marriage and working, and encouraged laziness. "Midnight raids" and "man-in-the-house" rules were outlawed. Since welfare payments were similar to minimum wages, the argument continued, women were rewarded for out-of-wedlock childbearing, single parenting, and unemployment. In conclusion, addressing poverty meant cutting costs. AFDC stopped benefits to several hundred thousand families (Secombe, 1999).

President George Bush, Reagan's vice president for eight years, continued these policies during his administration. Conservative wisdom was that hard work and initiative is the best way to eliminate poverty. Traditionalist policy called for government to cut back on welfare. Unfortunately, this perspective does not detect the structural constraints (e.g., changing economic and employment conditions) involved.

By 1996, approximately 14 million persons, the equivalent of 5 million families, received AFDC (Committee on Ways and Means, U.S. House of Representatives, 1996: 471, table 8-27). Republicans and Democrats clashed over welfare reform. Conservatives maintained that welfare only hurts a free economy and undermines the traditional family structure (Abramovitz, 1996b). Poignantly, welfare policy no longer aimed to help the poor improve their economic situation substantially. Instead it attempted to reduce the number of recipients.

In 1992, some states (e.g., Wisconsin and New Jersey) expanded AFDC benefits to married women but restricted benefits to single mothers (Secombe, 1999). Only married women were eligible for full benefits. The idea behind this was to intervene in the transfer of power and authority away from men in traditional family settings to the welfare state (Thomas, 1995). Other states (e.g., New Jersey in 1993 and Arkansas in 1995) capped welfare benefits, denying greater benefits to women who have additional children while on welfare. The idea that women have babies in order to get more money is extremely dubious. In fact, increments are meager, ranging from $24 to $147 per child (Secombe, 1999).

President William J. Clinton tried to prevent long-term dependence on welfare and focus on job training. Moreover, he felt health insurance should be accessible to support lower wage earners. Skyrocketing health-care costs contribute to welfare dependency. In 1996 (an election year), President Clinton signed a Republican-led welfare reform bill into law.

Public Law 104-193 (Temporary Assistance to Needy Families, or TANF) replaced AFDC. The changes now gave individual states the authority to determine eligibility, sought to transform welfare recipients to wage-earning workers, temporarily provided health care and child care, and enforced child support payments by absent parents. But nutritional assistance for working families with children was gashed and benefits for legal immigrants were disallowed.

The 1996 law required recipients to transfer their child support rights to the state and cooperate in establishing paternity in cases where this was an issue. Child support by fathers would be ordered and enforced. No one could receive more than five years of benefits (Secombe, 1999). Those who were physically able to work were required to after two years. The federal government required three-fourths of all two-parent families to either have jobs or train for one. But one-half of the states were unable to obtain such lofty goals (Deparle, 1997). If it is that difficult to find thirty-five hours of work between two adults, it must be that much harder for single mothers.

In 1997 welfare was reformed. Provisos included:

1. An increase of $3 billion over a two-year period to help states pay for employment training for persons who lacked marketable skills or other types of significant employment barriers.
2. Victims of family violence may be exempt from TANF work and time limit provisions. Moreover, the General Accounting Office emphasized studies on domestic violence.
3. Social Security Income benefits were restored to disabled elderly (legal residents).
4. Eligibility requirements for food stamps was loosened for adults ages 1–50 who are not caring for minor children.
5. Twenty billion dollars were set aside for health insurance for uninsured children. (Center for Law and Social Policy, 1997)

LABELING THE POOR "UNDESERVING": THE LEGITIMIZATION OF SOCIAL INEQUALITY

I'll always be poor. After all, I come from a broken family and I'm a fourth-generation welfare mother.

—A 35-year-old single welfare mother

Following the lead of Jürgen Habermas (as discussed in chapter 1), I am interested in rules for raising and redeeming "validity claims" about the poor and poverty in ordinary language. Consequently, the philosophy of language can be used to ground the claims about the "deserving" and "undeserving" poor. By deconstructing the language we use to discuss the poor and to frame social policy, we necessarily expose the hidden values so often based on blind tradition.

Language is political; it determines how we construct our reality and has direct implications for social justice. Language and beliefs shape our views of others and our behavior toward them. Language has become a method of legitimating social inequality and perpetuating poverty. Through labeling, we construct a social phenomenon, such as poverty, the words we use to define and describe it, as well as stereotypes of the people to whom it refers. Media images, sound bites, vilifying rhetoric, and assumptions behind welfare policy convey the dichotomy between the affluent and the poor as well as mainstream culture's messages of good, authority, influence, and power.

The functionalist paradigm proposes that poverty is inevitable. Since the poor are without a collective voice and are not organized, agents whose interest may be self-serving represent them. While disastrously deleterious on its victims, poverty, nevertheless, is functional for creating and maintaining economic, political, and social advantages and growth for a sizable majority of the population. Current opinions on poverty reflect our views about human nature, about the importance of hard work and our dislike of idleness, and our expectations of appropriate roles for men and women in society (Trattner, 1989). This, essentially, legitimizes social inequality.

Contrary to popular opinion, welfare recipients do not live extravagantly and are not typically irresponsible. This hostile attitude assumes that the poor do not deserve help. In fact, historically, we have labeled people "deserving" or "undeserving" of help. Labeling is important because it compartmentalizes people, often in negative ways. Once degraded individuals are labeled "underclass," they are viewed as hopeless and undeserving of assistance. Policy recommendations based on social justice recognize and compensate for large-scale economic forces that create and maintain the structural conditions in which poverty occurs.

WHO ARE THE POOR?

Poor people are often undercounted; nearly all industrialized countries exclude homeless and institutionalized populations (Daly, 1996). The U.S. Census Bureau first tried to count homeless people in the 1980s (Sarlo, 1992: 154). But even aggregate statistics gloss over inequalities between groups. Since public resources are finite, it is important to direct funding to where it is most needed. To examine rates of poverty over time, it is fruitful to look at income distribution for particular groups.

Poverty is correlated with changes in family structure (e.g., divorce, single women having children). In 1960, most poor families contained both men and women. By 2000, 53 percent of all poor families were female-headed

(U.S. Census Bureau, 2000c). This has been referred to as the "feminization of poverty." One-half of all children in the United States will live with a single parent at some point before reaching the age of eighteen (Macionis, 2002; Ellwood, 1988: 45–46). The increase in female-headed households is related to increasing rates of divorce, separation, and single parenting. These smaller households result in a large number of little, poorer households competing for a restricted number of affordable homes.

Poverty in the United States is strongly connected to racial, social, and spatial factors, being inexorably concentrated among blacks, Latinos, and Native Americans, among single parents, and in large areas of the city where poverty is the norm (Logan et al., 1992). One-third of all black children grow up in poverty (U.S. Census Bureau, 2000c). The rate of child poverty is high in households headed by nonelderly parents, especially those headed by women—54.8 percent (Ross et al., 1994: 111; Forster, 1994). These high rates of poverty remain even after women have received welfare payments.

Poor women who are single parents tend to be quite young, have much less formal education than their counterparts without children, and have more young children than do nonpoor single mothers (Daly, 1996). The number of single mothers with children below the poverty line more than doubled between 1970 and 1986 (Daly, 1996). Thirty-six percent of all single mothers live in poverty (U.S. Census Bureau, 2000c).

Labor force participation rates for women are high. The proportion of mothers with children under the age of six who were in the labor force rose from 20 percent in 1960 to over 50 percent in the mid-1980s (Daly, 1996). Women earn only 73 percent of what men earn (U.S. Census Bureau, 2000c).

Women in poverty are confronted with the possibilities of alienation and homelessness. In 2000, approximately one out of every three families with children under eighteen years of age had just one parent in the household, a 100 percent increase since 1970 (Macionis, 2002). Eighty percent of all single-parent families are headed by females. Their income is less than half of the national average. A single mother in a minimum-wage job earns 20 percent less than what is defined as poverty-level income for a family of three.

A mother on welfare receives benefits that average approximately 55 percent of the poverty level. Over half of the nation's low-income single mothers have housing problems in terms of crowding, affordability, and/or physical inadequacy. Female homeowners, many of them elderly, are twice as likely as other homeowners to have affordability problems. This feminization of poverty results from the failure to equalize women's employment opportunities and responsibilities in the family (Golden, 1992). High poverty rates for female-headed households are linked to low incomes, high unemployment, and barriers to job entry or advancement.

Twenty-five percent of the U.S. population are children; yet they account for 40 percent of those who reside below the poverty line (Daly, 1996). One out of eight children undergoes substantial food shortages. By 1992, 20 percent of all U.S. children lived in poverty (Daly, 1996). In 1999, the rate was 16.9 percent or 12.1 million children (Macionis, 2002). Out of the 18.5 million children who reside in America's central cities, nearly 30 percent live below the poverty line.

One child in eight has no health insurance (Daly, 1996). Only one in five has adequate day care. One in seven will drop out of school. One in six lives in a family in which no one has a job. Only 16 percent of those eligible for Head Start (a federal program that provides schooling and breakfast for poor children) in the mid-1980s were enrolled in the program (Edelman, 1987: 29–31).

Because of broad political and ideological support, much of the funds for housing and social programs in the United States are targeted for the elderly. The success of such welfare programs clearly shows that poverty can be significantly reduced by social intervention. Because of deliberate attempts to reach the elderly, their incidence of poverty has substantially dropped over the previous three decades.

Many families have members who work full time, yet they are still poor. Extremely low wages, particularly in the service sector, meager benefits, involuntary part-time employment, seasonal employment, underemployment, and recurrent unemployment often result in poverty for working households. A large ratio of the working poor is female-headed households. Half of the heads of households in poverty in the United States worked in 1986; over one-quarter of them worked full time throughout the entire year (Ellwood, 1994). These are "the poorest of the poor [who] play by the rules but lose the game" (Ellwood, 1994: 147–148).

Many are too proud to accept handouts from the government even though they are eligible. Even these low-paying jobs are vanishing and real wages are slipping. The working poor represent an enormous category of people who are not on welfare but could be tipped over the edge by structural and economic forces beyond their control (Bane & Ellwood, 1994).

Technological advances have led to replacing workers with machines or robots, creating greater unemployment, underemployment, and involuntary part-time employment. Although such technological advances have led to some high-paying high-tech jobs, most are menial positions, with low wages and scarce benefits. People are often required to work from their homes where they have no face-to-face contact with coworkers. This saves the employer a large portion of overhead costs. Since many of these workers are on contract, they are not, technically, employees and, therefore, do not receive any benefits or job security.

Several examples follow:

- A person who worked at home telephoning to find replacement teachers when regular instructors are ill, now is employed only three hours a day feeding information to the voice-activated computer that replaced her.
- Order-takers for fast food chains work from their homes, earning low pay, working part-time and split shifts to accommodate the peak demand periods. Most workers are not unionized and earn money only on a piecework basis; some are required to rent the computers, which must be used for order taking. Other firms are now accepting orders on the Internet, thus eliminating the need for order-takers altogether.
- Technicians at the telephone company, who once diagnosed and repaired equipment malfunctions, have been replaced by a central computer system that they helped to program. The computer operation only requires a few, low-paid clerical employees. (Gooderham, 1995)

The most important variables in the unequal distribution of income in industrialized countries are ethnic background and gender. Blacks are three times more likely than whites to be poor (Macionis, 2002; Daly, 1996). They have a lower life expectancy than other ethnic groups, are almost twice as likely to die in infancy, will receive less education, are six times as likely to be murdered, and are four times as likely to be imprisoned. They also earn less than other Americans do.

One-third of all black youngsters (U.S. Census Bureau, 2000c) and 37 percent of Latino children (Daly, 1996) grow up in poverty. Elderly blacks are over three times more likely to be poor than their white counterparts, Latinos two and one-half times (Ropers, 1991: 45–48). Native Americans have high rates of poverty, unemployment, and disease and illness, including alcoholism and drug abuse. Nearly 26 percent of them reside in poverty (U.S. Census Bureau, 2000c).

Aggregate rates of poverty are misleading. For example, while the incidence of poverty in Boston is not unusually high, the rates for particular groups are substantially above average. If Latino poverty is combined with those of single parents, the rates reveal that eight out of ten Latino single parents are poor and nearly 75 percent of Latino children are growing up poor

(Boston Foundation, 1989). In Boston women are three times more likely than men to be poor. Only 6 percent of singles are poor, but 41 percent of single mothers resides below the poverty line.

It is a misconception that all poor people are on welfare. In Boston, 37 percent have never received assistance. Moreover, one-third have not received welfare in the past five years. Fewer than one-third have received welfare continuously for the past five years. Forty-four percent of the poor do not receive food stamps, welfare, or general relief. One-half do not receive public housing or rent subsidies. Those who do not receive financial assistance pay an astonishingly high (60 percent) of their total income for rent.

Of those on welfare, 20 percent work, and two out of every three would like to work if they could acquire jobs. Those who do not work are ill, have sick relatives or small children whom they care for, or speak little or no English. At least 25 percent do not have any health coverage. The poor are four times as likely as the nonpoor to have health problems or disabilities. Twenty percent of all poor men are permanently disabled.

Another myth is that the poor are highly dependent on public institutions and community organizations. In reality, 75 percent are not aware of any such organizations that could help them. Most do not know what types of groups are available to assist children in trouble. The overwhelming majority (90 percent) of Latinos in public housing is not familiar with any community agency or group.

THE UPWARDLY MOBILE AND THE DOWNTRODDEN

As people become more upwardly mobile, primarily through education, there is a concomitant exodus of housing and employment from the inner cities to the suburbs. Although these processes tend to leave the central cities in financial straps, as I have mentioned, there is a strong reluctance to support, or even tolerate, government intervention through social welfare programs. In 1960, one out of three Americans lived in the suburbs (Daly, 1996). By 1970, most of the urban population lived in suburban communities (Macionis, 2002). By the end of the 1990s, a majority of the entire population lived in the suburbs (Peterson, 1999). Suburbanites represent a majority in six of the ten most populous states (California, Florida, Michigan, New Jersey, Ohio, and Pennsylvania) and are a majority in fourteen states (U.S. Census Bureau, 1990).

Nineteen of the twenty-five fastest growing cities in the United States are actually suburbs. Moreover, 40 percent of the 435 congressional districts are primarily suburban (U.S. Census Bureau, 1990). Suburbanites are typically white middle-class homeowners; they tend to be well educated, independent, and moderate on social and civil rights issues. They have little, if any, interest in chiefly urban problems such as poverty. They are fiscally conservative and favor cuts in social welfare programs, with the possible exceptions of Social Security and Medicare. For suburbanites, gated communities, sometimes with their own private security guards and surveillance systems, are now the residential trend. There are now more of these types of private guards than publicly employed police officers in the United States (Daly, 1996).

Among the industrialized nations of the world, the United States has:

- one of the highest per capita poverty rates;
- the most children living in poverty;
- the greatest gap between the rich and the poor;
- the largest infant mortality rate (due to disproportionately high rates for blacks, Latinos, and Native Americans);
- one of the highest rates of adult illiteracy (approximately 20 percent);
- and the highest per capita prison population.

The United States ranks second to last among major industrialized nations in the rate of income tax (Daly, 1996).

Only one out of eight federal benefit dollars reaches Americans in poverty. More than 40 percent of the poor do not receive public housing, welfare, school lunches, Medicaid, or food stamps (Daly, 1996). Nearly 43 million Americans (approximately 15 percent of the population) have no medical coverage (Macionis, 2002). At least another 40 million have such insufficient coverage that serious illness or disease could translate into financial ruin. For many, physical or mental incapacity or old age results in poverty. Unlike other First World nations, the United States does not have paid maternity leave for working mothers nor does it provide medical care and financial assistance to pregnant women.

In recent decades, income inequality in the United States has steadily increased. The gap between the haves and the have-nots is widening. Between 1980 and 1999, the annual income of the highest paid 20 percent of U.S. families soared by 48 percent (Macionis, 2002). The economy is expanding and globalizing; yet this matched with substantial increases in poverty. The wealthiest 20 percent of U.S. families earn almost as much as the remaining

80 percent of families combined; the wealthiest 5 percent of U.S. families own 60 percent of all privately held property (U.S. Census Bureau, 2000b).

Poverty has become more enduring in the United States (as well as around the globe) since the mid-1970s. The prospects for climbing out of poverty diminished in the 1980s (Adams et al., 1988). The concentration of the poor in the nation's fifty largest cities increased by 50 percent (from 16 to 24 percent) from 1970 to 1984 (Bane & Jargowsky, 1988).

The greatest problems regarding poverty affect the underclass, "poor people who live in areas with high concentrations of poverty and few opportunities to improve their lives" (Macionis, 2002: 39). Blacks are five times more likely than whites to live in neighborhoods where at least 40 percent of the people reside in poverty. Since 1970 there has been a significant concentration of minorities in urban areas, increases in unemployment and poverty, and increases of female-headed households (U.S. Department of Housing and Urban Development, 1995: 5).

POWER, JUSTICE, AND POVERTY

Mainstream discourse about poverty, whether liberal or conservative, largely stays silent about politics, power, and equality. But poverty, after all . . . results from styles of dominance, the way power is exercised, and the politics of distribution.

—Katz, *The Undeserving Poor*

A civil society is based on a conception of community. To be sure, we have individual rights and freedoms. But we also have a social responsibility to ensure the welfare of others. We must make sure that societal resources are distributed so that all people have enough to live a minimally acceptable standard. Distributive justice entails the equitable allocation of resources among members of society. This necessitates the decentralization of administrative decisions about funding social programs. There should be strong teamwork between local governments and voluntary sectors in social intervention. Nonprofit organizations with a minimum of bureaucratic structure and an understanding of local problems are particularly valuable.

Our history highlights how poverty has tenaciously harried our society. Since our cultural values include "justice for all" and "compassion for others," the concepts "distributive justice" and "social responsibility" are relevant. Distributive justice requires us to ensure that societal resources (e.g., quality education and health care, good jobs, equal protection under the law, affordable housing, child-care facilities, and so forth) are distributed fairly among individuals and categories of people (e.g., ethnic minorities, the elderly, women). In the 1950s, when American industrial cities were at their peak, most adults in inner-city communities were working and supporting their families. By the 1990s, however, two-thirds of these men and women had no jobs (Wilson, 1996). Social responsibility requires us to care for those not able to care for themselves. But to what extent do we have such a responsibility?

Poverty is essentially a work problem, not a welfare problem. Current policies that reduce families on welfare may create favor for politicians but do little to eliminate poverty. In fact, they may increase the number of families at risk. Welfare must be morally motivated and constructed, not politically motivated. We should use secure employment opportunities to base welfare reform. Instead of blaming welfare programs for social problems, we should be blaming the insecurity linked to low-paying jobs.

INEQUALITY AND URBAN POVERTY

My wife and I both work full time. . . . We have three children at home. In winter time the children are in school so we don't have a large amount of child care expense—around $100 per month. . . . In the summer we are just paying over $500 a month childcare (that's with a reduced fee to the YMCA). If we ever lose momentum, we're in trouble. Just a simple set of circumstances could make us homeless. We are treading water all the time . . . there's little room for a breather.

—Terry McClintic, Portland, Oregon

By examining concentrated urban poverty in the United States (e.g., the McClintic family), I hope to contribute to public discourse on ways to defeat indigence. Looking at the geographic spread of the nation's ghettos, we see how economic shifts have devastated particular regions, particularly in the Rust Belt states of the Midwest. Widespread urban trends demonstrate changes in the labor and housing markets that have fostered income inequality and segregated the rich from the poor.

When we consider employment sources for inner-city dwellers, it is evident that poor educational opportunities and family structure further limits their life chances. Poor neighborhoods have trapped members of poor minorities, who account for nearly four out of five ghetto residents. I hope to increase public understanding of the growth of urban poverty and confront basic issues about how the urban decay in our country's cities can be inverted.

It is important to understand what it is like to be poor and live on welfare. In a time of great debate over welfare, we hear from politicians and policy "experts," but rarely from the voices of the poor, especially single women with children. We should understand the stigma of poverty, low-wage jobs, and "welfare moms." Beneath the data and concepts are real live human beings trying to make sense of their lives and environment. I use a hermeneutic perspective that stresses the primacy of subjective meaning and its importance and connection to the larger social structure.

Reforms have been based on a patriarchal understanding of women and their roles within the family and the paid labor market. In postmodern society, traditional gender roles have been challenged. Poor women, for example, are expected to work outside the home besides raising their children. Our laws, social policy, and culture value their cheap labor often at the expense of care for their children.

We demand that poor women settle for the growing number of minimum-wage service sector jobs that offer no benefits, such as health insurance or subsidized child care, and ignore the fact that employment of this type does nothing to lift women and their children from poverty. The insecurity of these jobs encourages poor women to have on-again off-again rounds with welfare. Our society is frustrated with these repeat spells of welfare use, and therefore has imposed strict time limits and work requirements.

The real problem with welfare, however, has little to do with lazy women, or the structure of the welfare system. Instead, the real problem is that the structure of low-wage work is so tenuous and insecure that it cannot support a family in any decent manner. The "welfare problem" is best conceptualized as a "work problem." Until we improve the structure and conditions of low-wage work, poverty will never be reduced or ameliorated, and welfare will continue to be a necessary fact of life for millions of poor families.

CONCLUSION

To understand the nature and complexity of poverty it is necessary to examine the political economy of the corporate sector and government and the nature of decisions made regarding resource redistribution. There are linkages between poverty, unemployment, welfare policy, and global economic changes. In many cases the poor are not served well by federal policy decisions that tend to benefit the affluent, media savvy, vocal, and political heavyweights.

In the United States, the rate of poverty declined in the 1960s but rose in the late 1970s, continuing in the 1980s because of cuts in social programs. Shifting public policy diminished the staying power of the poorest families. The highest income group received at least nine times as much of the "national income pie" as their counterparts in the lowest 20 percent of income earners. The average after-tax incomes of families in all income groups except for the top 20 percent fell in the late 1980s and early 1990s.

From 1980 the number of poor households grew in the United States. The rate of poverty increased for specific groups: female-headed households, ethnic minorities, inner-city residents, younger workers, and disabled persons. These indicators reflect substantial differences in social policy, reflected in government welfare to the poor. As a result of globalization and technological change, economic and social boundaries became more avowed, actual wages for the working poor diminished, and the gap between housing rent and income widened.

Welfare policy reflects the belief that poverty could be eliminated if poor people are taught the moral values of work (Handler & Hasenfeld, 1991). The most consistent notion is to strengthen the work ethic. Only those who cannot work are considered deserving of help. Consequently, welfare was designed to be less desirable than lowest-wage work (Katz, 1986). Critics (Gilder, 1981; Mead, 1986; Murray, 1984, 1988), however, argue that now welfare has become more desirable than low-wage work.

Our attitude toward single mothers illustrates this concern. Critics caution that welfare enables mothers to raise children without the help of father or a job. Welfare policy questions whether single mothers are worthy of assistance. Should they be required to work? Should we provide welfare to single mothers, enabling them to stay home and care for their children? Does welfare undermine their motivation to work, encourage immorality, and destroy their desire to marry, and therefore continue their poverty?

The primary beneficiaries of welfare are children. These children generally live with their mothers, who alone are trying to take care of their children's physical, emotional, and spiritual needs. Pushing single mothers and their children off of government assistance and forcing them to accept low-wage and insecure jobs will not eliminate poverty. Welfare states have produced new forms of relative deprivation rather than social solidarity.

POLICY RECOMMENDATIONS

In the late 1980s and early 1990s, global economic changes led to high levels of poverty, rising unemployment (especially among particular groups), and to a prevalent dearth of decent affordable housing. Consequently, intervention to poverty must address these important issues. Poverty problems vary from region to region, from city to city, and from neighborhood to neighborhood. Thus, locally constructed, grassroots community programs are most appropriate.

Special attention should be given to the working poor because they are at risk and because the provision of work incentives will harvest long-term rewards. Work has actual as well as symbolic importance, especially for individuals who reside below the poverty line. I propose:

- raising the minimum wage high enough to provide an incentive to get off welfare;
- providing adequate medical coverage;
- providing credits to partially offset the cost of day care;
- instituting refundable tax credits to raise the level of take-home pay;
- increasing the value of earned-income credits.

Job creation could vary from using inner-city residents to improve the substructure in their neighborhoods to practical training for service and technical jobs. Nevertheless, not everyone will be able to obtain employment in the new world order. Mothers with young children should not be forced to work; rather, they should be encouraged to care for their children (Jencks, 1994; Secombe, 1999).

Welfare policy should reflect the relationship between shifting family situations and the risks of being poor. If we are to significantly lessen poverty, there must be both short- and long-term changes. We must invest in the human capital potential among members of society, including remedial education for those members of our population who currently possess limited education and job skills. Germany and Japan have moved toward the creation of a skillful underclass (Wilson, 1996).

Second, we must work toward creating secure and full employment for all persons who want jobs. There are a growing number of voices (Wilson, 1996; Kaus, 1992, Regan, 1994; Danziger & Gottschalk, 1995) calling for government public works jobs to rebuild society's crumbling infrastructure. The working poor and welfare recipients would be eligible. Their work would service financially weak cities and counties. These jobs would provide economic stability within the family; medical, dental, and retirement benefits; Earned

Income Tax Credit; perhaps a transportation allowance; and a child-care program with a flexible emergency family leave policy. I add the last requirement to address the special needs of single mothers.

It is important to note that these types of policies target the working poor as well as those on welfare. They need to be federally funded for two reasons: It is inadequate resources at the local level that exacerbate the problems; and to ensure that new jobs are created and not just the redistribution of resources in existing positions. Newly created jobs should not be segregated by gender.

Historically these jobs have ranged from after-school child care to construction—rebuilding roads and bridges. Traditionally, those occupations with high concentrations of male workers are paid higher than occupations with higher concentrations of female workers. While all positions should be available to anyone who seeks them regardless of gender, history suggests that we must take affirmative action to ensure that both men and women are paid fairly.

If these job programs were open to everyone, the welfare stigma could be eliminated. Wages should be above minimum wage; otherwise, they will not attract capable candidates. Despite its cost, the investment in our decaying infrastructure and ineffective social services would significantly contribute to the betterment of society and enhance economic development. If we do not take such steps, I predict higher crime and poverty rates and greater problems in the quality and accessibility of health care.

A massive investment in our society's substructure and social services would significantly contribute to the betterment of our society, and would ultimately enhance future economic growth (Secombe, 1999). Thus, it is in our best interest to distribute all of society's resources equitably—to reduce the tragic plight of poor children; violent and property crime; unnecessary deaths from treatable diseases; and racial, ethnic, and gender inequality.

Demographic trends display the ever-growing numbers of single mothers. Accordingly, intervention must account for their special needs. Sometimes part-time jobs are most efficacious. Moreover, the enforcement of child support payments by absent parents would help financial matters for TANF recipients.

WHAT YOU CAN DO

A single mother lives in a small, low-income apartment with her two young children (ages one and five). The father has deserted the family; no one knows where to find him. The mother dropped out of high school because of her first pregnancy. She has no employable skills or work experience.

- Complete a family profile based on what you already know.
- Contact the social services office that administers financial help to poor people in your city. Find out this family's eligibility for assistance. Find out what kind of help is available (e.g., child care, medical coverage, rent subsidies, TANF). How much will they receive? What is required to qualify and continue to receive this assistance?
- Create a budget for monthly expenses and figure out how this family is going to survive. Estimate as accurately as possible. Include rent, medical expenses, medicine, food, clothing, utilities, school supplies for the older child, and other needed expenditures.
- Realistically analyze this family's hopes for getting out of poverty. What can the mother do to help herself and her children have a better quality of life? Consider education and employment for the mother. Include child-care costs, tuition, and other related educational expenses. Does employment have any effect on her eligibility for welfare? If her benefits were eliminated, how much money would she need to earn to merely survive? How much money would she need to earn to improve her family's living conditions and social position?
- Is welfare in your city intended to help families like this escape poverty? Why or why not? What are the social characteristics (e.g., gender, race, and ethnicity) of those who qualify for welfare? How are applicants screened? Why is welfare so controversial? How is poverty a result of society's arrangements rather than merely a statement about individual differences?

FOUR

SIDEWALK STORIES: THE FORGOTTEN HOMELESS PEOPLE

If Society Can Provide Housing for a Man Like this [Charles Manson], Can't We Do More for the Homeless?

—Protest poster pointing to a glaring inconsistency in public policy: Why we take better care of convicted mass murderers like Charles Manson than the homeless.

IF YOU TAKE THE TIME or have the courage to look into the faces of homeless people, you will see single mothers and battered women, children and youth, the mentally ill, military veterans, people with disabilities, the elderly, refugees and new immigrant ethnic minorities, and even people who are employed full time but simply cannot afford the exorbitant cost of housing in some areas. Some people are chronically homeless; others are only recently homeless. Still many other people are on the verge of being homeless, yet they are not eligible for assistance. It is socially and economically advantageous to prevent a family or an individual from becoming homeless than to attempt to intervene after becoming homeless.

It is estimated that approximately 500,000 people are homeless in the United States on any given night; approximately 1.3 million people are homeless at some point during a year (Kozol, 1988; Wright, 1989; Wickham,

2000). Homelessness is clearly an urban problem. Homeless people are heterogeneous, ranging from full-time workers who cannot afford the excessive cost of housing to individuals and households who simply require temporary financial assistance to those in need of longer-term care. Most are somewhere in between, requiring several types of help, counseling, and occupational and organizational training. They can eventually become independent and take charge of their own lives.

Ronald Reagan won the presidential election in 1980. The Republican platform was based on undoing the social welfare policies of his democratic predecessors: Jimmy Carter, Lyndon Johnson, and John Kennedy. President Reagan was dogged in his attempts to reduce government spending, deregulate the economy, cut inflation, and lower taxes. The tax breaks, however, seemed to benefit only the affluent. Reagan slowed inflation by raising interest rates as the nation began a major economic recession. He started a deluge of deregulation plans and cut funding for social programs, stopping assistance to eligible recipients. In short, the administration petitioned for the largest ever cuts in social service programs, including federally assisted housing.

Homelessness emerged during the 1980s as a disturbing social problem and difficult social policy dilemma. During that decade, the federal government spent billions of dollars to house and treat the homeless (Maciones, 2002). During the 1990s, however, public sentiment regarding the homeless ranged from apathy to hostility. Social programs that served the homeless were eliminated or drastically cut. Law enforcement became intolerant of the homeless. Three dozen U.S. cities began enforcing anti-vagrancy laws to ticket the homeless for sleeping in doorways, begging for money, carrying open containers of alcohol, and other deviant behavior (Maciones, 2002). Additionally, many local police departments conduct nightly "sweeps" to get the homeless off the streets and out of public view.

The federal government does not play a strong role in social policy aimed at the homeless. There is limited funding through state and local agencies that may attack the web of problems or ignore them. Local governments concentrate on emergency shelters, assisting people only after they become homeless. Some cities confront homelessness only when it is required by the courts.

Nonprofit organizations operate shelters, missions, and food banks. Some are now developing or renovating housing. A few have been successful with self-help initiatives. The major players who work the most with homeless populations are city governments, philanthropic organizations, and ethnic groups. Innovative programs include transitional homes for women and health outreach programs.

The major causes of homelessness include poverty, unemployment, deinstitutionalization, and economic dislocation. Other reasons include cutbacks in social programs, a severe shortage of affordable housing, and the failure of emergency shelters and food banks. International migration has also negatively affected the U.S. economy in terms of resource allocation and employment.

OVERVIEW

Wait till the sidewalk shivers the beggars
Wrapped in their blankets they try to hang on
Light from the street lamp seems to shine bitter
After the autumn has been here and gone.

—Steve Forbert, "Wait"

There is much debate about the characteristics of the homeless, the causes of their condition, their capacity for restorative action, and the types of intervention that might be effective in reducing homelessness. What are the physical, social, and psychological implications of being homeless? To provide a constructive solution to the problems of homelessness, problem solving should be expanded to include those who are at immediate risk of losing their shelter. Like many social problems, if homelessness is to be effectively dealt with, it is better to confront it before it happens—rank and file intervention and self-help programs aimed at helping people before they lose their homes. Prevention is less costly both in financial and human terms than in intervention or treatment. Nevertheless, since so many people are already homeless, social policy must address the ever-increasing problem.

People who sleep in doorways or live under bridges or in cardboard boxes are a sign of our public policy's failure to adequately respond to the needs of people without homes. Unlike much of the literature on homelessness that covers the "pathology" of street life or the demographic characteristics of homeless persons (see Bachrach, 1983; Watson & Austerberry, 1986; Burt & Cohen, 1989; Niner, 1989; Greve & Currie, 1990; Golden, 1992; Liebow, 1993), this chapter examines the institutional and social policy contexts of homelessness.

There is a close relationship between poverty, homelessness, and the political redistribution of societal resources. This chapter also describes the human experience of homelessness, including health and health-care delivery, deinstitutionalization, and the perilous nature of living on the streets and in emergency shelters. This is to present people who are homeless in humanist rather than statistical terms.

The present analysis also includes:

- responses to homelessness and the nature of innovative programs constructed by voluntary, public, and self-help organizations;
- cleavages between public policy and practice;
- the effectiveness of public policies;
- the relationship between the federal government and local governments.

LANGUAGE AND CONTEXT

The actuality of homelessness depends on how people define it. Symbolic interactionism and labeling theory require that we take the nuanced view of the homeless, social workers, and social policy makers to understand the range of beliefs and attitiudes about homelessness. It is important to look at how society conceptualizes and responds to the homeless.

Homeless people are resigned to the margins of society and the perimeters of public consciousness because by ceasing to conform, they break social norms and insult public sensibilities. The public disassociates themselves from them, usually to avoid feeling contempt, guilt, shame, conflict, or resentment. In this way, society avoids collective responsibility. Even the term: *homeless* (instead of *homeless people* or *people without homes*) helps us disassociate ourselves from them. In the public eye, homeless people lack individuality, even humanity. A sense of social welfare, civility, and community is lost. These notions of the homeless expose our ideologies and personal beliefs and values.

It is important to examine the nature of the institutional and bureaucratic context of homelessness where social policy is formed and the arenas in which political and power dynamics play themselves out. The context determines what is newsworthy and what is not. It sets what gets discussed in the public arena as well as what gets kept out of the agenda.

The correlation between language and action is especially substantial in analyzing homelessness. Any framework is based on ideology, or a system of ideas shared across a society, culture, or subculture. Ideologies construct our worldview and justify existing social arrangements. Such ideas, taken from each culture's popular ideology, are captured in language and, taken as acquired wisdom, become implicit in social policy (Livingston, 1994: 177).

If we look at public housing policy, it is clear how ideology shapes public discussion and resulting decisions and collective action. By constructing and controlling the agenda, politicians, lobbyists, and interest groups frame the discourse and determine the rate and direction of social change. Consider how the federal government and activist organizations define homelessness. Public agencies of the U.S. government use a narrow definition.

"The fragmented nature of the American federal system, division of powers, and multiplicity of agencies all work to the detriment of a broad definition of the public good and have undermined welfare reform initiatives" (Daly, 1996: 248). Homeless social policy is narrowly interpreted and vulnerable to reduction. Makeshift reforms for homelessness are probable candidates for retrenchment (Slessarev, 1988: 377).

Cultural ideology defines the behavior and survival techniques of the homeless as bizarre, illogical, random, ill conceived, paradoxical, or impetuous. Yet value-laden judgment of this type reveals the biases and ignorance of the dominant culture. This cultural baggage fails to understand the sorts of adaptation that homeless people are sometimes forced to take. Even though their survival strategies may be logical within the context of homelessness, the behavior of homeless people still falls outside mainstream social norms.

"The environment of homeless people, then, while apparently characterized by disorder and chaos, has an order of its own" (Daly, 1996: 11). For people who live a comfortable lifestyle, the behavior of homeless people may appear schizophrenic. Although homeless people are forced to spend much of their time trying to meet their basic needs, for example, some of their behavior appears to be quite self-destructive. Still such apparently disparate activities could somehow link together to form a coherent pattern.

SOCIAL DEATH AND INVISIBILITY

This Bench has been Removed in Order to Deny the Poor and Homeless a Place to Sit.

—Faux plaque attached to bricks where park benches
were removed from a Seattle public park

The term *social death* is sometimes used to emphasize the disenfranchisement and social isolation that homeless people experience. Alienation, powerlessness, and invisibility also characterize their lives. The homeless are victimized by being treated as outcasts (Lifton, 1992). It is important to understand the perspectives of homeless people and realize their desire to shape their futures. Homeless people have sometimes demonstrated their empowerment by manipulating mass media and politicians to bring attention to their plight, contending for space in urban areas, and successfully brandishing political power.

There is a stigma attached to being homeless. Homeless people are often labeled "dysfunctional," "lazy," "immoral," or "psychotic." In essence, the homeless are blamed for their condition. It follows, then, that if homelessness is their fault, society is not obligated to help them. The causes of homelessness, however, are largely complex, economic, social, and powerful. Homelessness results from the recent increase in low-paying jobs and sparse affordable housing (Ratnesar, 1999).

Perspectives that blame the victim will point to alcoholism, drug abuse, and other forms of social deviance. After all, 40 percent of all homeless people abuse alcohol and 25 percent have some other drug problem (U.S. Department of Housing and Urban Development [HUD], 1999). Clearly, a person who abuses themselves with drugs or alcohol is only making matters worse. Still we must recognize the link between poverty and homelessness that pushes people over the edge. Moreover, the connection between homelessness and mental illness or clinical depression is also significant. Forty percent of all homeless people have mental health problems (HUD, 1999). Depression often leads to self-hatred and self-doubt.

Women are more successful than men at avoiding homelessness and succumbing to drugs or alcohol despite greater social disadvantages. Half of homeless men and 20 percent of homeless women have a serious problem with alcohol (Baum & Burnes, 1993). Women drink less than men for social, emotional, and physiological reasons. Women are physiologically less tolerant of alcohol than men; typically, women begin drinking at a later age than men. There is also a great social stigma for women drinkers than men.

Because of gender role socialization, women are more likely than men to be caregivers and have more emotional attachments to children, family, or friends. This means that women have greater access to housing than men and are less likely to be homeless. Males are socialized to be independent, women interdependent. Women often remain in abusive relationships with men because they lack other options.

PROBLEMS WITH RESEARCHING THE HOMELESS

Despite the visibility of homelessness, extensive media coverage, intensive advocacy efforts, widespread voluntarism, government programs, and our familiarity as a people with this recurrent social problem, homelessness persists and an industry has grown up around it. How do you explain all this expenditure of energy with virtually no social transformation and none on the horizon?

—Benedict Giamo and Jeffrey Grunberg, *Beyond Homelessness*

Homelessness affects a wide range of social categories, cutting across ethnic, racial, gender, and class divisions. Single mothers, minorities, and the poorest of the poor are disproportionately homeless. Researchers who study homeless people have their own sets of stereotypes and preconceptions. The relationship between the researcher and the homeless is affected by sharp power and status differences. Researching the homeless may also be very intrusive. All these dynamics may contribute toward miscommunication and misunderstanding between the researcher and the homeless, making scientific validity and reliability more problematic.

To be sure, homelessness is not a new or even recent phenomenon. However, homelessness reached a twenty-seven-year high in 1991 (Daly, 1996). Although private or public funding is necessary to ensure that adequate housing and basic services are available for the poor, communities can only be created by the people who live in them. Thus, research on homeless people should contain a significant self-help component. Finally, it is important to realize that the homeless are diverse. Research must recognize those who are at risk of losing their shelter, those without shelter on a temporary or episodic basis, and those who are chronically homeless.

CAUSES OF HOMELESSNESS

Even as the numbers of homeless people increase, little attention is being directed at addressing the underlying causes of homelessness (Morse, 1999). Homelessness is caused more by a lack of public resources than by individual shortcomings or behavioral disorders. In part, homelessness is a result of social policy and, consequently, cannot be separated from the political economy. Recent increases in homelessness are attributable to global economic changes, a severe shortage of affordable shelter for low-income families, and cutbacks in social programs (Maciones, 2002; Daly, 1996).

Some categories of people are particularly vulnerable to homelessness: single mothers, battered women and children, abused youth, disabled and fragile elderly, military veterans, and the households of workers whose jobs have been lost. The typical response to homelessness has been to provide emergency shelters and food banks. Such attempts have failed miserably because they do nothing to address the underlying questions of poverty, employment, housing, and resource reallocation.

Since many people who are inadequately sheltered will lose their housing for at least a short time, homelessness must be broadly interpreted to include those at risk. Most homeless people live on the street, less in the open areas in rural America. Others live in some sort of shelter but lack basic safety, security, and amenities such as heat, water, and a bathroom. It is not surprising that homeless people are often on the move. "Their deprivation depends on the extent to which the absence of shelter is combined with social isolation and economic poverty" (Daly, 1996: 1).

For people who are labeled "undeserving," intervention to homelessness has not changed much in the past century. Human warehouses, better known as emergency shelters, eliciting memories of poorhouses and jails used for lodging at the close of the nineteenth century, remain the main way of taking care of transients or chronically homeless people.

COUNTING THE HOMELESS

As I have mentioned, there are approximately 500,000 homeless people in the United States. HUD (1984) determined that 250,000 to 350,000 people were without shelter in 1984. Previously it was believed that homelessness in rural areas was not a major problem. Studies of rural regions, however, suggest that the number of homeless people is quite high (Daly, 1996). Although homelessness may emerge in a variety of forms, the rural homeless are less visible than those in urban areas. Since many homeless people move frequently, they are difficult to count. A nationwide random sample (Link et al., 1994) found that six to eight people per thousand were homeless. More than 8 percent of male Vietnam veterans had "no regular place to live for at least a month or so" (Rosenheck & Fontana, 1994: 421–427).

The extent of homelessness increased throughout the 1980s at a rapid rate (Daly, 1996). In the 1990s, the homeless rate continued to grow—although at a slower pace. There are sometimes reliability problems, however, since officials of metropolitan areas tend to exaggerate statistics in order to receive more federal funding. Moreover, as the number of emergency shelters increase, the official number of homeless people also increases.

TYPES OF HOMELESSNESS

The homeless can be characterized by their residence, work record, degree of disability, health status, shelter history, familial characteristics (e.g., single, married, divorced, single mother), and demographic characteristics (e.g., age, ethnicity, race, gender). Other times homelessness is described in terms of assumed causes or precipitating factors: social (those who are marginalized or discriminated against; e.g., the handicapped); political (refugees from countries with political, tribal, or ethnic conflict); economic (unemployment or involuntary part-time employment resulting from deindustrialization); structural (e.g., pertaining to health problems or poverty); or accidental (based on natural disasters or external events).

Their degree of vulnerability or the length of their homelessness also categorizes people without shelter. This includes those at risk (refugees, the elderly, single mothers with young children); those who are temporarily homeless as a result of an extraordinary event (loss of one's home, death of or abandonment by the household head); those who are periodically without homes (women escaping domestic violence, youth, migrant farm workers); and those who are chronically homeless.

The homeless may also be depicted along a range on the basis of their needs:

1. Those who need continuous residential care in an institutional setting. Some may eventually be able to live in shelters or halfway houses with appropriate services and counseling.
2. Those who have considerable and, often, multiple problems but, with help could live independently or with others. This includes those who have been institutionalized or abused and require a period of time in transitional housing before they are ready to live autonomously.
3. Those who can become almost autonomous but need housing as well as other types of assistance such as employment training, literacy education, and budgeting and life skills assistance to enable them to manage their own lives.
4. Those who only need housing. This often includes the working poor who are temporarily homeless. They require financial help to return to their regular way of life but they do not have other serious problems as long as they receive assistance in a timely fashion.
5. Those who are at risk of losing their homes in the near future. They need short-term help to prevent them from being homeless. (Daly, 1996)

THE STRUCTURAL CONTEXT OF HOMELESSNESS

The problems of homelessness cannot be properly understood or treated without an understanding of the contextual framework from which homelessness arises in the United States. Our centralized form of bureaucratic government is largely mistrusted. We favor solutions at the local level. Ethnicity, race, and narrow-mindedness heavily influence the dynamics of political power. Our approach to solving social problems is individualistic. We expect individuals to remedy their own negative conditions and problems. Self-help is paramount. We are skeptical of collective-oriented intervention.

We disfavor welfare, particularly its dramatic growth, but will tolerate it for short-term or emergency situations. There is great opposition to long-term dependency, especially when it is intergenerational. Welfare benefits are being privatized. There is a prominent laissez-faire attitude—an aversion to any socialist tendencies in intervention. There is a heavy reliance on charity and, recently, job training initiatives. In short, cost containment is a key issue.

Inequalities in the health-care delivery system abound (see chapter 5.) Those who can afford it receive high quality care. Those not covered by employer-provided or private insurance are very vulnerable to catastrophe; this may lead to homelessness.

There is an important link between homelessness and poor health. A HUD (U.S. Department of Housing of Urban Development, 1999) study of poor people (most of whom were homeless at the time they were interviewed) revealed that half reported significant problems of physical health. Homeless people cannot afford adequate nutrition. Forty percent of the homeless people surveyed by HUD said they had gone without food for at least one day in the previous month.

Access to quality education is problematic for many residents of the United States. Although it is widely available, it is evolving into a two-tiered system of public and private education. Education is the major basis of social mobility for individuals. Consequently, educational stratification results in a wider gap between the haves and the have-nots (see chapter 2).

Globalization is strongly influencing our economy, particularly employment. There is a dearth of programs for skill development and job training as we forge into a new millennium. Globalization has been accompanied by deindustrialization. This translates into marginalized, low-paid workers with few benefits. There is rising involuntary part-time work for low-wage earners.

WHO ARE THE HOMELESS?

Homelessness affects a wide variety of people: recent immigrants and refugees; deinstitutionalized people (the physically or mentally ill, ex-convicts, those recently discharged from detoxification or detention centers); poor single mothers; runaways or abused youth; victims of domestic violence; workers displaced by economic recession; victims of natural disasters; elderly on low fixed income; substance abusers; people who are transient because of personal crises, domestic strife, or seasonal work; military veterans; and Native Americans who have migrated to urban areas to find work and escape the abject poverty life on reservations.

Many of these people have nothing in common except homelessness. Many have multiple problems that are economic, social, psychiatric, or physical in nature that cause them to be marginalized. Many are alcoholics or substance abusers. Some have mental problems that lead them to drug addiction. Others are both unemployed and disabled. A large number have been institutionalized, ranging from psychiatric hospitals to prisons. Once they have been returned to the community they have few support networks or social and employable skills. While some are educated, many are functionally illiterate, traveling from town to town and grabbing whatever temporary jobs they can find. Their deep sense of isolation leaves them with nowhere to turn for assistance.

Now I will examine the homeless in terms of ethnicity, age, education, health status, gender, income, and length of time they have been without a home. Ethnic minorities are disproportionately homeless. Fifty-five percent of all homeless people are nonwhites, 2.5 times their representation in the total population (HUD, 1989: 1–2). Eighty percent of all homeless ethnic minorities is blacks. In our largest cities, the majority of homeless people are blacks, in rural areas, whites (Daly, 1996). In western (primarily Mexican Americans) and northeastern (primarily Puerto Ricans) states Latinos are a sizable minority of the homeless. For example, in New York City, Latinos comprise approximately 30 percent of the homeless population.

The median age of homeless persons is approximately thirty-five (Daly, 1996). The average age has been decreasing over time. Homeless women tend to be younger than males without shelter. In some areas the average age of mothers with young children in emergency shelters is twenty-seven; 75 percent of the population is under forty (Institute of Medicine, 1988).

Today's homeless people in the United States have more education compared to those in previous decades. Nonetheless, their educational attainment is lower than the general population. Nearly half are high school dropouts. A substantial number are functionally illiterate; they are unable to complete employment application forms and questionnaires and/or cannot read written directions (Momeni, 1989).

Approximately two of three homeless people have been previously institutionalized in mental hospitals, detoxification units, prisons, or jails (Daly, 1996). Only one of three men living in shelters does not have illnesses or injuries. The most frequently occurring health problems are associated with alcoholism (e.g., seizures, hallucinations, and delirium tremers), blackouts, respiratory illnesses, and dental problems. Not surprisingly, the frequency of ill health increases with age and length of homelessness (Schutt, 1992). This pattern is greater among men than women, and is somewhat higher for military veterans than for nonveterans.

At least half of all homeless persons in the United States are single males (Daly, 1996). The rates of homelessness among women is higher in large cities because of the shortage of shelters for women and the prevalence of poor female-headed households living under precarious conditions. The U.S. Conference of Mayors found that 36 percent of the homeless were comprised of families with children (Daly, 1996). Females head the vast majority of these households (Institute of Medicine, 1988; Reyes & Waxman, 1989).

Many homeless are totally dependent on charity, social assistance, emergency shelters and soup kitchens: "There are 4 to 7 million extremely poor people, persons whose income is below two-thirds of the official poverty line and who are thus at high risk of becoming homeless. . . . [The] pool of extremely poor persons with incomes under $4,000 and that the literally homeless are drawn from has increased enormously (i.e., doubled) since 1970" (Rossi, 1989: 79-81). A nationwide random sample found that Americans with annual incomes below $20,000 are almost three times as likely to be homeless during their lifetimes as those with incomes above $20,000 (Link et al., 1994: 1910)

The character and magnitude of problems encountered by homeless people are related to the length of time they have been without adequate shelter, which in turn depends on their living conditions. A nationwide sample (Link et al, 1994: 1910) found that a majority had been homeless for more than one month. Peter H. Rossi and his colleagues' (Rossi et al., 1987: 1336) study of Chicago homeless discovered that roughly one-quarter were homeless for less than three months, one-half were without shelter from four months to two years, and the remaining one-quarter had been on the street for more than two years.

GLOBALIZATION AND INDUSTRIALIZATION

As the U.S. economy globalizes and deindustrializes, a scarcity of jobs and affordable yet adequate housing exasperate inequalities between primarily ethnic minorities, deprived inner-city residents, and primarily wealthy whites in gentrified urban or suburban areas. The number of homeless people grew in the

1980s and early 1990s as the federal government decreased its role in housing policy. Rates of homelessness are closely connected with economic shifts, government policies, and demographic changes. Globalization has resulted in a loss of manufacturing jobs, increased automation, and growth in involuntary part-time, low-paid employment in unskilled service sector jobs, along with streamlining of companies, accompanied by layoffs and decreases in real wages.

Public policy reflects a shift in budget priorities by recent federal administrations determined to cut spending on housing and social services, considering rapidly escalating financial deficits. Government housing policy emphasizes privatization and tax subsidies for middle- and upper-income homeowners. Such policy results in a sharp shortage of low-rent public housing, a drained inventory of private rental units, and reduced housing choices for poor people.

Social policy changes reflect a shift from a welfare state to a determination to decrease spending on social programs. This trend is clear in the considerable number of people living in poverty, declining social benefits relative to the cost of living, and an inability to afford available housing. Demographic changes are evident in the formation of smaller households—many of them made up of elderly or poor single mothers with young children—and in the prevalence of nonfamily households. Widespread gentrification in downtown areas has led to the loss of single-room occupancy units, the transformation of rentals to condominiums, and residential displacement. Changes in housing need attributable to demographic trends affected demand for affordable shelter. At the same time as demand increased (especially for smaller, low-cost units), prices rose.

HEALTH ISSUES OF THE HOMELESS

The homeless probably harbor the largest pool of untreated disease left in American society today.

—James D. Wright and Eleanor Weber, *Homelessness and Health*

Why do you wait until I'm sick until you give me the housing and stability I need to keep healthy?

—Homeless man with AIDS in Boston

Homelessness is . . . unhealthy for children, . . . their parents, and for other living things. In the extreme, it is a fatal condition.

—J. D. Wright, "Address Unknown"

Homeless people have a great deal of obstacles in obtaining proper health care and related services. Certainly, this is important to the physical and mental health issues linked to homelessness. The homeless suffer from a variety of health problems. Of course, economic hardship is one of the most grave health risks. Additionally, tuberculosis, hypertension, respiratory problems, skin ulcerations, and a range of other infectious diseases are prevalent among homeless people. There are institutional and attitudinal barriers to the delivery of health care for the homeless.

There are physical and psychological anxieties from exposure to the elements and from having to inhabit a dense, disordered, deleterious, and often hostile environment. There are also psychological problems corresponding with poverty and the stigma of living on the streets. The homeless are very vulnerable to a host of viruses and bacteria. Many lack the psychological comfort of having a home base and support network. In short, homelessness is often both the source and the outcome of poor health.

As I have mentioned, poor physical health affects one-half of all chronically homeless people (HUD, 1999). The majority of those for whom poor health was the single most important factor in homelessness was considered unemployable (Wright & Weber, 1987). Shelters, soup kitchens, missions, alcohol detoxification and drop-in centers, and juvenile courts are all related to health care for the homeless.

HEALTH PROBLEMS OF THE HOMELESS

Among the health problems commonly encountered by the homeless are the following:

Cold Injury. In much of the United States homeless people are more vulnerable to frostbite and hypothermia due to exposure to the elements. They also lack adequate housing, clothing, and health care. Often they sleep in shelters requiring that they leave every morning to look for a job, irrespective of inclement weather.

Cardiorespiratory Diseases. At Health Care for the Homeless clinics, one-third of the patients have upper respiratory problems As many as 30 to 40 percent of homeless people suffer from such chronic physical ailments as coronary artery disease, high blood pressure, or emphysema. The homeless are disproportionately represented among those with hypertension, gastrointestinal disorders, skin disease, dental problems, and injuries such as fractures, bruises, sprains, and lacerations. Injury and illnesses frequently become disabling for the homeless because many are continuously moving and do not receive regular health care.

Tuberculosis (TB). From 1987 to 1992, the United States experienced a 20 percent increase of TB (Daly, 1996), a highly infectious disease common among residents of shelters and those living on the streets. The rate of TB among the homeless is at least one hundred times greater than average for the general population. Nearly 17 percent of the homeless have "an infectious or communicable disorder that poses some potential risks to . . . public health" (Wright & Weber, 1987: 110). These diseases spread quickly among the homeless. A man with TB infected more than four hundred others in a shelter in Maine. It is difficult to control contagious diseases such as TB in mobile populations such as the homeless.

Skin Diseases. Homeless persons are inclined to get skin problems resulting from malnourishment, poor circulation, ill-fitting shoes, cuts, and dirty clothing. The homeless typically do not have access to washing machines. Because of these unsanitary conditions, homeless people often get lice, scabies, and intestinal worms. Consequently, homeless shelters continue to delouse their guests.

Nutritional Deficiencies. Because of poor nutrition and lack of health care, a high percentage of homeless persons have dental problems and suffer from malnourishment, which increases the risk of infectious diseases and gastrointestinal disorders. In addition, the nutrients of greatest concern—vitamin C, thiamin, and folate—are not in the foods provided by most shelters because such facilities do not have either satisfactory refrigeration or a regular supply of fresh fruits and vegetables. People without these necessary nutrients experience weakness, fatigue, depression, and emotional disturbances.

Sleep Deprivation. For most people, sleeping is hard in the loud, disorderly environment of emergency shelters. Sleep disorders cause irritability, apathy, and/or behavioral impairment. Stress and lack of sleep, especially, negatively affect children in shelters.

Health Problems of Children and Youths. Children in emergency shelters often have behavioral, emotional, and developmental difficulties. Most are unable to do well in school. It is not unusual for these children to move from one school to the next as their family moves from shelter to temporary housing to permanent housing, sometimes in different parts of the city.

Children in homeless families are twice as likely to develop chronic physical disorders than their counterparts with shelter. Approximately 16 percent of homeless children seen in health clinics already have chronic health problems. Poor health and chronic physical illness "[c]ontribute to the cycle of poverty . . . interfere with, if not preclude, normal labor force participation, and with it, the ability to lead an independent adult existence. . . . Poor health may be one mechanism by which homelessness reproduces itself in subsequent generations" (Wright, 1989: 77).

The rate of chronic disease among youth is nearly twice that of their peers in the general population. They are subject to upper respiratory infections; traumas and skin disorders; lice infestation; chronic problems with eyes and teeth; and along with malnutrition, gastrointestinal disorders, genital-urinary infections, and sexually transmitted diseases. A substantial percentage abuse drugs and alcohol.

Mental Illness. There is a strong correlation among homelessness, mental illness, and public policy on the delivery of mental health care to mentally ill people (Belcher & DiBlasio, 1990). As I have mentioned, 40 percent of homeless people have mental health problems (HUD, 1999). It is commonly believed that one-third of all homeless people have severe and chronic types of mental illness. About one-half are depressed about their futures. The predominance of depression is demonstrated by the notable number (one of six) who attempt suicide (Rossi, 1989).

Such obstacles only get worse by the anxiety of homelessness or institutionalization. Many homeless people rotate between mental hospitals and life on the streets. Approximately 25 percent of homeless persons in the United States have been in a mental institution at least once. This is more than five times the rate for the general population. One study found that 28 percent of the homeless people examined were chronically mentally ill: "Both substance abuse and schizophrenia were elevated among the individuals who had been homeless many times or for long periods of time" (Koegel & Burnam, 1988). "About two-thirds of the homeless are either alcoholic, drug abusive or mentally ill; nearly one in four of them have two or more of these disorders" (Wright & Weber, 1987: 94).

Physical and Sexual Assault. Life on the streets is often violent. Physical assaults are common; these attacks hasten health problems. Women and young people are especially defenseless. Homeless women often undergo trauma. The rate of sexual assault among homeless women is twenty times higher than for other women (Kelly, 1985).

Drug Dependency. As I have mentioned, 25 percent of all homeless people are drug abusers (not including alcohol; HUD, 1999). Among those who are regular users, there are high rates of liver disease, HIV/AIDS, sexually transmitted disease, skin problems, bruises, lacerations, and injuries attributable to violence. One study found that 6.5 percent had been in a drug treatment facility, 15 percent use intravenous drugs, one in eight has drug-using partners, and almost one in ten indicates that drugs are a problem; between 4 and 8 percent of these young people are HIV positive (Sherman, 1992). One study at New York City homeless shelters found that 80 percent of single homeless men tested positive for some drug (Cuomo, 1992).

Mortality. The death rate for homeless people is about four times greater than that of the general population. Among young homeless men, the incidence is even higher. Generally, homeless adults die twenty years earlier than their nonhomeless counterparts. More than one-half die violently; one-quarter of those who died were murdered, a rate more than twenty times higher than the U.S. average. This was preceded by deaths directly attributable to alcohol and drugs (16 percent of deaths), car accidents (13 percent), and by cancer and heart disease (11.5 percent each) (Wright & Weber, 1987).

HIV/AIDS. AIDS patients represent from 5 to 11 percent of all homeless people. Because drug use is common among street people, they are susceptible to HIV/AIDS and to sexually transmitted diseases. Sharing needles is the most high-risk activity since injections go directly into the bloodstream. In one study, researchers found that 78 percent of the patients with HIV or AIDS had a history of intravenous drug use; 18 percent were women. In addition, some homeless are gay, bisexual, or engage in sex to earn money.

Alcohol Abuse. Some of the health problems I have mentioned are exacerbated by chronic alcohol abuse or drug addiction. As I have stated, 40 percent of homeless adults chronically abuse alcohol (HUD, 1999). This contrasts with 10 percent of the general population. The poorer an individual is, the more likely problems with alcohol will expedite homelessness. Substance abuse worsens other problems. "It is a precondition for vulnerability; it increases the probability that non-economic factors also lead to homelessness" (Conrad et al., 1993: 36). It is commonly accepted that the severity of alcoholism among homeless adults is a result of their impoverished conditions. It is less severe among the newly homeless than among those who have been on the streets for some time. Some individuals "may cope with the deprivation of homelessness and their damaged self-esteem by drinking yet more heavily" (Koegel & Burnam, 1988: 21).

While it is foolish to focus only on the problems of individuals, and to ignore the systemic problems responsible for recent increases in homelessness, it is impractical to overlook the reality that alcoholism touches many homeless people. Consequently, intervention should include effective and sensible alcohol rehabilitation programs (Koegel & Burnam, 1988: 18). However, it is probable that alcoholism will continue among homeless adults, despite the large amount spent on detoxification, unless intervention successfully addresses the causal factors of homelessness. People on the street drink alcohol to cope with cold weather, depression, isolation, and physical or emotional pain. Because it dulls pain, generates euphoria, and fills insignificant time, alcohol is accepted as the drug of choice and as a way of boosting fellowship among homeless men and some homeless women.

Clearly, alcohol assists or worsens health problems, hastens the death of some homeless individuals, and is a factor in accidents and traffic fatalities (e.g., drunken street people hit by cars). Drunken people create large problems for police, caregivers, medical practitioners, and others. This topic denotes an ongoing quandary for the directors of shelters, soup kitchens, and group homes as they attempt to care for people who are inebriated, troublesome, and a threat to other shelter residents, especially women with children and other adults who are unable to protect themselves.

In conclusion, the link between homelessness and health is direct and evident. Many people lose their homes after experiencing serious illness or injury that results in hospitalization, income loss, and eviction. Homeless people are susceptible to illness and injury as a result of physical and psychological stress. As I have indicated, half are in poor health (HUD, 1999) and at least one in three is too disabled to work (Daly, 1996). People who lack adequate shelter and bathing and laundry facilities find it difficult to maintain personal hygiene. Their illnesses, skin diseases, and nutritional deficiencies are exacerbated by their lifestyle. They also encounter problems in obtaining access to proper health care and, for those who are visible minorities, disabled, or have AIDS, difficulty in finding housing as well.

The difficulty in ascribing an illness to heavy drinking is that heavy drinkers differ from nonheavy drinkers in other ways. They smoke more. They often eat less. They often lead irregular lives—staying up all hours, never exercising, sleeping it off on park benches. These potentially harmful influences cannot be separated from the effects of alcohol (Goodwin, 1994: 46).

THE MYTH OF A CARING COMMUNITY: DEINSTITUTIONALIZATION

Beginning in the early 1960s, the federal government began closing institutions for the mentally ill on the presumption that patients would do better outside mental hospitals. Deinstitutionalization was based on an optimistic belief in the compassion and nurturing of the community, the discovery of psychotropic drugs and on the belief that large medical and psychiatric hospitals fell short of furnishing perceptible benefits to most patients.

It is hard to guess the extent of mental illness among homeless people. Some of the uncertainty is distinguishing between drug abusers and others. As I have indicated, 40 percent of homeless people have mental health problems (HUD, 1999). Many mentally ill people became homeless after being deinstitutionalized. But homelessness is not primarily a medical issue. Focusing on personal illnesses ignores the underlying social and economic factors of homelessness.

Those who have been deinstitutionalized are hopelessly dependent on society in a relationship rooted in illness and the disbursement of generosity. Once these people reenter the community, most are not proficient—initially at least—of functioning on their own. In some cases, deinstitutionalized patients are sent home too soon, without proper investigation, and to the custody of their families or foster family members; many of these people are not ready to assume the responsibility of taking care of mentally ill children or spouses. The concept of a caring community, conjuring images of fellowship and support networks in a neighborly backdrop, is ill founded.

Nonetheless, as deinstitutionalization continues, this marginalized population continues to grow. Many of those discharged or refused admission have no place to go (U.S. Congress, 1983: 903). Government agencies perform a major part in this procedure. Deinstitutionalization, government policies of financial restriction, and judicial findings limiting agencies' capability to institutionalize individuals have made admittance to psychiatric institutions questionable.

This hands-off policy is especially unsuitable for poor, uneducated, and mentally ill military veterans who neither understand their rights nor how to use the system. More than 275,000 veterans are homeless at any given time with approximately 500,000 being homeless for some time during any given year (National Coalition for Homeless Veterans, 2000). Veterans without a high school diploma are 25 percent less likely to have contact with the Veterans Administration than are veterans with college degrees. Only about one in eight homeless veterans receive benefits of any kind from the Veterans Administration (U.S. Congress, 1983).

Some cities have criminalized homelessness. Others run the homeless out of town. New York City officials believed that the homeless mentally ill were slowly killing themselves. Consequently, Project Help began. The homeless were forcibly taken off the streets, evaluated, and confined for treatment without their approval. This program raised serious ethical questions.

ALTERNATIVES TO INSTITUTIONALIZATION

Community care alternatives largely fail to meet the needs of those discharged from or denied access to psychiatric institutions. Our government continues to cling to policies implementing deinstitutionalization—without much success. These people need physical and mental health care, proper housing, educational opportunities, vocational training, community services, and recreational programs. Synthesizing these different modules is the versatile Community Services Model, which aims to provide support and develop self-esteem and determination.

The "clients' movement" questions the hierarchical character of the relationship between medical staff and patients, the sequestration of patients, and excessive reliance on medication to treat conditions. Emphasizing talent, personal gifts, and the possibility contributions rather than concentrating on disabilities is known as "valorization of the subject" (Messina et al., 1992: 69).

In summary, the United States has severely reduced the number and size of psychiatric institutions. This was often done for financial reasons. However, the accumulated funds were not rerouted to community services nor made accessible for housing to assist those released from psychiatric hospitals.

Deinstitutionalization is based on two shortsighted assumptions: First, community care is better than institutional care. Second, psychotropic drugs could secure clients, resulting in immediate autonomy. Deinstitutionalization has become part of a more general trend toward privatization. Some are released too early. Others are refused admittance. All seem to lack adequate mental health support service. For many, an emergency shelter is the only opportunity.

Individuals typically improve more in community-based programs than in institutions. They become more independent and manifest fewer signs of mental illness. Additionally, in the long run community-based programs are less expensive than institutions.

POSTMODERN HOMELESSNESS

If the structural roots of homelessness presented thus far (the political economy, gentrification, globalization, privatization, poverty, unemployment, institutional discrimination, poor education, deinstitutionalization) are not convincing, I offer the following analysis. There are a growing number of homeless people who work full time in nontechnical jobs and make $50,000 annually in the lavish Silicon Valley (Nieves, 2000). This image stands in sharp contrast with media images of homeless people: unemployed drunks who sleep on park benches; beggars at busy urban intersections; and mentally ill foul-smelling people who talk to themselves. The increasing number of high-tech jobs and the decreasing number of skilled and semiskilled jobs has resulted in regentrification and an expanding gap between rich and poor throughout the nation's urban areas, including the Silicon Valley.

For example, in Santa Clara the number of homeless people who work full-time rose from 25 percent in 1995 to 34 percent (or 20,000 people) by 1999. Of course, this does not count the growing number of families who share a single apartment or house or individuals who pay $400 per month to sleep on the floor in the houses of strangers. In one case, twenty-six men lived together in one house, each paying $400 a month.

This new breed of working homeless goes beyond those who earn minimum wage; they include teachers, police officers, firefighters, salespeople, and even people in entry-level high-tech jobs. There are also a growing number of poor immigrants who work in fast-food restaurants, construction, landscaping, or service jobs. The Silicon Valley "poor" family of four has a household income of $53,100 per year, while working homeless individuals earn an average of $37,200 annually.

More than half of the people in shelters are employed. Fewer than 30 percent of the households can afford to buy a house. People must wait several years for subsidized housing. Housing consumes an average of 80 percent of family incomes. There is not much left over for food and other basic necessities. Consequently, acquiring an illness, having an accident, getting laid off, or losing a second income is catastrophic.

The working homeless seek help from homeless shelters, churches, and other organizations. In the Silicon Valley, they ride public buses called "rolling hotels" throughout the night in order to get some rest. The median family income in the Silicon Valley is $82,000 per year, the highest in the nation. Sixty-three people become millionaires every day. It has arguably the most expensive housing in the country; the median house costs $410,000 (more than twice the national average). A two-bedroom apartment rents for $1,700 per month. A studio or efficiency apartment in a bad neighborhood rents for $1,000 per month.

The moneyed in the Silicon Valley bid on scarce real estate offerings. A four-bedroom house in Palo Alto priced at $2.2 million sold for $3.2 million. A one-bedroom cottage listed at $495,000 sold for $750,000. In Santa Barbara, real estate is increasing at the rate of 1 percent per month (Mimi Greenberg, Coldwell Banker, personal correspondence, 2002). This is primarily due to the virtual ban on new housing developments. A three-bedroom ranch-style house without air-conditioning in Santa Barbara, built in 1961, in desperate need of repair and updating, 1,100 square feet, single-car garage without automatic door opener lists for $545,000. Because space is so scarce, garages rent for $300 a month in Santa Barbara. Clearly, the exorbitant cost of housing is beyond the reach of many people—not just the unemployed.

SUMMARY AND CONCLUSION

The way that policy makers define homelessness sets the tone for intervention by both the government and the voluntary sector. Currently, the definition is narrow and generally limited to absolute or chronic homelessness. The idea that everyone is entitled to adequate housing has not caught on. It is important that broad definitions of homelessness are used to ensure that those most in need of assistance, including those at risk, are not excluded from social assistance. This definition would help focus public spending on preventing homelessness, a far more cost-effective approach than attempting to deal with people who are already homeless. Prevention is less costly, socially and economically, than treatment.

A fruitful definition would include those temporarily without shelter, those who are without shelter in the long term, and those who are at a substantial risk of being on the street in the immediate future. Overcrowded, inadequate, or extremely expensive housing (relative to household income) that lacks basic facilities does not constitute satisfactory accommodations. People who are placed in emergency shelters, hostels, or welfare hotels lack privacy, security, and rights of tenancy. They also should be considered homeless or vulnerable. Temporary assistance should be provided before they become absolutely homeless and their need for social assistance multiplies.

Homelessness in the United States can be traced to a punitive nineteenth-century ideology (see Henshel, 1990) that carries into the twenty-first century. We still label people "undeserving" or "deserving" of assistance. Similarly our historical commitment to the principles of individualism is the basis of our distaste for both undiscriminating openhandedness and government intervention.

It follows from individualism that government should not force social or economic change. Despite the events of September 11, 2001, privatism—the attitude that one should be uncommitted to or avoid involvement in anything beyond one's immediate interests—still prevails. There is also hegemony to privatize business or industries. Transportation, utilities, health-care delivery, security and law enforcement, education, and housing have transformed from public to private control and ownership.

Intervention on behalf of homeless people has not been prevalent for several reasons. There are rigid eligibility requirements for social welfare programs; consequently, only a small group of low-income and minority Americans are helped. These underclass beneficiaries are neither organized nor represent a vigorous political constituency. Housing programs that attempt to help low-income and homeless people are more costly (per household) and notably more contentious than other programs such as Medicare. Such social welfare programs eventually become closely connected with ethnic minority issues and, when combined with affirmative action regulations, are perceived as threatening the independence of local political, social, and economic institutions.

A bold step in helping the homeless is supportive housing, a program that combines low-income housing with on-site social services (Maciones, 2002). People with physical or mental disabilities, alcohol or drug problems, or emotional scars from stressful and unstable living on the streets find they can live independently as well as hold jobs with the assistance provided by these programs.

Such programs based on care, distributive justice, and social responsibility build bridges and tear down walls between poor homeless people and mainstream society. They are also financially efficacious. In New York City, the cost of supporting an individual with affordable housing and social services amounts to $12,500 per year. Compare this to the $40,000 per year we pay for one person in prison (HUD, 1999).

The street offers its children the spectacle of society without integration into is values: proximity, but not participation. It becomes symbolic of their distress. It replaces school, and has a very different syllabus. It belongs to everybody and nobody, and puts everyone on the same footing. It cancels out the past and makes the future uncertain: only the present moment counts (Agnelli, 1986: 9).

While existing in a high-risk environment, many street children demonstrate healthy, competent behavior (Felsman, 1984). They have much to teach us about strength, resiliency, and healthy adaptation as it exists in childhood. Lack of shelter is one of the most basic elements of human adaptation now experienced by many Americans. Apparently, shelter is not a basic human right in the world's richest, most advanced nation. Meanwhile, homelessness and a crisis in low-income housing continue.

WHAT YOU CAN DO

Talk with some homeless people. Find out why they are homeless and how long they have been homeless. How is their health? Where do they sleep? Where do they eat? What is their worldview? Do they have family, and if so, do they keep in contact with them? Ask about their future plans: where they will live and whether they plan to work.

FIVE

MEDICAL APARTHEID: THE UNEQUAL DISTRIBUTION AND QUALITY OF HEALTH CARE

There are communities in the very shadow of America's finest medical institutions where infant mortality rates rival those of Third World nations.

—Durado Brooks, David R. Smith, and
Ron J. Anderson, "Medical Apartheid"

THE MOST FUNDAMENTAL social problems regarding health care are ultimately issues of power and justice. The delivery of health care depends on scientifically reliable ways for improving the quality of life and decreasing unnecessary death and premature death. As American medical technology—the best in the world—advances in leaps and bounds, the amount of cases for which potential public health activity might be taken on is proliferating quickly. Moreover, scientists use various innovative strategies to implement new and existing technology.

This chapter examines the relationship between health care, minorities, and discrimination. I raise the issue of why poor people seem to lack equal access to good health, and I consider alternative explanations. Minorities are dying unnecessarily, and at much higher rates than the general population, yet the bulk of medical research and technological advancement appears to focus on fulfilling the desires of a rather small elite class of people. Interventions in the social environment and continued research on social factors such as environmental racism must become a priority in public health planning and program development.

I examine health care for two reasons: Because health care resources are finite, the question of distributive justice—the equitable distribution of scarce resources among the various segments of our population—is crucial; and medical responsibilities have sharply increased. There are rising public and patient demands for medical help to address social and behavioral problems. A virtually unlimited range of social issues are becoming at least partially dependent on medical intervention: AIDS, drug addiction, genetic counseling, unwanted pregnancy, unwanted childlessness, suicide, sagging body parts, laziness, and crime, to cite just a few.

OVERVIEW OF HEALTH-CARE PROBLEMS

Health care is very expensive and, therefore, not equally accessible to all. Although technically competent and highly esteemed, medical care is unequally distributed. The typical physician sees more patients than she/he should, yet more go untreated. Medical powers and decision making have increased because of technological innovation.

The authority and the power of physicians have been challenged with demands for the control and regulation of their activities. An increasing number of physicians are being forced to defend their behavior and decisions by the American Medical Association. Medical malpractice insurance has become both alarmingly scarce and excessively expensive (Kass, 1985). Groups opposing government control of medicine advertise to demand physician's control of their treatment of patients.

Health-care reform has emerged as an important social issue. Analysts have noted the sharply rising costs of health care and an increasingly large number of uninsured. Spending on health care grew from about $12 billion in 1950 to about $1.2 trillion by 1998 in dollars controlled for inflation (U.S. Department of Health and Human Services, 2000). Moreover, the number of U.S. residents who lack health insurance is greater than 40 million (Maciones, 2002). The rejection of high-risk patrons by health insurance companies (at first viewed as unacceptably deviant) has become business as usual.

The causes and effects of the crisis in health care have been studied widely. A broad range of solutions has been offered. But health-care problems cannot be approached in isolation to the economy. Corporate merging, restructuring, and downsizing have fanned the flames of the health-care crisis. Thousands of workers laid off in recent years have lost their income and health insurance at the same time. Those who could afford health insurance have had their benefits cut by employers and are forced to invest a greater portion of their income. Consequently, health care is a social problem, not just a problem for the poor.

Does our health-care system actually help the mental and physical well-being of patients? Advances in medical technology, as well as increases in government regulation and consumer demands, have threatened to reduce a physician to merely an engineer or technician who sells services on demand. Although health is the goal of medicine, the ambiguous concepts of happiness and pleasure are crowding in. Physicians are called to satisfy the desires of their patients in attempts to produce contentment. In the area of mental health, anxiety and unmet desires are signs of an illness and, consequently, necessitate a cure or a solution.

Physicians are being asked more and more to gratify their patients:

> A woman gets a surgeon to remove a normal breast because it interfered with her golf swing. An obstetrician is asked to perform amniocentesis, and then abortion, if the former procedure shows the fetus to be of the undesired gender. (Abortion is now the most common surgical procedure in the U.S. Over 1.5 million abortions were performed in 1980—a year in which there were 3.6 million live births.) "Dr. Feelgood" devotes his entire practice to administering amphetamine injections to people seeking elevations of mood. To these real but admittedly extreme examples one could add, among others, the now generally accepted practices of performing artificial insemination or arranging adoptions, performing vasectomies and abortions for nonmedical (i.e., family planning) reasons, dispensing antibiotics or other medicines simply because a patient wants to take something, and some activities of psychiatrists and many of cosmetic surgeons (e.g., where the surgery aims to appease patient vanity and fantasy, not to correct inborn or acquired abnormality or deformity). I would also add the practice, now being advocated more and more, of directly and painlessly killing a patient who wants to die. (Kass, 1985: 159)

Such procedures are aimed at appeasing a patient's desires, not maintaining or improving health. A growing segment of the medical profession caters to the pleasures, conveniences, luxury, and gratification of the affluent at the expense of the underprivileged. It is not the responsibility of doctors to satisfy the desires of patients as consumers. The goal of the physician is not to make the patient happy, but rather healthy. Health may be defined as a state of complete physical, mental, and social well-being. Health is a state of being that reveals itself in activity as fitness. Accordingly, health care should prevent or treat diseases. The elimination of heart disease, cancer, and stroke (currently the major "killers") falls clearly within the objectives of the medical profession.

Health should be viewed from both the patient's and the physician's perspectives. It is also relative to the patient's age and cultural and natural circumstances. Health is strongly related to the marvelous power of self-healing. Virtually all living organisms heal wounds or breaks and tend to restore wholeness. Health depends on the cooperation of the body and the mind. Some disorders are related to problems with the mind: nervousness, tension headaches, depression, and insomnia.

Others are the result of a patient's lifestyle: sexually transmitted disease in prostitutes, lung disease in coal miners, hepatitis in drug addicts, and cirrhosis of the liver in alcoholics. In short, we are much more responsible for our own health than we care to admit. Physical neglect, drunkenness, laziness, and gluttony are often paid for through illness. The wages of poor health habits during youth are often paid for much later, so much later that it is difficult to establish the relation of cause and effect, let alone make it vivid enough to influence people's actions. If it is not likely to rain for twenty or thirty years, few of us are likely to repair our leaky roofs.

Many years ago, Socrates made the link between human ability to produce self-illness and human desire beyond self-preservation. Socrates, Sigmund Freud, and Émile Durkheim realized that social welfare depends on constraining and moderating the often-hazardous urges and aspirations of individuals. Our lifestyle is an important part of our health status. Our overindulgence and shortcomings contribute to our illness. The majority of physician visits in the United States result from risky patient behavior and/or unhealthy lifestyle.

Most chronic lung diseases, much cardiovascular disease, most cirrhosis of the liver, many gastrointestinal disorders (from indigestion to ulcers), numerous muscular and skeletal complaints (from low-back pain to flat feet), sexually transmitted diseases, nutritional deficiencies, obesity and its consequences, and certain kinds of renal and skin infections are in important measure self-induced or self-caused—and contributed to by smoking, overeating, overdrinking, eating the wrong foods, inadequate rest and exercise, and poor hygiene. To these conditions we must add the results of trauma—including automobile accidents—in which drunkenness plays a leading part, and suicide attempts, as well as accidental poisonings, drug abuse, and many burns (Kass, 1985: 176).

SHOULD WE LIMIT BIOMEDICAL TECHNOLOGY?

Medical powers and decision making have increased because of technological innovations. Such breakthroughs have allowed new ways of diagnosis and treatment, as well as new methods to change the functions of the body. The limits of biomedical technology are also being questioned (Beauchamp and Childress, 1989). For example, research shows DNA engineering can improve memory in mice.

What does that mean for humans, and should we use genetics to make ourselves, our children, and our aging parents smarter? Many of us would like this. But who will have access to it? What are the trade-offs of giving this "Viagra of the mind" to children? In addition to the financial costs, what about the emotional well-being of our children? How will heightened intelligence affect personality and human development? Undoubtedly, with greater intelligence comes greater expectations and stress. What problem, if any, are we solving? What new problems would be created?

Memory may be found to be affected by genes, but genes have not been found to have even a small causative correlation with normal "intelligence." What does intelligence actually mean and can it be measured? Intelligence is more than the highly specialized, arbitrary, narrowly defined and largely learned skills measured by American-designed IQ tests. Why do we not measure skills in second-language acquisition and the physics of a thrown object—both fundamental skills in our culture. IQ measures literacy but not evolved skills.

If scientists begin to implement genetic engineering in humans, how far would it go? If genetically engineered humans intermarry, how do we evaluate their children? When do engineered genes begin to dominate and infuse themselves into the gene pool? What about potential health problems linked to massive inbreeding?

Could genetic engineering for intelligence lead to children being reared in emotionally barren environments? There is a thin line between medical achievements for neurological diseases and manipulating nature's way. Intelligence has been nurtured through curiosity and creativity, not tampering. It is quite possible that any gains through the genetic engineering of humans would be short-lived.

HEALTH, RACE, AND SOCIAL CLASS

In the United States, most legalized discrimination has been eliminated. The Civil Rights Act of 1964 ensures equal protection under the law for all citizens. There have been significant advances in some parts of life for ethnic minorities. Of special note is the emergence of a very sizable African American and Latino middle class in the past several decades. The removal of legal impediments, unfortunately, does little to change the ravaging effects of centuries of racial bigotry and institutionalized discrimination.

In addition to health status, income and educational attainment are especially significant arenas of relative deprivation for people of color. Ethnic minorities continue to lag far behind the economically and politically dominant white majority. The social reality of economic and educational oppression is tightly linked to the continuation of de facto apartheid for an increasingly large number of our minorities. Economic oppression of the poor and minorities combined with the ever-increasing cost of health care has created a major social crisis.

Due to socioeconomic disparity, American residents of color and poor whites suffer excess death and disability. Black and Latino males, for example, have the highest risk of being murdered (Centers for Disease Control, 1986). Measurements of health in the United States confirm the failure of existing health care to recognize or respond effectively to the unmet needs and the barriers that exist. Health-care delivery in the United States has become excessively rationalized, increasingly fragmented, and too costly for those who need it the most: the poor, the elderly, children, women, and ethnic minorities.

The poor tend to become crippled, blinded, or killed by preventable illnesses such as diabetes or renal failure. They have higher rates of hypertension and suffer cervical cancer twice as often as the nonpoor. Poor people in the United States have been struck with infant mortality rates as high as in Guatemala, a Third World nation.

It was not until the 1960s that important studies of African American health care were published. Concentration on Latinos came even later—during the 1970s. Even so, there has been little research on Latinos except for Mexicans Americans in California and southwest Texas. Social scientists, more recently, have begun to study Native Americans and Asian Americans. From these studies, we know that ethnic minorities have the following problems:

1. a generally lower life expectancy than their white counterparts;
2. linguistic and cultural barriers that hinder access to social, legal, and health-care services and to public transportation;
3. less education than their white counterparts;
4. lower-paying blue-collar jobs, many without Social Security/retirement benefits;
5. inadequate income;
6. poor housing conditions;
7. poor access to health care, social services, and preventive health services;
8. inadequate representation in policy and legislative bodies;
9. underutilization of long-term care and mental health services.

Ethnic minorities also have many strengths, including:

1. strong kinship bonds, family unity, loyalty, and interfamily cooperation (ability to provide for the physical, emotional, and spiritual needs of the family);
2. strong work and achievement orientation (ability for self-help and mutual help);
3. adaptability of family roles (ability to perform family roles flexibly);
4. strong religious orientation (ability to discern spiritually).
5. emotional attachment to their ethnic communities.

Good health is often taken for granted. The absence of such—especially when it limits our daily activities—has a significant impact on our sense of well-being. It also affects our social relations and economic earning power. Good health is socially variable and, perhaps, socially structured. Given a pattern of gradual reduction in public spending, there is a move toward making people more responsible for their own health. Nowhere is this more evident than in the deinstitutionalization of people with long-term health and mental-health problems. Do these types of policies make people healthier or simply permit us to ignore a growing social problem? Inequitable resources in health care have not received adequate attention.

HEALTH-CARE DELIVERY REFORM

Health care is a significant political problem. A health system based on national insurance is controversial. A major goal of reform is health security. Accordingly, all U.S. citizens are guaranteed access to quality health care. Universal health insurance coverage is promised despite lack of income, preexisting health conditions, or job loss. Consumers would be able to choose their own providers.

States would create regional health alliances—purchasing cooperatives to pool health insurance premiums into large financial bodies. This permits alliances to effectively negotiate with health providers who bid to provide care. Plans would include health maintenance organizations, fee-for-service, and preferred provider. Competition between providers would keep costs down. Costs would be controlled through a centralized budget, set for an alliance by the state. Individuals would be able to change plans every year; data would be available to help make more fully informed decisions. States would have considerable freedom to develop and regulate regional health-care alliances. The president could appoint a national health board to establish federal and state budgets, monitor the performance of the total system through evaluation research, and implement guidelines as they become available through medical or policy research.

With national health insurance, the government would set prices for reimbursing physicians for their services (just as for Medicaid and Medicare). The medical profession is fighting against government control of their activities. In 1992, physicians contributed more to President Bush's reelection campaign than any other category except law, securities, and the retired.

In addition, there are the distinctive tensions of postmodern urban life that contribute to or cause illness as we will see in the next section.

COMPARING SOUTH AFRICA AND THE UNITED STATES

The oppressive policies and practices of apartheid in South Africa have directly contributed to preventable disease and mortality in black Africans (Brooks, Smith, & Anderson, 1991). Correspondingly, functional apartheid in the United States, based on social stratification, has resulted in often preventable but serious health problems for America's poor and ethnic minorities. Not surprisingly, the changes in social policy needed to improve the health status of black South Africans are similar to those that are necessary to remedy the bleak situation in the United States. For example, a health service provision model called "Community-Oriented Primary Care" has begun to address some of the pitfalls of our current medical-care systems (Brooks, Smith, & Anderson, 1991).

The Republic of South Africa has been the target of international protests, boycotts, and contempt based on the treatment accorded their black and mulatto populations. Many of the most strident demands for the elimination of institutionalized racial discrimination have come from the United States. Ironically, the health care of U.S. ethnic minority citizens is in dire need of attention.

Most Western and many Eastern nations consider health care to be a right, similar to education for all children and adolescents. The United States and the Republic of South Africa share the dubious distinction of being the only industrialized countries in the world that continue to view health care as a privilege. This failure to guarantee access to basic health care for all citizens results in substantial economic and human losses for these countries.

While the segregated nature of South Africa's health system (see Nightingale et al., 1990) is not surprising, it's similarity to health-care delivery in the United States is startling. Both systems are characterized by "inadequate (or totally absent) care for large segments of their population, gross inequities in the allocation of health care resources, and poorly coordinated and economically inefficient bureaucracies" (Brooks, Smith, & Anderson, 1991: 2746).

In the United States, there is a strong positive correlation between health and socioeconomic status. Since racial minority groups comprise a disproportionate portion of our nation's underprivileged, these minorities, the primary victims of economic and political oppression, tend to have the worst health. Latinos and blacks are more likely to be uninsured and less likely to have access to health care than the rest of the population (Trevino et al., 1991). A lack of insurance has been linked with significantly fewer expensive diagnostic tests among hospitalized patients and an increased risk of in-hospital death (Hadley, Steinberg, & Feder, 1991).

Despite the differences in the dynamics and institutions between South Africa and the United States, the manifestations are strikingly similar. For example, the United States has virtually eliminated legal discrimination but not institutional discrimination. The wide gaps in life-expectancy rates, preventable disease incidence, socioeconomic status, and quality of lifestyle between dominant and minority groups signifies a plethora of inequalities inherent in the existing social and health-care delivery systems of both countries.

In South Africa, many narrowly focused agencies have been created to address different aspects of health care (Nightingale et al., 1991). Consequently, there are a large number of competing authorities that add bureaucratic paralysis and expenses, and prevent the efficient delivery of health care. This factionalism is similar to that found in metropolitan areas in the United States. A multitude of city, county, and private agencies provide a narrow range of services at various times and locations. For example, "well babies may be seen at one location, but immunizations must be obtained at a different site, while ill children must travel to different clinics or the county hospital" (Brooks, Smith, & Anderson, 1991: 2746). Services often overlap; but sometimes there are gaps. Sites for comprehensive health-care services are rare. Attempts to develop comprehensive health networks are typically met with opposition because of the vested interests of affected agencies, without concern for the medical needs of the population to be served.

Apartheid rigidly cut the population of South Africa into four categories based on race (white, black, Asian, and mulatto or colored—mixed race). Socioeconomic level and standard of living strongly correlates with skin color. The darker one's color, the lower one's social class. The poor health of South African blacks can be traced to hazardous living conditions that relegate blacks to urban ghettos and rural "homelands" (Nightingale et al., 1991). They live in separate and sharply segregated areas characterized by miserable housing, poor sanitation, and inadequate or nonexistent health care. Impoverished blacks in South Africa are handled by overcrowded hospitals with outdated equipment and facilities, limited staff, and grossly inadequate budgets (Abkiewicz et al., 1987).

This description is hauntingly similar to the living conditions of our nation's poor and minorities. Like much business and industry, the medical profession has largely abandoned America's urban neighborhoods. Medical services, including primary care, have left the community and are transformed into inaccessible "medical centers." Barriers have created and cultivated growing chunks of our population who are continuously searching for ways to get over, around, or through them.

Public hospitals are the only access to health care for the poor in many parts of the United States. Most of these serve a population that is overwhelmingly underprivileged and minority. Much of the inequality described in the South African medical system is reflected in the delivery of health care to the indigent population in the United States. The occupancy rate of some public hospitals in the United States often surpasses functional capacity, requiring diversion of ambulances away from emergency wards. In 1990, at Parkland Memorial Hospital in Dallas, there was a 30 percent increase in trauma volume (due mainly to drug- and gang-related violence), which threatened to overwhelm an already swamped situation and thereby lessen medical resources dedicated to the care of victims of automobile accidents, industrial mishaps, and other trauma (Brooks, Smith, & Anderson, 1991).

A tremendous amount of volume flows through public hospitals. At Parkland, 150,000 people annually are treated in the emergency department alone; 1,500 scheduled patients are seen in its outreach clinics each day

(Brooks, Smith, & Anderson, 1991). An additional three hundred patients per day are processed through a walk-in ambulatory care clinic where waiting times average seven to eight hours. Due to the lack of accessible primary care for the underprivileged, public clinics are the only option for many patients.

Inappropriately viewed as "free care," the burden imposed on the working poor by the loss of a day's wages is anything but free. A day's pay can sometimes make a difference between the patient's family eating or not eating. Moreover, the long waits cause approximately one of every nine of these non-scheduled patients to leave the clinic prior to receiving care (Brooks, Smith, & Anderson, 1991). Such patients may never come back or may return later in a more advanced stage of their illness, necessitating more involved and costly treatment, or hospitalization.

Conditions are even worse for rural citizens in South Africa and the United States. Medical care is primitive or nonexistent for rural South Africa and a similar situation is emerging in our own country. For example, more than 20 percent of Texas's 254 counties have no acute-care hospital, and 119 counties do not have hospital obstetrical or newborn services (Texas Hospital Association, 1991). While only 8 percent of all U.S. births occur in Texas, they account for one-third of all out-of-hospital births nationally. (These births are disproportionately among minority women.) This contributes to infant mortality rates in some urban areas that are seven times greater than the national average (Texas Hospital Association, 1991).

While choices in medical care are diminishing for many rural Americans, health-care delivery for the poor (especially the poor of color) has always been problematic. Even for those with Medicaid, a private physician willing to treat them is difficult to impossible to find. (There is no profit with Medicaid patients.) In a wealthy county with thirty-three obstetrician/gynecologists, a woman with Medicaid was unable to locate a physician willing to accept her for pregnancy care (Klein, 1991).

Both South Africa and the United States have disgraceful records for preventable diseases in their indigent populations. Both have alarmingly high rates of black infant mortality, and a greater prevalence of diseases such as tuberculosis, pneumonia, and measles (Brooks, Smith, & Anderson, 1991). Such diseases have virtually been exterminated among the white population of South Africa via immunization programs, nutrition, sanitation, and quality health education. Correspondingly, blacks in the United States die from preventable diseases at much higher rates than whites (Schwartz et al., 1990). Latinos and blacks suffer disproportionately higher complications from diabetes and hypertension (Council on Scientific Affairs, 1991); African American men in Harlem have a shorter life span than men in many impoverished Third World countries (McCord & Freeman, 1990).

A traditional indicator of the health status of a population is infant mortality rates. They tend to reflect the quality of medical service and the sociopolitical environment. Adverse social situations have been strongly correlated with increased rates of infant mortality (Molteno & Kibel, 1989). The United States is, arguably, the world's most affluent country. However, the infant mortality rate in the United States is embarrassingly high when compared to rates of other industrialized countries. The U.S. rate of ten infants lost for each ten thousand births (twentieth in the world; Children's Defense Fund, 1991) is a national scandal.

Black infant mortality rates as high as 282 per 1,000 births have been documented in rural South Africa (Knutzen & Bourne, 1977). The U.S. mortality rate for black infants is estimated to be between 94 and 124 deaths per 1,000 live births (Yach, 1988). This sharply contrasts with the nationwide average of 13.5 deaths per 1,000 births among white South Africans (Rip & Bourne, 1988). Data from South Africa suggest the potential benefits of improving access to even substandard health-care services (Rip & Bourne, 1988; Wyndham, 1986). While the ratio of black-to-white infant deaths remains approximately 3:1, black infant death rates as low as 27 per 1,000 births have been achieved. This rate is actually better than current black infant mortality rates of up to 38 per 1,000 births in some urban areas (D. Bacchi, unpublished data, 1990).

Hypertension is prevalent in the black and white populations of both nations. Complications of hypertension such as end-stage renal disease (ESRD) can be prevented through early detection and adequate treatment. South African research on patients with ESRD in two urban areas reveals hypertension to be responsible for 32 percent and 33 percent of kidney failure among blacks, but only 10 percent of the disease in whites (Seedat et al., 1984; Gold, Isaacson, & Levin, 1982). Likewise, 42.5 percent of black patients with ESRD in the United States have hypertension as the primary cause of their renal disease, while hypertension accounts for only 17.4 percent of ESRD in the U.S. white population (Eggers, Connerton, & McMullan, 1984). The risk of ESRD from hypertension in Jefferson City, Alabama, is reported to be nearly eighteen times higher in blacks than in whites (Rostand et al., 1982).

The poor of South Africa and the United States also suffer disproportionately from yet another preventable disease: measles. Black children in South Africa continue to experience significant morbidity and mortality from this disease, while it has been largely eliminated among whites through immunization (Bourne, Rip, & Woods, 1988; Kettles, 1987). To be sure, conditions related to poverty such as malnutrition, poor sanitation, and overcrowded living conditions are associated with the disease. Nevertheless, the lack of immunization of minority infants and children is the major factor in the continuance of this pestilence.

In 1990, the United States experienced a measles epidemic, the epicenters of which were Los Angeles and Dallas. Predictably, primarily ethnic minority and poor children contracted the disease. But the entire communities of both metropolitan areas were adversely affected. The financial and social costs of more than twenty-five hundred cases of measles and the tragedy of twelve young lives lost to a completely preventable disease will not easily be forgotten. The failure to provide a $3 immunization in some cases resulted in thousands of dollars in hospital expenses.

National health insurance, health-care financing, and access to care are common topics in the major medical journals of both South Africa and the United States. The National Medical and Dental Association and the Progressive Primary Health Care Network labored assertively against apartheid and toward a health-care plan for post-apartheid South Africa (Nightingale et al., 1990; Mji & Vallabhjee, 1990). Unfortunately, the medical profession in the United States has not been as responsive. Finally, the Medical Association of South Africa (the nation's largest organization of physicians) supports the development of a social and health-care system without racial and economic discrimination ("Policy Statement on Discrimination in Medical Practice," 1989).

HEALTH CARE AND THE POLITICAL ECONOMY

The U.S. health-care system cost $1.2 trillion in 1998 (U.S. Department of Health and Human Services, 2000). In 2003, health care will likely cost $1.6 trillion. Consequently, whether to reform health care is not the issue, how to reform it is. The contemporary crisis in health care is a situation that even the most traditional supporter of the status quo cannot afford to ignore.

The cost of health care has become the major factor of small-business and personal bankruptcy (Ehrenreich, 1990). Health care is now 12.4 percent of our gross national product (Kosterlitz, 1992). But we are getting a poor return for our investment. Our system is analogous to cancer—uncontrollable growth (financially speaking) and more dysfunctional with every jump. More than 40 million Americans have no health insurance in spite of per capita medical expenses that socialized systems cannot touch. Twenty-eight percent of the U.S. population is either uninsured or underinsured (Ehrenreich, 1990). For these people, a laboratory test or diagnostic workup can mean not being able to pay rent, going without food, or not filling a child's prescription.

Even with Medicare, the elderly must put more than 15 percent of their income toward health care. Infant mortality in the United States is higher than Singapore, with life expectancy lower than Cubans (Ehrenreich, 1990). Tragically, as many as 50 percent of inner-city infants and toddlers go unimmunized. The current AIDS crisis, our first major epidemic since polio, is dependent on expensive and, therefore, unavailable for most medical technology. Public hospitals are overcrowded with victims of AIDS, tuberculosis, and poverty.

With health care too expensive for so many, it is not surprising that three out of every four Americans support a government-financed national health-care program (*New England Journal of Medicine*, cited in Ehrenreich, 1990). Moreover, because of increasing financial burdens for employers (especially companies with less than one hundred employees) in providing health care for employees, unions are lobbying for a national program. Even a majority of physicians now support national health insurance (Ehrenreich, 1990). Yet, the American Medical Association opposes it; the medical profession fears the centralized intervention of the federal government that a national program would bring. The association would lose relative power and control of the medical industry. Private practitioners have a great deal of freedom to charge their patients whatever they decide. With a national program, physicians would set medical fees only for those affluent enough to not need the program.

Over the years, the private insurance industry has contributed to the rising costs of health care by remaining uncritical to uncontrollable increases in physician and hospital fees. As insurance overpaid the medical profession through reimbursements, insurance companies overcharged its policyholders: the individual, family, or employers. The current crisis in health care has pushed the insurance industry to more drastic measures: They price out the poor and drop the sicker clients. People who are rejected in this manner are, of course, the most expensive to insure.

The nightmarish financial burden then falls into the hands of the federal government that is forced to implement cost-control measures. But the government's control of health-care costs is limited to Medicare, Medicaid, and its other programs. Private insurers, meanwhile, simply convert their costs into premiums for the insured individual to pay. This sheds the poor and the sick that continues the cycle. While private practice snares the most profitable share of the health-care market, the public domain is served leftovers.

Only when fee-for-service (FFS) plans are legislatively permitted to follow health maintenance organizations (HMOs) in contracting with hospitals on the basis of price can HMO market penetration be expected to reduce hospital cost inflation (Robinson, 1991: 2719). However, market forces did not work well enough to curb the increase in hospital costs. The average hospital cost, per case, expanded 74.5 percent in only six years (1982–1988), in spite of the development and prevalence of HMOs.

Too many obstacles remain for healthy competition between health-care providers. Most employers do not offer an option that includes one of the most cost-effective health plans and then require employees to pay the difference in premium if they select the more expensive coverage. Employers, consequently, subsidize the most costly plans (usually FFS), at the same time blocking the chance for those of most value to compete. FFS plans typically counter HMO market penetration by competing for consumer loyalty established on actual or imagined differences in quality, while increasing costs.

Approximately half of the workforce is employed by companies with one hundred or fewer workers (Enthoven, 1991). More and more, the insurance industry underwrites these small companies by charging higher premiums to the sick or refusing to cover them at all. Administrative costs are approximately 30 percent of contracted claims for companies with ten to nineteen workers, but only 5.5 percent for companies of more than ten thousand (Subcommittee on Health of the Committee on Ways and Means, 1990). This radical fragmentation permits insurance companies to divide markets and negate price competition.

Information control is one form of power. The prospective client cannot make a fully informed decision without comparative information on the quality and costs of health-care services and goods. However, in many states there are significant barriers to obtaining data in a form easily comprehensible and accessible to potential purchasers (Enthoven, 1991). Hospitals take the position that information on their value and effectiveness is confidential; they have generally succeeded in protecting what they claim to be their turf (Singer, 1991).

Physicians and private health-care delivery systems have lobbied their concerns so successfully that a cost-competitive market has not been able to flourish. An enormous and uncontrollable growth in the cost of health care has resulted. Much of the rise in the cost of health care can be related to inflation and the increase in the number of patients. Much of the increase is mainly the consequence of the rising use and technological state of the art of health-care delivery.

There are at least five key factors related to the rising cost of health care: (1) unnecessary care; (2) medical technology; (3) availability and affordability; (4) longevity increases; and (5) medical fraud, abuse, and waste.

1. *Unnecessary Care.* There is much health care that is actually not needed (Kosterlitz, 1992). Physicians who are paid for each service they provide are motivated to order more tests, consult with patients often, and perform more service activity in order to make more money. The elimination of unnecessary medical procedures could cut $50 billion per year from the nation's medical bill (Robert H. Brook, Rand Corporation, cited in Kosterlitz, 1992). When individuals, the government, or the insurance industry pay physicians and hospitals for each service, an economic incentive (to do more rather than less) is created for the provider.

The power in the health provider–patient relationship leans heavily on the side of the provider. Hospitals and physicians, much more often than patients, make the chief decisions regarding the quality and quantity of health-care services. Health-care providers remain largely unchecked in their ability to charge whatever they do. Physicians in the United States receive among the highest salaries when compared to their international peers (Kosterlitz, 1992). To be sure, there are factors other than greed that motivate physicians to provide more care than less, including patient demand and the fear of malpractice suits. When private insurance or government programs pay for health care, neither the provider nor the patient are motivated to become cost-conscious.

2. *Medical Technology.* Medical treatment has become considerably more complex and sophisticated and, consequently, more expensive. How else does one explain rising health-care costs despite Americans not going to physicians more often? In addition, hospital stays (which account for the bulk of the costs of health-care services) have sharply declined in the past ten years. Innovations in medical procedures, the emergence of new drugs with high expectations, and technological advances have meant, for the most part, better (albeit more costly) health care. Total costs generally increase even when the new procedure is less expensive than the previous one since the new procedure is more widely used.

3. *Availability and Affordability.* National health-care consumption tends to rise with national wealth. What this means is that people who can afford to buy better or more health care will do so. The widening coverage and availability of insurance since, at least, the middle of the twentieth century has helped to bring more people to the physician while keeping actual costs away from them. Generous tax breaks have motivated employers to provide health coverage for their employees. This has resulted in a $60 billion per year subsidy for health care (Kosterlitz, 1992). Needless to say, the people who need the most help paying for health care are the least affected by such programs. The affluent disproportionately benefit because they are most likely to have generous employer-provided health coverage.

4. *Longevity Increases.* People are living longer and the use of health-care services increases with age (Kosterlitz, 1992). Nevertheless, population aging is a fairly small factor in rising health care costs (approximiately 10 percent).

5. *Medical Fraud, Abuse, and Waste.* Everyone favors the elimination of fraud, abuse, and waste. Some hospitals and physicians overcharge or charge for health services that were never provided. Such deceitful practices resulted in expenses estimated at $20–30 billion in 1991 (National Health Care Anti-Fraud Association, 1992). Money is also wasted through bureaucratic regulation and advertising. There are high administrative and marketing costs related to the seemingly infinite number of private health insurance plans, each with its own set of rules. An estimated $58 billion could be saved each year if administrative costs for insurers, hospitals, and physicians were reduced.

It seems clear that excessive health-care costs are related to inadequate insurance coverage. Americans generally are not happy with the health-care system. One problem is cost shifting: Hospitals and physicians charge insured individuals and their employers the additional cost of those unable to pay their medical bills. Underfunding exacerbates the chronic problems of inner-city hospitals and emergency centers.

The insurance industry has rejected poor-risk individuals and overcharged small companies. The U.S. health-care system, consequently, is not only slighting the poor but the recently uninsured middle-class family. Health clinics, public hospitals, and the emergency centers of some private hospitals act as a hastily assembled safety net for those who cannot pay for medical care. The uninsured typically receive poor and less care. Additionally, health-care providers do not see them on a regular basis. Those who lack insurance also have the greatest danger of economic devastation. Health-care costs are now a major factor in individual bankruptcies.

Why do so many people in the richest nation in the world lack adequate health care? The overwhelming majority of the uninsured simply cannot afford it. Some can but choose to take risks. The majority of uninsured Americans are full-time workers (and their families), most of whom work for small companies who must pay more than their large counterparts for health coverage for their employees—particularly since financial risk and administrative and marketing expenses cannot be diffused as broadly. A small company with fewer than twenty-five workers pays 16.7 percent more than a large company employing more than one thousand people for the same medical coverage (Kosterlitz, 1992).

DISTRIBUTIVE JUSTICE AND HEALTH CARE

On what basis do we distribute limited medical resources? Given that the need for medical services and products is greater than what is available, who should receive an artificial heart or a lung transplant? What is the fairest way to assess need—First-come, first-served?

There is a great deal of inequality in health care. Too much attention, effort, research, technology, and financial resources are geared toward costly cures for the rich at the expense of basic, preventative health care for the poor working and middle classes. Medical schools train too many specialists and not enough primary-care physicians. Australian medical schools instruct three-fourths of their students in primary care; in Canada, one-half; but in the United States, only one-third. Growth in specialization has also resulted in an overabundance of hospitals and physicians concentrated in the affluent suburbs. Consequently, inner-city communities and rural areas are stranded with unsuitable access to health-care delivery.

The problem of distributive justice also emerges at a more basic level: How should resources be distributed that combat new diseases (e.g., SARS) or that develop particular types of new procedures at the expense of others or that acquire new knowledge in some areas while ignoring others? "Personnel and facilities for medical research and treatment are scarce resources. Is the development of a new technology the best use of the limited resources given current circumstances?" (Kass, 1985: 26). We must consider that the resources used in medicine and biology are also needed to reduce gender and ethnic discrimination, urban decay, environmental pollution, and poverty and to improve the quality of education.

American society is experiencing an internal "brain drain" that squeezes our brightest youth into rigid careers focused on the search for biochemical defects in rare genetic diseases, while the much more fundamental issue of social inequality is chiefly ignored. These judgments are usually made within a framework of conflict between competing interests. The sociolegal system in the United States is based on a complex that is inherently power- and conflict-oriented. Institutional arrangements are grounded on the balance of power and checks and balances. The question starts as How should X be justly distributed? But it ends up as Who will decide how to distribute X? Consequently, a moral issue is often turned into a power play.

Some people, with knowledge of medicine as their instrument, exercise power over others. It is the marriage of science and politics that makes this possible. Science and politics combine to decide the limits of population growth. Fertility control is typically coercive, including brute force as well as the imposition of forceful sanctions. During the Nixon administration, a high-level psychologist–adviser called for the psychological testing of all six-year-olds to detect future criminals and misfits. The suggestion was rejected because current tests lacked the required predictability. What would have occurred had valid and reliable tests been available?

Technologically induced dehumanization, the abuse of power, and the distribution of scarce resources are topics that provide a window for defining and implementing an ethically based health program. Technology has increasingly come to be the primary rationale for scientific inquiry. Science has come to be associated with power, and less with knowledge. We hold the power to manipulate most of the unfavorable consequences of technology; yet we lack the ethics to decide what technology should be developed in the first place.

SUMMARY AND CONCLUSION

Approximately one-third of uninsured people live in poverty. In addition, nearly all of the remaining uninsured are in families who earn less than twice the official poverty level. It has been estimated that a centralized health-care program would cut $58 billion annually in administrative expenses (approximately 8 percent of total costs) (Kosterlitz, 1992).

Moreover, the American Medical Association admits that $15 billion per year (2 percent of total costs) could be saved by stopping physicians from performing unnecessary procedures in the hopes of avoiding malpractice suits. Finally, 4 percent of total costs could be obtained by eliminating fraud.

Reformers have not, however, taken into account monitoring and transitional costs. Even if such expenses were modest, the net effect would be a one-time decrease (less than 15 percent) in national health-care expenses.

We must eliminate financial rewards that tempt hospitals and physicians to supply more health service than is actually necessary. HMOs, for example, could drop the traditional fee-for-service practice of medicine. Such plans, rather, could require a total per-person fee to cover all care. HMOs usually put their physicians on salary, monitor referrals to expensive specialists, carefully check hospital admissions, and ensure that hospital stays are kept to a minimum. There are also health-care networks through which needed services are provided at discount. Patients who select physicians outside of the network must pay more. Health-care networks allow more patients a greater range of choices than HMOs but are more expensive.

While it may cost less for HMOs than for traditional health insurance, HMO costs rise at approximately the same rate as other health costs (Kosterlitz, 1992). This implies that cost saving is only a one-time reduction. If cutting prices and unneeded care is not sufficient to slow down the price of health care, what is? Most people simply cannot afford even a short stay in a hospital. For those who can, medical bills cut into their standard of living. More and more income must go for health care.

Cost sharing—collaboration among two or more health providers to share capital-intensive medical technology—is a feasible solution. This reduces cost without impairing care. There could also be limited protection from antitrust violations to defend facilities that share costly medical technology or other high resource-intensive services. The overall objective is to encourage hospitals and other health-care providers to share some of the expensive high-tech technologies, especially when sharing would not inconvenience patients. This assumes that health-care providers are willing to be team players in offering a comprehensive array of affordable health-care services. This would make health care more affordable and cost-effective.

To cut health-care costs, the introduction and use of new technology, drugs, and procedures must be carefully monitored. The implementation of scientific advances cannot proceed unrestrained. We must ask ourselves the question How much of what science makes available do we really need? As long as a new diagnostic machine or a new surgical procedure offers some benefit, there is sure to be consumer demand. In a sense, supply creates demand. Think about magnetic resonance imagers, for example. These high-tech diagnostic machines, which give physicians elaborate pictures of what is going on inside the body, were first used in 1984. In 2001, there were 949 new magnetic imagers sold in the United States for $1.2 billion (National Electrical Manufacturers Association, 2002). Some of them run nonstop, at a cost of between $600 and $1,000 per hour.

A limit must be placed on what people want or, at least, what they can have. However, the issue is much more problematic for politicians, who must satisfy their constituency. Reformers call for a greater role for government in limiting spending on the introduction and deployment of new health-care technology. Without such limits, health costs will soar even higher if the latest fads become accessible to everyone with private insurance or government coverage. Alternatively, only the affluent will be able to afford them. Neither option is acceptable. National medical committees could make well-informed choices as to what level of health care people need and can afford, and guarantee that health-care delivery is equitable. In short, the health-care system should have a moral basis, not just a focus on profit.

Others support free-market health care. Theoretically, increased competition in the health-care marketplace should result in lower costs and improved quality and efficiency. The elimination of subsidies for employer-sponsored health care, it is argued, would force most Americans to become more cost-conscious in choosing health programs. The rich would no longer receive tax subsidies that pay as much as 40 percent of the cost of their health plans. Only the underclass would be covered, and then, only enough to cover the basics.

If price-conscious consumers begin selecting the best values, health providers and insurers would have to become more competitive and more useful. If patients are forced to pay their own way, they will become more health cost-conscious. Individuals would also be forced to make difficult decisions about the quality and quantity of health care they are willing to buy.

Yet health care lends itself poorly to market competition. The consumer has very little knowledge and a minimal capacity to judge what type of health care to buy, and how much. Without price regulation, the task is even harder. Employers do not always make ethical decisions when selecting health-care programs for employees. Competition would probably eliminate only the most extreme types of unneeded care and waste. It would not decrease the desire for features that assure some degree of enhanced care. In a free-market economy, consumers decide how much of their incomes to spend on health care and how much to spend on other consumer services and goods. But people do not always make ethical decisions; sometimes they do not even act in their best interests.

The health-care debate is not about regulation versus competition, but in synthesizing the two strategies. The proposed changes to improve the health conditions of black South Africans are similar to those that are needed to solve the condition of U.S. citizens. The splintered health system that unsuccessfully serves the underprivileged should be removed and replaced. The present health-care delivery system is woefully inadequate. It seems to only create obstacles for people—obstacles that result in expensive delays and duplication of effort. Immediate and inexpensive access to comprehensive primary care centers is needed.

The lack of such centers have already been associated with disease and excessive deaths (Schwartz et al., 1990; Dana et al., 1990; Council on Ethical and Judicial Affairs, 1989). In addition, health promotion exercise and community education are sorely needed. A significant increase in the number of ethnic minority individuals pursuing careers in health-related fields is also necessary. Certainly, this entails aggressive affirmative action programs on the part of medical schools, as well as the availability of scholarships to medical schools for deserving minority candidates.

In the Community-Oriented Primary Care (COPC), the health status and medical needs of a delineated population or community are appraised. A health-care delivery plan is then developed and implemented based on these identified needs. This method of health-care service synthesizes basic public health issues, individual patient care, and epidemiology (the study of the spread and control of diseases in a particular population). The Institute of Medicine has positively evaluated the COPC (Conner & Mullan, 1983).

COPCs could become the new federal models. This type of health-care delivery has been tried in the United States (Nutting, Wood, & Conner, 1985; Conner & Mullan, 1983). They are designed to provide frontline, primary care—not to replace hospitals. The COPC is the model for public health in Dallas. Preventative clinics in eight targeted "incubator" communities should fundamentally improve the quality and quantity (and lower the costs) of health care in the city, on a wide range of services from birth wards to trauma rooms. It is ironic that the fundamental ideology and format of COPC originated in South Africa more than forty years ago. In collaboration with the indigenous community in Polela, South Africa, Dr. Sidney L. Kark and his associates are credited with the organization of the first successful COPC models (Kark, 1981).

Today in the United States, networks of health centers conveniently located in economically deprived neighborhoods are starting to spring up. They provide a full spectrum of health-care services, promote healthy lifestyles, and stress preventive medicine at accessible sites. Providers are on call twenty-four hours a day, available to respond to calls from worried parents, authorize prescription refills, and decrease expensive, unnecessary visits to emergency centers in hospitals. Moreover, health care is provided in nontraditional settings, serving needy people in recreational centers for the elderly, schools, churches, and homeless shelters. There are weekend and evening office hours that guarantee accessibility for the working poor (for whom losing a day's pay because of a trip to the physician may have seriously adverse consequences). This type of health-care structure is aimed at providing underprivileged people with something they have never had: a family physician.

An essential component of the COPC is community health education. Programs are designed to make at-risk populations sensitive to the advantages of reducing or eliminating risky behavior for many diseases, the significance of routine preventive care, and early signs of diseases. When communities are empowered by this kind of knowledge, individuals are encouraged to pursue a much more active part in their own health care.

Ideally, physicians, nurses, and other health-care providers of COPC should be of diverse ethnic and social backgrounds, equivalent to the communities that they serve. When this is not possible, full-time translators should be provided to facilitate communication and avoid misunderstandings. Health-care providers should be encouraged to take an active role in community matters, and serve as much-needed role models for the youth of the community.

The dynamics of evaluating the beliefs, risk factors, and health status of communities, and then constructing intervention programs based on this protocol, is also undergoing a sorely needed resurgence in South Africa. Programs such as the Mamre Community Health Project (Klopper & Tibbit, 1988) and a door-to-door study of cardiovascular risk factors among urban blacks ("Heart Disease Study Launched in Western Cape," 1990) are applying methods pioneered over fifty years ago.

The creation of similar health-care delivery systems should continue. Such systems hold the potential for dramatically improving the health of indigent people. Medical care, nevertheless, does not exist in a social vacuum. Health-care programs are part of the sociopolitical environment; consequently, even if economic oppression and racial discrimination were eliminated, their effects on health and education would remain for many years. Social policy must take into account the relationships among the access to economic opportunity, education, housing and residential patterns, and health status. Poverty acts as an independent risk factor for premature death in African Americans (Otten et al., 1990). Similarly, for Latinos, poverty and the lack of health insurance are the greatest barriers to health care (Council on Scientific Affairs, 1991). Institutional discrimination persists to hamper any meaningful economic empowerment and political participation by blacks and other minority or marginal populations.

POLICY IMPLICATIONS

Physician and hospital fees should be harnessed by an externally generated regulatory schedule. Private insurance should not be permitted to drop the poor and the sick. The essential component of insurance is risk sharing. The private health insurance industry must accept and practice risk taking. This involves not only the healthy and wealthy, but also the sick, poor, elderly, and children.

To alleviate health problems, there must be a combined effort. A "play-or-pay" plan would require employers to either provide insurance for their workers or pay into a public plan that also serves the poor and unemployed. Small businesses could provide better health coverage through pooling their financial resources and insurance reform. Health-care costs could be monitored by a federal board that sets spending targets, controls hospital and physician fees, and approves the purchasing of high-tech equipment.

There is emphasis on HMOs and other group model systems, phased-in benefits for long-term care (starting with home and community-based care), and alternatives to malpractice litigation. How can our political system provide health care for citizens without raising taxes or restricting access to services? Individual patients need to pursue healthy lives. Physicians need to put the health of their patients before self-interest or patient vanity. Legislators and health officials need to develop and implement health policy that best maintains or attains the health of citizens. Finally, a more equitable distribution of scare resources must be realized.

The range of physicians' responsibilities should be limited. Medical associations can play a very key role in this. There is far too much medical technology that can be used for nonmedical purposes and nontherapeutic ends. Examples include the use of medical technology to help parents determine or select the sex of their future child or the destructive brain surgery to modify behavior. Many of the procedures that physicians use for nonmedical/nontherapeutic purposes (abortion, artificial insemination, mercy killing, vanity surgery, mood elevation, eugenic counseling) could be learned by fairly bright and dexterous high school graduates with six months of technical training.

Consumer control of medicine renders the physician a mere technician or public servant. If this were eliminated, physicians could place greater attention on keeping their patients healthy, particularly preventative medicine. The medical profession spends too much of its effort and resources on treatment at the expense of prevention and health consciousness. Medical scientists need to better understand what damages and improves health. Reliable studies in the following areas are needed: particular resistance to particular diseases; personal hygiene and individual health habits; adaptations to stress; relaxation and sleep; exercise and fitness; and diet and nutrition. The American Medical Association and the National Institutes of Health should foster quality research on disease prevention and healthy living.

An effective plan for national health insurance would drop the no-fault principle found in most current health-care packages. The significance of personal responsibility for one's health would be stressed, not ignored or treated as irrelevant. Accordingly, both positive and negative inducements can be built into the insurance payment plan (e.g., refusing or reducing benefits for chronic respiratory disease care to persons who persist in smoking).

WHAT YOU CAN DO

How do social class, race, ethnicity, and gender affect health and health care? Visit the Web site for the U.S. Centers for Disease Control and Prevention: www.cdc.gov. Examine information about them as well as statistical data, health news, and traveler's health advisories.

SIX

CRIME AND PRISON: THE SOCIAL CONTROL OF DEVIANCE

If the purpose of imprisonment were to socialize men to become as violent as possible—both while they are there, and after they return to the community—we could hardly find a more effective way to accomplish it.

—James Gilligan, *Violence*

THE UNITED STATES has more prisons and more people in prison (over 2 million) than any other country. Yet we still have more violent crime than any other postindustrial nation in the world. The data present a very bleak picture of our society and our criminal justice system:

- The state of California has opened only one college since 1984—and twenty-one prisons.
- There are five times as many Americans in prison today as in 1970.
- The national incarceration rate in 1997 was twice that in 1985.
- California has the third largest prison system in the world.
- Young black men in the United States are more than one hundred times as likely to suffer a violent death than are young men in France or Great Britain.
- Forty percent of Los Angeles residents personally know someone who has been killed or seriously injured in a violent attack.

- There are more homicides in Los Angeles (population 3.5 million) than in all of England and Wales (population 50 million). (Yet we incarcerated six times as many people as the British.)
- A shoplifter with two previous convictions for burglary can be sentenced to prison for life without any chance of parole.
- Nearly three out of every ten black men have been or can expect to be locked up in federal or state penitentiaries sometime during their lives.
- Currently there are seven times as many inmates in California prisons than less than twenty years ago. (Currie, 1998)

Clearly, we are not winning the War on Crime. Some think we are too lenient on crime and demand stiffer sentences, more prisons, and harsher treatment of juvenile offenders. This chapter argues against this approach for three reasons: it is too expensive, it is unethical, and it does not significantly decrease violent crime. Furthermore, the data will suggest that we are not, in fact, lenient on crime. In fact, sentencing has become more severe for those who have been arrested and then convicted of crimes.

A SOCIAL ETHICS APPROACH TO CRIME PREVENTION POLICY

The possibilities for preventing violent crime are great and still fundamentally undeveloped. On the other hand, the possibility of stopping crime by building more prisons, incarcerating younger offenders, and handing out longer sentences is not only ineffective and tremendously costly but also unethical.

There is a substantial gap (with a few notable exceptions) between what social-scientific research tells us about alleviating crime and what our criminal justice policy actually is. Current policy debate does little to address the sources of crime, crime prevention, the rehabilitation of criminals, and the functions and limitations of punitive intervention. While our prisons swell from overcrowding, violent crime has not been substantially reduced.

The media have provided the public with half-truths, misconceptions, myths, and often-conflicting coverage of crime. Moreover, the 2000 presidential debates did not seriously address issues about crime. The myths also continue because they support the political and economic status quo. The control of crime is big business. The recent and dramatic increase in the number of those who have been incarcerated in some states has manufactured a large and politically powerful constituency of people whose employment and status rest on maintaining or expanding current levels. Of course, a tough-on-crime position by politicians is always viewed favorably by the public. Scholars, as well, have often benefited tremendously from this approach.

Perhaps most important, these myths serve a deep ideological function. They support a Social Darwinian approach to society that justifies social inequality. This punitive and impressionable response to crime is a harsh assault on the poor ethnic minorities and those who deviate from mainstream culture. It is an indirect attack on social welfare policy and an explicit blaming the victim for his own poverty and misfortunes.

Our social policies emphasize personal responsibility but do not recognize the structural constraints of a capitalistic system that prevents a sizable portion of the population from attaining even a minimal level of economic stability. If we admit that our criminal justice system has fallen short in providing a reasonable level of safety to our streets, neighborhoods, and cities, then it forces us to also recognize that we failed as a democracy to provide equal protection under the law.

We are a nation that imprisons a large and rapidly growing segment of our population. Yet we continue to endure the most violent crime of any developed society in the world. What is wrong with this picture? We are floundering in a profound way. We use ideologically inspired prevarication disguised as science to guide our crime policies. It is no wonder we are losing the war against crime.

As we enter the new millennium, we are standing at the crossroads. There is a unique opportunity to eliminate the violence that pervades our society. There are new research findings that tell us what has worked and what has not worked in our fight against crime. If we set aside our preconceptions and vested interests, we can figure out which course to take. There is even evidence of hope because the high levels of violence so prevalent in the late 1980s and early 1990s have subsided somewhat.

As with virtually every social problem, prevention is far more effective than intervention. "The best prevention programs aimed at vulnerable children, youths, and families can be much more effective in reducing crime than further increases in incarceration" (Currie, 1998: 9). In the United States, violent crime is closely correlated to the endurance of absolute poverty and social inequality. It follows then that increases in social support and employment opportunities for the most vulnerable segments of our population will substantially reduce violent crime. If we shift crime policy to preventing harm and reintegrating ex-convicts into society instead of merely reacting to crime, violent crime rates will plummet.

We need to focus on public safety and not do just what is popular. Current crime policy is ineffective and wasteful; it squanders the hard-earned dollars of taxpayers, breaks up families, cripples human potential, and destroys lives. The decisions we make are not merely technical; they are also moral judgments. We must ask ourselves not only whether our policies work well but also whether they reflect our fundamental values as a democratic civilization.

If we build more prisons, it is inevitable that we will fill them. But what does it say about a society in which a continuous condition of civic erosion is momentarily prevented by the expansion of an enormous prison system that is unrivaled in human history, especially in any other democracy?

IS THE UNITED STATES SOFT ON CRIME?

On Tuesday, May 16, 2000 at 2:00 AM, a female was walking in her neighborhood in the xxxx block of xxxxxxxx Drive. The victim saw the suspect standing on the side of the street as she walked by and then as she walked by a second time, she saw the suspect walking the same direction that she was. When the victim reached xxxxxxxxx, she was grabbed from behind by the suspect and taken between two houses.

The suspect punched the victim several times until she fell to the ground and then the suspect sexually assaulted the victim. The suspect then ran in an unknown direction and the victim was able to call 911. The police were unable to locate the suspect in the area when they arrived. The victim suffered bruises on her face and head.

SUSPECT: White male, unknown age, 5' 11," 180 pounds, wearing a T-shirt and jeans, wedding ring and has a pointed nose.

—City of Dallas Crime Alert

The definition of a *social problem*, in its broadest sense, is a political issue involving opposing ideologies (e.g., pro-choice versus pro-life). Negative conditions must be collectively labeled as "social problems" before intervention is taken. However, what seems negative for one group may seem positive for another. Social problems are not solved primarily because of people's unwillingness to change the basic conditions from which they emerge. In recent times, the media and politicians have labeled crime the "major social problem in the United States."

Particularly, in the past two decades, illicit drug use has also been considered more serious and treated more harshly. Violent crime, including domestic violence and hate crime, is receiving widespread attention by the media and activist organizations. We have always had hate crimes. But now Web sites on the Internet readily provide violent ideology to encourage and corroborate lone individuals otherwise not linked to a group that supports such extreme viewpoints. Web sites also provide opportunities to exchange ideas, and receive information and technical knowledge needed to commit violent crime.

Violence is a potential danger that has crossed socioeconomic lines and lessened the quality of life in urban areas. The sexual assault described in the City of Dallas Crime Alert occurred in an affluent residential subdivision in North Dallas. Nevertheless, crime has recently been dropping. In 1998, 2.88 million crimes were reported in the Bureau of Justice Statistics *National Crime Victims Survey* (1998). This contrasts with an all-time high of 4.19 million in 1993. Nevertheless, violent crime rates in the United States remain higher than those of other advanced industrial societies—even despite obvious increases in the number of persons who have been incarcerated.

Many people feel that the courts and juries have been extremely lenient with criminals. However, data suggest that this is a myth (Currie, 2000). In truth, our criminal justice system, compared to most others, is quite punitive with the underclass persons who are arrested and brought to trial. There are approximately 2 million people in prison in the United States. That figure is larger than the population of five states. There is also a misconception that prisons are cost-effective.

The well-known "three strikes, you're out law" that mandates twenty-five-years-to-life sentences for criminals convicted of three felonies are used as quick fixes and vote-getters for politicians. This is because they give the impression that the supporter is tough on crime and has provided a seemingly effective deterrence to crime. In some states, the third felony may be a relatively minor offense, such as bicycle theft or possessing a small quantity of marijuana.

While these "one-size-fits-all" laws contain muscle, they lack efficiency and flexibility. They are overly rigid and eliminate judicial discretion for context and situation in sentencing. Accordingly, they result in a vast and costly expansion of the prison system into a home for aged and low-level criminals (Skolnick, 2000). Others (DiIiulio, 2000) argue that we are soft on criminals, allowing the most dangerous to turn state's witness and plea-bargain at the front end of the system, while releasing them early on parole and community supervision in the back end of the system.

From 1994 (the original year of the law) to 1999, the courts have sentenced 47,861 felons under its provisions. Out of all those who were sentenced, 5,419 were given at least twenty-five years to life under the law. The three-strikes policy has also generated clear racial unevenness. Police arrest blacks for felonies at a rate 4.7 times greater than that of whites. Judges and juries also imprison blacks thirteen times the rate of whites, hinting that district attorneys prosecute these "strikes" differently depending on the ethnic background of the defendant.

By 1995, the criminal justice system oversaw almost one in three young (i.e., twenty to twenty-nine) black men. This represents a hefty increase since the almost one in four rate in 1990. Much of the rise is attributable to an increase in convictions for drug offenses (Mauer & Huling, 2000). Illicit drug use in the inner city is, on the one hand, a symbol of a profound "social marginalization and alienation" (Bourgois, 2002). On the other hand, drug dealing has become the occupation of choice for poor young men (Davis, 1992). It provides a higher income than low-wage dead-end jobs—the only legitimate work most of them have ever had (Lusane & Desmond, 1991). Displays of economic success bring high honor or status. Trafficking in drugs actually brings in relatively low wages for small-time dealers. It is young men like these that increasingly make up our bulging prison population.

As I have mentioned, it is commonly believed that we are lenient with criminals. Yet this belief does not resonate with the fact that we have the world's highest rate of incarceration. The notion that serious, violent criminals are treated leniently in the United States is a myth; we are not "soft" on criminals. Data show a huge growth in punishment in recent years (Currie, 2000). Those who argue that we do not punish criminals and that we follow confused and progressive policies of leniency simply ignore the inordinate increase in incarceration rates. For example:

> Today and everyday the "justice" system permits unknown, convicted, violent and repeat criminals, adult and juvenile, to get away with murder and mayhem on the streets. Criminals who have repeatedly violated the life, liberty, and property of others are routinely sent free to do it all over again. (Council on Crime in America, cited in Currie, 1998: 38–39)

It is readily accepted that only one in one hundred violent crimes result in a prison sentence. Accordingly, even when convicts are punished, the courts hand down ridiculously light sentences for despicable crimes. Another misguided attack on our criminal-justice policies is the misconception that most of our criminals are not put in prison; rather they are all on probation, parole, or pretrial release. The Council on Crime in America, for example, points to misguided leniency and "the failure to restrain known violent offenders" and has argued that:

> America needs to put more violent and repeat criminals, adult and juvenile, behind bars longer, to see to it that truth-in-sentencing and such kindred laws as are presently on the books are fully and faithfully executed, and to begin reinventing probation and parole agencies in ways that will enable them to supervise their charges, enforce the law, and enhance public safety. (Council on Crime in America, cited in Currie, 1998: 38–39)

In conclusion, it is presumed that leniency is the root of America's ongoing problem with crime. If we are so easy on crime, then why is the prison population growing? Let us examine the evidence.

Violent crime rates have declined since 1994, reaching the lowest level ever recorded by the "National Crime Victimization Survey" in 2001 (U.S. Bureau of Justice Statistics, 2002). While only a relatively small proportion of violent criminals go to prison, that is extremely misleading. First, the majority of violent crimes are not life threatening. For example, in 1995, 6.2 million were "simple assaults"; almost 5 million (more than half of all violent crimes) were simple assaults without injury.

Most simple assaults are comprised of schoolyard fights or petty squabbles in establishments that serve alcohol. Most would agree that such minor crimes should not carry prison sentences. Moreover, most assaults are "attempted" or " threatened," and not "completed." The bark is worse than the bite. The relatively low incarceration rate is also misleading because it does not include juvenile institutions, federal prisons, or local jails.

The biggest distortion, however, is the overwhelming majority of crimes do not even enter the criminal justice system. Out of the more than 10 million violent crimes reported in the *National Crime Victimimization Survey* in 1992 (U.S. Bureau of Justice Statistics, 1993), only slightly more than 4 million were reported to the police. Of course, serious violent crimes are reported more often. However, even for robbery and assault, the rate of reporting is relatively low. They are lower still for sexual assault and domestic violence. Often the victim still loves or is dependent on the assailant and refuses to tell the police.

More than nine in ten motor vehicle theft victims file a report with police (insurance requirement). However, only two out of every three robberies, one out of every two aggravated assaults, and one out of every three sexual assaults are reported to police (U.S. Bureau of Justice Statistics, 1993). The majority of violent crimes that are reported do not culminate in an arrest of a suspect. Nearly half of the thirty-two homicides in a sampled week in Los Angeles during the summer of 1994 did not lead to an arrest. Of those arrested, one in five were either acquitted, released, or had their cases thrown out.

Only 641,000 out of 10 million violent crimes even resulted in an arrest. In conclusion, the infamous "one-in-ten-thousand" statistic is meaningless since only six in one hundred even enter the criminal justice system. Once they are in the system, prosecutors dismiss some charges for lack of evidence (or other reasons) or the defendant is acquitted. The outcome is that the 10 million crimes are preceded by only about 165,000 convictions. Consequently, most violent crimes never get to the juncture of sentencing.

In gang murders, the police seldom discover murder weapons or arrest suspects. These homicides often involve drug sales. Witnesses may initially identify suspects but often recant or contradict their statements made earlier to detectives. Other witnesses become uncooperative or vanish.

Murders that occur in the dark realm of urban gangs and drugs are difficult to solve. In addition, racial profiling by police has led to deteriorating community relations and mistrust among ethnic minorities and immigrants. If police investigation results in arrests based on substantial evidence and prosecutors convict those brought to trial, successful intervention against violent crime is possible.

Where sentencing occurs, it is firm—not lenient. Criminals who are caught and convicted are generally imprisoned. In the United States, the likelihood of a prison sentence for violent crimes has climbed steadily in recent years. Repeat offenders are virtually guaranteed prison time. In 1994, 77 percent of offenders convicted of felony robbery went to prison. Another 11 percent went to jail, making the total incarcerated almost nine in ten. Likewise, 88 percent of felons convicted of rape were incarcerated, four out of five of them are in prison. Prison time for violent crimes has been increasing significantly since the 1970s.

Do we give convicts long enough sentences to fit their crimes? The myth is that judges and juries typically hand down ridiculously short prison terms to criminals. Some politicians have used misleading data to condemn what they consider to be "soft sentencing." According to data from 1990 (Graham, 1993), murderers serve only 1.8 years behind bars, rapists 60 days, robbers 23 days and car thieves 1.5 days.

There is no consensus on whether to examine the average time served by prisoners who have been released or by estimating the time that will be served by offenders now being sentenced. In 1994, the estimated time to be served in prison for murder was 127 months, or approximately 10 years (Currie, 2000). This figure, however, understates the penalties for murder for two reasons: The statistics include "nonnegligent manslaughter," a less serious offense that carries a far lighter sentence than murder, thus lowering the average; and, more important, the statistics do not include the approximately 27 percent of murderers who are sentenced to life imprisonment or death, which reduces the average far more.

The same disparity holds true for other violent crimes as well. The average expected time to be served for a convicted rapist in 1994 was not sixty days but eighty-five months, or more than seven years (Currie, 2000). For robbery the average expected time to be served was not twenty-three days but fifty-one months, or more than four years.

Critics have also argued that opportunities for parole and reduced sentences for good behavior result in convicts serving sentences that have been vastly reduced. In 1994, the Justice Department estimated that offenders sentenced for violent crimes would serve, on average, approximately 46 percent of their sentences; 54 percent for rape (Currie, 2000). However, whether this indicates leniency depends on what the original sentence is. If a first-time robber is sentenced to forty years, the fact that he ended up serving only half of that sentence would probably not be considered lenient even by the most punitive observer. In fact, we do impose very harsh sentences when compared to other countries. In 1994, robbers received an average term of nearly ten years; they could expect to serve four years and three months (Currie, 2000). Rapists received sentences of more than thirteen years; they could expect to serve more than seven.

In recent years, sentencing has become more severe; and parole and reducing sentences for good behavior have come under attack. Consequently, the length of time served has swiftly increased:

- In just four years (from 1990 to 1994), the estimated time to be served in state prison for murder went up by two years.
- During that same period, the estimated time to be served in state prison for sexual assault increased by eleven months.
- The estimated time to be served rose from an average of thirty-one months in 1985 to forty-three months in 1995. (Currie, 2000)

These statistics refute the myth that we are becoming more lenient with criminals.

In short, time served has risen for homicide, robbery, and sexual assault. It has fallen, however, for less serious crimes, notably drug offenses and larceny. This decrease in sentencing for lesser crimes explains the overall decrease in time served (since they represent the bulk of criminal convictions). Drug offenders were only 8 percent of the inmate population in 1980, but 26 percent by 1993; violent offenders decreased from 57 percent to 45 percent of the total (U.S. Bureau of Justice Statistics, 1998). Since drug offenders were being handed shorter sentences (with some notable exceptions), this resulted in a lower average for time served among all inmates.

Another reason for the myth of leniency is the low rates of arrest and conviction for most crimes. If one takes the average time served by robbers who are arrested and convicted by the total number of robberies committed, irrespective of whether anyone is ever caught, much less convicted, of course it will come out to a short (but meaningless) time served. The average robbery does not lead to an arrest. In 1994, approximately 1.3 million robberies occurred (based on self-reported surveys), of which only 619,000 were reported to the police. There were fewer than 46,000 adult felony convictions for robbery, most of which (more than 40,000) resulted in incarceration. (Recall that the average length of time served is more than four years.) Of course, catching and then convicting more robbers would increase the overall average for time served. Nevertheless, we are not lenient with the ones we do catch.

Deterrence does not appear to be working. We already impose rather stiff sentences to violent criminals (especially repeat offenders). Perhaps we need to focus more on prevention. The popular three strikes, you're out law in many states has not helped to put away many violent offenders. Instead, primarily low-level property and drug offenders have been given sentences of twenty-five-years-to-life imprisonment. By 1995, more people had been sentenced under California's three-strikes law for simple marijuana possession than for murder, sexual assault, and kidnapping combined, and more for drug possession than for all violent offenses (Currie, 2000).

Most violent offenders would have been severely sentenced even without the three-strikes law. There is already five-year minimum sentencing for second felony offenses. There is also a "habitual offender" statute requiring life imprisonment (with a minimum of twenty years before the possibility of parole) for violent offenders who have caused "great bodily harm" to victims and had already served two prison sentences for similar offenses. In conclusion, California's prisons have not been filled with repeat violent offenders by the three-strike law, primarily because these criminals were already being imposed tough sentences based on earlier laws.

To be sure, punitive sentencing is efficacious for all violent offenders. Moreover, some truly dangerous people sometimes are released from prison prematurely; unfortunately, some are never sentenced at all. Nevertheless, the data show that the criminal justice system is not lenient with violent offenders. In fact, the release of violent criminals back into society has sometimes occurred because overcrowded prisons have had to make room for far less serious offenders especially drug offenders imprisoned under new mandatory sentence statutes.

In Florida, an enormous inflow of drug offenders during the 1980s overcrowded the state's prisons despite the addition of twenty-five thousand new prison beds. This forced an early-release program that put a great number of violent criminals (including rapists and robbers) back into the community; most of them received little supervision while on parole. Realizing this serious mistake, the state has now sought to reverse this policy, targeting violent offenders for prison and searching for alternatives for nonviolent offenders.

HISTORICAL BACKGROUND TO CURRENT DRUG POLICY

More people are now incarcerated in the nation's prisons for marijuana than for manslaughter or rape. Marijuana gives rise to insanity—not in its user but in the policies directed against it. A nation that sentences the possessor of a single joint to life imprisonment without parole but sets a murderer free after perhaps six years is in the grip of a deep psychosis.

—Eric Schlosser, "More Reefer Madness"

The laws of at least fifteen states now require life sentences for certain nonviolent marijuana offenses. In Montana a life sentence can be imposed for growing a single marijuana plant or selling a single joint. Under federal law the death penalty can be imposed for growing or selling a large amount of marijuana, even if it is a first offense (Schlosser, 2000).

Teenage marijuana use has increased sizably since 1992. The number of Americans arrested every year for marijuana crimes has increased 43 percent since that time. In 1995, a record six hundred thousand arrests were made for selling, buying, possessing, and growing marijuana. Police arrested more Americans for marijuana offenses between 1992 and 1995 than during any other three-year period in our nation's history. More Americans are incarcerated today for marijuana crimes than at any other time (Currie, 1993). Despite severe penalties, marijuana use flourishes (Nadelmann, 1992).

In 1968, Richard M. Nixon ran for president based on a campaign promising to restore law and order. This was largely a reaction to several consecutive years of widespread racial unrest and rioting, large-scale anti–Vietnam

War demonstrations, perceived failures in welfare policy, and rampant illicit drug use. Nixon used the term *War on Drugs* during his successful campaign and, after he was elected, began the contemporary trends in drug policy. To his credit, President Nixon believed that rehabilitation could keep addicts off drugs and, thus, invested federal dollars in drug treatment programs.

Federal spending on illegal drugs rose from 68 million in 1968 to 1.1. billion in 1980. Moreover, in states such as New York, passage of the rigid Rockefeller Drug Laws anticipated the federal laws of the late 1980s and beyond (McCoy & Block, 1992). Major federal agencies were created during President Nixon's time, such as the Drug Enforcement Administration (Larner, 1991).

In 1982, President Ronald Reagan and his wife Nancy ("Just Say No"), initiated the War on Drugs, specifically targeting marijuana use. It is clear that conservative organizations and parents against not only the use of but also the image of marijuana sparked the War on Drugs. Marijuana symbolized the weakness and dysfunctions of a permissive liberal society. It also represented rebellion and disrespect for authority. It was blamed for the lack of motivation in and grungy demeanor of teens.

What the Reagans created (or helped make possible) was a climate that moralized recreational drug use in absolutist "good/evil" terms (as would be expected given their Religious Right constituencies). This, in turn, made possible the hastily passed, almost entirely punitive, policies from the death of Len Bias (a popular young basketball star) onward. The frenzy did not abate with President Reagan; it continued into the Bush administration (1988–1992). In the fall of 1990, shortly after President George Bush appeared on national television waving a bag of crack cocaine, the public perceived drugs as the most significant threat to the nation. Illicit drug use as a social problem peaked in the polls at 60+ percent; a year later it had dropped off to approximately 10 percent.

Carlton Turner, Reagan's first drug czar, said that marijuana use was related to "the present young-adult generation's involvement in anti-military, anti-nuclear power, anti-big business, anti-authority demonstrations" (cited in Schlosser, 2000). A public health approach to drug enforcement was left behind in favor of a punitive criminal approach. Drug addiction lost its label as a medical illness and took on a label of immorality. Consequently, drug offenders should be severely punished; drug rehabilitation was no longer favored.

The drug war quickly became a bipartisan issue, with support from all sides. Within the prevailing ideology of zero tolerance to drugs, nothing could be gained politically by defending drug users from harsh punishment. The effects of this misguided policy are reflected in the shift and increase in prison populations. In 1980, there were almost twice as many violent offenders in federal prisons as drug offenders. There are now far more people in federal prisons for marijuana offenses than for violent crimes.

During a time when fear of violent crime is prevalent, the courts are sentencing low-level marijuana sellers to prison for life without parole, while violent criminals are being prematurely released—usually to commit more violent crimes. Federal prisons and more than three-fourths of all state prisons (thirty-eight) are now over their recommended capacity. Federal and state drug laws have indirectly led to dangerous overcrowding in correctional institutions. Nonviolent drug offenders with mandatory minimum sentences without the possibility of parole fill our country's prisons. In 1992, prison boards released violent offenders who served, on average, less than half of their original sentences. A convicted murderer spends less than six years in prison, a kidnapper about four, according to a study by the U.S. Department of Justice (U.S. Bureau of Justice Statistics, 1995, 1997).

Nearly one in three violent offenders released from prison is arrested for another violent crime in less than three years. Of course, we do not know how many violent crimes these released convicts commit without ever being apprehended. In 1992, the average time served for a violent crime was forty-three months. The average punishment, under federal law, for a marijuana-related offense was approximately fifty months for that same year.

Even laws enacted to deter violent crime have been undermined by the War on Drugs. California's three-strikes policy has incarcerated twice as many people for marijuana than for homicide, sexual assault, and kidnapping combined.

The concern for public health alone cannot explain the severe penalties for marijuana use. The courts have imprisoned AIDS victims, cancer patients, persons with multiple sclerosis, epileptics, and paraplegics for medicinal use of marijuana. The condemnation of marijuana, since its beginnings early in the twentieth century, has been a cultural war based on the ability of moral entrepreneurs to tout and lobby for legislation representative of their particular ideologies.

In an unsuccessful try to vastly cut marijuana smoking, federal and state legislators have given prosecutors a huge increase in their power to try to convict those arrested on drug charges. This sharp increase of prosecuting power has resulted in a class of professional informants and the prevalent seizure of private property by the government without due process—institutional tactics reminded ful of those used in the former Soviet Union. Mandatory long sentences for convicted marijuana farmers and sellers has resulted in a marked increase in prices, spawning an underground industry with yearly profits that now compare favorably with those of our major legal crops such as corn, soybeans, and cotton. As these traffickers increase their distribution and profits, their capacity to bribe corrupt federal officials also grows. This is a problem in the United States, Mexico, Colombia, and many other countries.

Millions of ordinary individuals in the United States have been arrested for marijuana offenses. This extremely high arrest rate shows us that lengthy sentencing does not deter marijuana use. Just as marijuana symbolized defiance to mainstream society in the late 1960s and early 1970s, current use is still based in a youthful counterculture.

THE INJUSTICE OF DRUG POLICY

The greatest tragedy in my professional life. . . .

—Eric Sterling, former counsel to the chairman of the House Subcommittee on Crime, on the 1986 federal drug law he helped enact

Those who love the law and good sausage should never see either one being made.

—Bismarck

Drug crimes are unique in the sense that, unlike other crimes, they are applicable to local, state, and federal law. Consequently, defendants can be tried twice for the same crime—even if they were convicted in their first trial. For example, in 1985 a watermelon farmer was arrested for growing marijuana, convicted, and given probation. In 1990, federal prosecutors chose to prosecute the same man for the same crime. The defendant was convicted and given a life sentence without parole.

This section addresses a continuing issue of fairness in the War on Drugs (Massing, 1991). In 1986, Congress enacted rigid mandatory minimum sentencing for drug crimes. The Anti-Drug Abuse Act represents a critical change in the criminal justice system, especially drug restriction policy. The law was not the result of a careful deliberative process. Policy makers did not appear to rely on the theories, methods, and findings of researchers in criminal justice.

It was mid-August and many academics and government officials were out on vacation. The law was written and enacted in several weeks without a single public hearing. There was no time to study the implications of this law for law enforcement, the courts, and prisons. This was the most significant drug provision in more than twenty years—and it was prompted by the drug overdose death of a popular young basketball star.

The federal law emerged during a time when the media and policy makers had labeled crack use "an epidemic." The law reflected a belief that judges are soft on crime. Speaker of the House Tip O'Neill had recently returned from July 4th District recess. His constituents were obsessed with the drug overdose in the death of Len Bias who at the young age of twenty-two had just been drafted by the Boston Celtics. O'Neill knew that if Congress passed a strict drug law, his chances of being reelected were virtually assured.

Len Bias had been a local celebrity in the nation's capital. His clean-cut image made his death seem even more shocking. He was an all-American athlete at the University of Maryland. Only two days after signing a contract with the Celtics, he died of heart failure, ostensibly brought on by smoking crack.

O'Neill was concerned that Democrats would be accused of being soft on drugs. With President and Mrs. Reagan pushing for tougher drug laws, the Democrats cooperated enthusiastically. The provision passed in the Senate by a voice vote; only sixteen members of Congress voted against the bill. The president signed the bill a week before Election Day.

The law requires a mandatory minimum sentence of thirty years to a maximum of life imprisonment; there is no possibility of parole in the federal courts. The mandatory minimum sentences were not based on the relative weight of an individual's role in a crime. In other words, a low-level dealer receives the same amount of punishment as a drug kingpin.

The 1986 national drug legislation has led to tripling the number of people in our federal prisons. Its harsh sentencing and tough-on-crime mentality has spilled over into similar state laws; it is not surprising that this has led to noticeable increases in state penitentiary populations.

During every congressional election year in the 1980s, politicians introduced drug-control legislation. Election years continue to spawn new drug legislation. In 1996, then-Speaker of the House Newt Gingrich proposed a call requiring either the death penalty or a life sentence without parole for anyone apprehended smuggling more than two ounces of marijuana into the country. Although the provision was not able to reach the House floor for discussion, it enticed twenty-six cosponsors. Also in 1996, Texas Senator Phil Gramm sponsored a provision denying welfare assistance (including food stamps) to those convicted of even a misdemeanor drug offense. This demonstrates a glaring disregard for the welfare of innocent indigent children.

President William J. Clinton signed a draconian welfare reform bill into law in 1996, the year of his reelection. The bill, with support from both liberals and conservatives, denied welfare benefits, including food stamps, to those convicted of a drug felony (even if they are disabled). It is important to note that possession of a few ounces of marijuana or growing a single marijuana plant is a felony in most states. Convicted murderers, rapists, and child molesters, nonetheless, continue to receive these types of federal assistance. This points to an unfair inconsistency in social policy.

INFORMANTS

America's War on Drugs has created a new breed of witness: the informant. With the prospect of a mandatory thirty-year-to-life sentence without parole for drug crimes, the only option for an arrestee to escape their fate is to render assistance to federal prosecutors. The extremely high rates of conviction in federal trials exacerbate this pressure to testify for the prosecution. Generally, witnesses will not testify unless there is a major incentive, such as reduced time. Often these snitches have their sentences commuted—through the 5K1 Motion—in exchange for their testimony. Supporters of the bill correctly note that informants help to solve crimes; they are part of our way of life. Prosecutors often depend on informants to testify to help convict defendants in drug cases.

A defendant hopes to reduce a lengthy prison sentence in exchange for testimony. The prosecutor alone (not the judge) decides whether the testimony justifies a reduced sentence. Accordingly, there have been occasions where a prosecutor blames an informant for losing a case and reneges on the commitment to reduce the informant's sentence.

The law also permits snitches to receive up to one-fourth of all assets confiscated based on their testimony. The U.S. government has sponsored a prosperous, busy, and growing class of professional informants. In 1985, the federal government paid informants $25 million for their testimony. By 1996, that figure had grown to $100 million.

Snitching on others has become not only a way to avoid or reduce punishment, but also a lucrative way to make a living. An informant may earn up to $1 million in a major drug case. The ratio of federal drug warrants depending only on unidentified informants nearly tripled from 1980 (24 percent) to 1993 (71 percent). This growing dependence on informants has resulted in a dramatic increase in the power of criminals who directly benefit financially from helping convict other people.

Informants have sometimes framed innocent persons through their false testimony. Informants have also fabricated evidence and solicited other dishonest people to corroborate their lies. Police officers have sometimes used fictitious informants to justify search warrants.

The legal and financial advantages of snitching has led to the new underground craft of selling valuable drug information to wealthy defendants who need the information to avoid lengthy sentencing. Some professional informants have sold their services for $250,000.

The eagerness of informants to testify has become more consequential than the severity of their crimes. Since drug smuggling executives have choice information on the large-scale purchase, transportation, and distribution of drugs, they have the most to offer prosecutors. Mules (transporters) and low-level dealers have little or no information of value to prosecutors. The overwhelming majority of people convicted of marijuana offenses are not rich or big-time drug dealers. They are ordinary folk. They do not have valuable information to provide about drug rings. Consequently, current informant policy often results in harsher sentences for minor players in the underground drug industry.

PROPERTY SEIZURES

In the 1980s Congress approved forfeiture provisions allowing the federal government to confiscate real estate, cash, securities, vehicles, jewelry, and any other property linked to marijuana consumption or distribution. The government does not have to prove that the seized property was purchased with drug money, only that it was "probably" used (or intended to be used) in an illegal activity. A house can be taken if smoking marijuana occurred within it—even just one time. Amazingly, a house can be confiscated if it contains books on how to grow marijuana plants (Steven B. Duke, cited in Schlosser, 2000). A farm could be seized for a single marijuana plant.

In 1996 the Supreme Court ruled that the government could confiscate property even when its owner had no involvement in or knowledge of the crime that was committed. When property is taken, its legal title passes immediately to the government. The original owner now has the burden of legal proof of "innocence." The government took approximately $1.5 billion worth of property and assets in 1994. Forfeiture provisions exacerbate social inequality by permitting affluent defendants to buy their freedom (or at least a reduced sentence) with their assets.

The proceeds from the seizure of property are divided among the involved law enforcement agencies. This policy is inherently a conflict of interest, inviting potential abuse and plundering. Financial motives rather than the guilt or innocence of a defendant sometimes guide forfeitures. In California, federal and state agents raided a ranch on the pretense that marijuana might be growing there. Agents "accidentally" killed the owner; no marijuana plants were found on the property. An investigation by the District Attorney's Office later revealed that the urge to seize the ranch was based on its $5 million value.

In New Jersey, a prosecutor seized land from a marijuana case and later assisted a colleague in purchasing the property at a greatly reduced price. In Connecticut, a prosecutor confiscated the home of an octogenarian couple after their twenty-two-year-old grandson was arrested for storing marijuana there. The couple had owned the home for approximately forty years and was unaware of their grandson's illegal activities. The prosecutor blamed the grandparents for not knowing. Soon afterward, police arrested the prosecutor's eighteen-year-old son for selling marijuana from the prosecutor's vehicle. Ostensibly, he also sold marijuana from the prosecutor's home. The District Attorney's Office quickly transferred the prosecutor out of the forfeiture unit; the government did not confiscate the house or the automobile.

CRITIQUE OF CURRENT DRUG POLICY

Current drug interdiction policy, including the 1986 Anti Drug Act, is objectionable for the following thirteen reasons:

1. The law was based on a combination of *politics and frenzy*. There was no hearing. No federal judges were consulted. There was no input from the Drug Enforcement Administration or prison and law enforcement officials. It seems as if politicians were arbitrarily picking numbers to create new and much more severe sentencing for drug crimes.
2. Federal prosecutors have an almost unlimited amount of discretion:

- When to apply mandatory minimum sentencing.
- What quantity of drugs to use in the indictment.
- Whether to prosecute at all—where to devote their resources, time, and effort. Theoretically U.S. attorneys could prosecute every marijuana bust in the country. Their discretion to prosecute some cases while ignoring others results in great disparity with local and state courts in terms of conviction rates and severity of sentencing.

This potentially permits legal favoritism (e.g., lenient treatment based on the notoriety or affluence of the defendant) or institutional discrimination (harsh treatment based on cultural, social, or physical characteristics).

3. The War on Drugs has created tremendous pressure to arrest, convict, and sentence drug offenders. The government holds a precious commodity to offer the potential informant: his freedom. The law requires that the only way to avoid mandatory minimum sentencing is to provide substantial assistance to the government. This means informing or posing as a drug buyer. Prosecutors sometimes pressure informants to endanger themselves by setting up and buying drugs from noted dealers and then by testifying against them. The federal government sometimes *misuses informants* in drug prosecution with devastating effects on individuals trapped in the judicial system (Public Broadcasting Service, 1999).

- A young black man with no prior arrest record was sentenced to three consecutive life sentences, concurrently, with no chance of parole after he was convicted of dealing crack based only on the testimony of convicts who received lighter sentences in exchange for their testimony.
- Prosecutors charged the mother of a renegade major drug dealer with conspiracy to traffic drugs in an unsuccessful attempt to pressure him to turn himself in. She was convicted, not on evidence but on the testimony of one witness, and served approximately eight years in prison.

4. The "conspiracy amendment" to the 1986 federal drug law, "an oversight" (Eric Sterling, cited in Public Broadcasting Service, 1999), promotes *disproportionately unfair sentencing* and creates a situation that *encourages informants to give false testimony*. It allows low-level drug dealers to receive as long a prison sentence as a so-called drug kingpin. It also allowed the bill's sponsors and supporters to appear tough on crime to their constituents.

5. The law deprives judges of discretion. They are no longer able to assess the defendant, the crime, and the potential harm to society to render justice. Consequently, this law has transferred power from judges to prosecutors.

6. Because *oral testimony* is enough to convict a defendant in federal cases, this results in *unfairness* because defendants are sometimes convicted without physical evidence. In short, because of this law a lot of people are receiving a lot of jail time based only on the testimony of an informant without any corroborating evidence.

7. The law has not resulted in many high-profile prosecutions of important narcotic dealers—as it was designed to do. *Only 11 percent of all 1995 federal drug trials featured defendants who were major drug traffickers.*

8. When law forces people to testify against family members and loved ones (especially if it is a lie) to save themselves, it *destroys families*. However, most people in trouble with the law will do about anything to avoid a thirty-year-to-life sentence without parole.

9. The snitch system has *destroyed the integrity of the courts system*. Someone serving a life sentence can falsely testify against a defendant in a federal drug case in order to receive a lighter sentence. Policy makers had the unrealistic assumption that prosecutors would always be honest and efficient. Prosecutors either do not care that *snitches lie* or naively assume that snitches always tell the truth and do not compare notes with other informants. Prosecutors have no idea if snitches are lying. New York police call this "testa-lying," while the Los Angeles police call it "the liars club." Prisoners can receive freedom by making up a story and informing on someone. Inmates have revealed that other inmates read newspapers looking for opportunities to give false testimony against someone in exchange for a lighter sentence.

10. The *forfeiture law* allows the federal government to seize the assets of convicted drug users or sellers. The law requires only a *low burden of proof*. If a person "more likely than not" used their house, car, or bank account to buy, sell, or use drugs, their property can be taken. This makes it easy to repossess a person's private property. Even if a drug dealer uses someone else's house to sell drugs, the homeowner could still lose her/his property even if she/he was unaware of illegal activities. The presumption of innocence in the courts system now appears to be nominal only.

11. Mandatory minimum sentencing has resulted in the *overflow of prisons*. The *cost to taxpayers* for holding one prisoner is $25,000 initially to build a prison cell and then $30,000 annually to feed and supervise each inmate. Violent inmates are prematurely released to make room for nonviolent drug offenders.

12. The mandatory minimum sentencing law has had *no benefit on society; drug use is still as prevalent* as before the law was passed. In fact, two relatively new types of dangerous drugs—methamphetamines and "ecstasy"—have flourished. Both can be manufactured easily and cheaply and then sold for high profit. According to former Attorney General Janet Reno, methamphetamines have replaced crack as America's number one drug problem. Chemicals used to make the drug are legally imported to make cold medicine. Ecstasy, a synthetic drug, is popular among the "Rave" set; and its use has increased sharply. In 1998, 105,000 teenagers reported using ecstasy; in only one year, that figure had climbed to 165,000.

13. The conspiracy amendment to the 1986 federal drug law that allows low-level drug dealers to receive as long a prison sentence as a so-called drug kingpin is *blatantly unfair*. The policy is logically inconsistent. The government desires to capture the drug kingpin, yet the policy allows the kingpin to inform on low-level dealers in exchange for lighter sentencing.

In conclusion, current drug policy is eroding our constitutional rights and the moral fabric of society. We are making criminals out of mere users and sharply dividing society along ethnic, racial, and social class lines (Lusane & Desmond, 1991). Additionally, we have not made much of a dent in our drug problem. Drug availability remains very high, its use still prevalent, despite punitive sentencing.

Hard-core addiction is still rampant. The War on Drugs is neither effective nor ethical. We are becoming a society of criminals and informants. People are either in prison or trying to put others in prison. If our present drug policy were a play or film, it could be reviewed as a tragedy or a satirical comedy.

CONCLUSION

Our national history is important not only because it tells us from where we are coming but also where we are going. During the turbulent 1960s our nation stood at a juncture in crime policy. President Lyndon B. Johnson's 1967 crime commission and the Kerner Commission on urban violence called for a balanced approach to the problem of crime instead of tackling the foundational bases of crime and violent behavior.

The consensus was that we needed more powerful law enforcement, a more efficient court system, harsher sentencing, and punitive prisons. However, "attacking violent crime [also] meant attacking social exclusion—reducing poverty, creating opportunities for sustaining work, supporting besieged families and the marginalized young" (Currie, 1998: 185). Finally, it also meant a commitment to reinserting offenders into the community and protecting our neighborhoods and cities from violent crime.

The other option would take us on a path toward greater incarceration, a deemphasis on the rehabilitation of offenders, and less emphasis on trying to help those who are economically disadvantaged. This approach was based on the following three notions: We treat criminals far too leniently; offenders could not be rehabilitated; and the social conditions consistently linked to violent crime in research should be ignored or considered inconsequential.

Critics maintained that the social programs designed and implemented to cut poverty, bolster employment, and end racial discrimination only exacerbated the problem. In particular, it was argued that welfare created "learned helplessness" and maintained a "culture of poverty" that was passed on from one generation to the next. Moreover, the criminal justice system overprotected criminals, creating an era of permissiveness and fabricating excuses for criminal behavior.

In the late 1960s and early 1970s, largely under the leadership of President Nixon, the second path was taken. The hard-liners had won the political contest over which road to take. The quest for social justice did not occur. Because of this, the consequences have been urban unrest, continued racial stratification, violent crime unparalleled in other developed countries, neighborhoods torn apart, and bursting prisons.

Here in the new millennium, again we stand at a fork in the road. Do we continue social neglect or do we make serious social investments? There have been recent favorable declines in crime, but they may be only temporary. Part of the decline in violent crime, since the early 1990s, is due to the ebbing of the crack-cocaine epidemic (Currie, 1998). However, now the epidemic revolves around methamphetamines and other dangerous synthetic drugs. Thus, the potential for increased violent crime remains because we have not addressed the underlying conditions that breed the demand for hard drugs; we have merely substituted one dangerous drug for another.

Another reason for the recent decline in violent crime in the late 1990s was a good economy (Currie, 1998). Although violent crime is less affected by the normal ebb and flow of the business cycle than by more fixed conditions of economic marginality, the recent economic boom lasted so long, and with substantial increased employment opportunities, it cut the crime rate. Unemployment decreased enough to lower the poverty rate. Even some of those marginalized persons outside of the labor force had taken up legitimate jobs.

The dip in violent crime since 1992 closely reflects the decline in unemployment for black males during the same period. From 1992 through 1996, the murder rate dropped by 20 percent and the robbery rate by 23 percent (Currie, 1998). The unemployment rate for black men aged twenty and over fell by 30 percent, and those for black teens by 12 percent.

The hypothesis that increases in employment may assist in explaining the decreases in crime is supported if one considers which crimes have declined the fastest. If decreases in crime were mainly based on increases in imprisonment, they should be greater for property crimes and less for violent crimes. This is based on the research findings that rehabilitation works better for property crimes than for violent crimes (e.g., murder, aggravated assault; Currie, 1998). However, the greatest decline has been in homicide, while property crime has dropped more slowly. This pattern jibes with knowledge about the effect of economic growth on various types of crime. People are more likely to commit property crimes than violent crimes for economic reasons. An economic buildup is likely to have a mixed impact on property crime. Increases in employment and income translates into less motivation to steal or use other illicit means to acquire money. However, good economic times also mean there is more to be stolen.

An enduring upturn in the economy can sink previously high rates of violent crime for several reasons. Providing employment opportunities for low-income people:

> 1. decreases the encouragement to commit robberies or sell drugs, crimes often linked to violence;
> 2. reduces the stress that often results in violence, especially violence in the family and in relationships;
> 3. simultaneously pulls people away from degenerate settings and situations (e.g., bars, street corners) where they are most likely to be involved in violent confrontations (either as assailants or victims). A continuation of the current sluggishness in the economy could nullify these positive trends. (Currie, 1998)

Perhaps there has been a shift among youth (especially ethnic minority youth) away from violence. They have witnessed the destructiveness of an epidemic that has claimed the lives and destroyed the futures of so many of their family members and friends. The juvenile homicide rate has dropped to a thirty-three-year low (Federal Bureau of Investigation, 2000). As the wave of violence that tore through teenage America in the past decade continues to ebb, FBI data show that approximately fourteen hundred children between the ages of ten and seventeen were charged with murder in 1999. This represents a 68 percent drop from the height of the crack-cocaine epidemic in 1993 and the lowest level since 1966.

The report cites prevention as one of the major reasons for the decline, as a range of police, social, and neighborhood programs across the country have targeted high-risk youth. Those programs, coupled with a booming economy in the mid- to late 1990s, apparently slowed the violence that accompanied urban crack wars in the early 1990s. For all violent crimes—

murder, forcible rape, robbery, and aggravated assault—the rates of youth arrests dropped 23 percent from 1995 to 1999, much faster than the 12 percent drop recorded for adults.

The greatest improvement was among young black men—the population that had been most contaminated by gangs, guns, and drugs. The rates of homicides for young black men tripled from the 1980s to the early 1990s. Correspondingly, their rate of arrest has dropped the most rapidly as crime has declined. The drop in youth violence mirrored a similar trend across the country. In all, 15,533 Americans were reported murdered in 1999, the lowest number since 1969.

After youth violence hit record levels in 1994, grassroots organizations across the country began working with police, prosecutors, and schools in an effort to stem the tide; 335 programs have been created in the last six years. In the District of Columbia—once the nation's murder capital—the drop in juvenile violence has been dramatic. Each year between 1992 and 1994, the worst years of the crack epidemic, at least 1,337 youth between the ages of ten and seventeen were tried for violent crimes. By 1999, that number had dropped to 719.

Police charged eight District youths with homicide in 1999, compared with sixty-nine in the peak year of 1994. By mid-December 2000, only five youths had been charged with murder. The District has fewer youth incarcerated than in 1995, yet the crime rate has dropped. This certainly questions the value and effectiveness of prison as the best means of intervention against violent crime.

Perhaps the decline of violence in our inner cities has little to do with the reorganization in law enforcement, the creation of special police units trained to stop gang activities, and new police tactics of zero tolerance toward youth. Perhaps it has more to do with the changing attitudes of a new cohort of youths who refuse to follow their predecessors down a futile path of lawlessness, disrespect, and violence. Even these new positive trends may be short-lived if we do not provide the educational and employment opportunities necessary to parlay those sentiments into productive and useful lives.

An increase in empowering community-based prevention programs has also probably contributed to a decrease in crime. Head Start, family support, and school-based social services that provided disadvantaged children and families after-school programs and family support groups have benefited tens of thousands of at-risk individuals in some of our nation's most crime-invested communities.

Our current situation has resulted from a number of fortunate developments but it may not endure. We desperately need greater investment of not only financial but also human resources to prevent future epidemics of violence. We hold the potential to curb violent crime to levels not experienced in the lifetimes of most Americans. We now have an unprecedented chance to use resources to construct a vibrant infrastructure if we take a path of social ethics. If we do not, we will surely lose this opportunity.

Let us not waste our resources on more prisons, tax breaks for the wealthiest 1 percent of our country, or the politically correct quest for balanced budgets. This path will only reap violent and drug-ridden communities, decaying and inefficient schools, unacceptable health-care delivery, neighborhoods without opportunity, support, or even hope and another generation of disenfranchised youth—the result of economically stressed and ineffective families.

The path we take to attack crime will affect all other aspects of public life. It will affect our likelihood of being a victim of violent or property crime. It will also determine the opportunities of our youth for quality and affordable education, a rewarding and decent-paying job, and access to quality health care. Our increasing dependence on putting people in prison for nonviolent offenses prevents us from facing a plethora of persistent social problems:

- inadequate education, especially for disadvantaged children;
- the scarcity of affordable and effective drug treatment;
- the practical breakdown of preventive public-health and mental-health care;
- continuous child poverty;
- persistent unemployment in inner cities;
- steadily increasing homelessness.

An exploding prison system may disguise these problems but it clearly will not eliminate them. This chapter has proposed a crime policy based on social ethics that nearly every other advanced country has already implemented.

Expanding our prison system is not the answer to how to prevent crime. We already incarcerate the most violent criminals who are arrested and convicted. We give them longer sentences. Clearly, improvements can be made in apprehending and convicting the most dangerous offenders. But aside from this, the only other way of increasing incarceration rates is by sending people to prison for less serious offenses and by sending younger offenders to maximum-security prisons with hardened criminals where they will only reject attempts at rehabilitation and learn to become better criminals.

This will exacerbate the already unbearable overrepresentation of ethnic minorities in our nation's prisons. Additionally, this drastically cuts into financial resources that could have been spent preventing crime. There is public support for these recommendations. The vast majority of Californians would prefer to spend money on programs to prevent youth violence than on further incarceration. Eighty percent indicated that the highest priority should be to invest in ways to prevent youth from being violent and ending up in gangs or prisons (Resources for Youth, 1997). Only 13 percent felt that the top priority was to build more prisons and youth facilities and enforce strict sentences. Sixty percent supported shifting money away from prison building to community-based violence-prevention programs.

It certainly does not speak well of a society that incarcerates such a large segment of its population, especially considering that we still endure the greatest levels of violent crime in the developed world. There are better ways. We could invest in the potential of our youth instead of discarding their lives. How we go about confronting criminal behavior is actually more important than merely reducing it for an enlightened and humane civilization. The integrity of our nation is on the line as we sincerely and genuinely face this challenge in the coming years.

How a society treats its lawbreakers or deviants provides a window on the civility for its populace. What we do to people while they are in prison is not inconsequential to us. Approximately nine in ten prisoners will one day return to our streets and neighborhoods. If our prisons make young nonviolent offenders violent, better criminals, more addicted, and incorrigible, we will surely suffer the consequences.

WHAT YOU CAN DO

- Investigate white-collar computer crime. What new types of crime are arising in the new millennium? How does computer technology allow new ways of catching criminals?
- Watch several documentary or otherwise real-life law enforcement programs. Describe the social characteristics of investigators, police officers, and criminals. Describe the ideologies expressed directly or indirectly by judges, policy makers, attorneys, investigators, police officers, and criminals.

SEVEN

SOCIAL ETHICS AND IMPLICATIONS FOR PUBLIC POLICY

IN THIS BOOK, I have examined some of the social determinants that have led to the development and continuance of social problems related to education, poverty, homelessness, health care, and crime. Critical thinking about these issues reveals their complexity and the difficulty in untangling and implementing effective solutions. There is no one correct answer; there are multiple routes to addressing these problems, including social policy and social activism.

Some problems are persistent characteristics of social dynamics and organization; others have emerged in modern society. Social problems cannot be eliminated or lessened simply with new technology or lots of money. Many people and groups have vested interests when social problems are attacked through social policy. For example, attempts to reduce air pollution through alternative sources of energy are opposed by oil-producing firms and cartels. The extent to which groups are cognizant of such interest will, in large part, determine their opposition to, or support for, policies that attempt to alleviate social problems.

The definition of a social problem ultimately rests on a subjective value judgment. Various people and groups do not fundamentally view the same events or conditions as equally problematic. To an environmentalist, air pollution is a serious social problem. To an oil producer, it is a trade-off—something bad that comes necessarily with something functional. A further example: Higher rates of unemployment are often correlated with low and steady rates of inflation. Conversely, higher levels of employment constrict the job market forcing increases in salaries and prices on good and services.

POLITICS, INEQUALITY, AND SOCIAL POLICY

Who decides what a social problem is? Who has a vested interest in protecting the status quo? Who stands to gain through social change? We have seen that politics plays a key role in welfare, education, health care, and legal reform.

Democracy in the United States is a facade. What we really have is a plutocracy—a government run by a small, elite class of people. There is one political party with two conservative alliances: the Democrats and the Republicans. Corporate America and, more and more, international conglomerates control both parties through enormous campaign donations, lobbyist organizations, and political action committees. The ostensible differences between the two are minimal. Even the American public does not seem to be able to distinguish between the two. Generally, immediately after each party's national convention, their candidate for president surges in public polls. The public seems to support whomever promises to improve conditions within the country.

At the present time, the military receives the majority of our federal budget. Since the terrorist attacks on September 11, 2001, the military has gained an increasingly larger share of the budget. The United States has spent $7 trillion on the military since the end of World War II. Our history has shown us that politicians who do not support the military do not survive politically and, sometimes, literally.

A constitutional convention would be a great opportunity to restore true democracy in this country. Thomas Jefferson, one of the principal authors of our Constitution, believed that we should have a constitutional convention every twenty to thirty years. This could help usurp political power from financial giants and restore it to "We the People."

In the early 1990s, the Clinton administration made a concerted effort to provide a national health-care program. Every First World country (except the United States and South Africa) has such a service. However, insurance firms, the majority of the American Medical Association, and pharmaceutical companies (each of whom has the most to lose because of the enormous profits they reap) firmly opposed and effectively prevented the implementation of such policy. They serve the same functions, belong to same sociocultural niche, and exert overwhelming influence on social policy. Any social policy proposal that threatens their political and financial hegemony has little or no chance of coming to fruition.

High-priority social issues do not directly affect everyone—at least, as we have seen, in the same way. At the present time, the federal government closely regulates inflation and unemployment fluctuations since they are viewed as the most substantial gauges of the overall soundness of the economy. Upper-middle-class people in stable employment are sufficiently invulnerable to the consequences of such symptoms since their jobs are not linked to the cost of labor in the same manner as is the predicament for low-level workers. Low unemployment is an economic obstacle for some portions of the population—employers who profit chiefly from paying low wages to entry-level workers. On the other hand, low unemployment is ideal for the working poor who have greater chances of employment to sustain their families.

Social problems often have latent consequences. Such unanticipated repercussions are the consequences of the interdependent attributes of social organizations, institutions, and groups. If a particular social problem becomes pervasive, it is likely to indirectly affect even socially advantaged portions of the population over an extended period even though they may not be directly affected by it. Upper-middle-class professionals, for example, will be affected by the probable rise in criminal activities that are commonly associated with the economic disengagement of low-level workers and rising rates of poverty. This is the case even though the economically advantaged would not suffer financial pressure that is the consequence of inflation, unemployment, and minor fluctuations in the economy.

Sometimes ventured solutions to social problems can emerge as problematic in themselves. For example, affirmative action has been used to attack the severe underrepresentation of ethnic minorities in higher education and professional occupations. Yet critics have come to view affirmative action as reverse discrimination against whites—especially white males. This characteristic of social problems results from the negotiated enterprises of various groups with often opposing vested interests.

A second example is economic inequality. The federal government taxes citizens to create funds that are made available for social services for the poor. Who gets taxed and how much as well as how funds are distributed are continuously at the center of much political controversy. Thus, persistent social problems, essentially, are old problems obscured by joint but often-conflicting attempts to alleviate them. This often occurs in a give-and-take cyclical process. What is regarded as a solution to a social problem during one particular period may be labeled as a "fresh new problem" at a later time. This is particularly true if the macro-level features that permitted the development of the original negative conditions are not satisfactorily accosted.

The intricacy of social problems has numerous causes:

- Viewing social problems in terms of individual responsibility. Too often explanations that "blame the victim" overlook structural factors that often contribute to the negative conditions individuals experience.
- The problem of defining social problems.
- The different and often conflicting interests among society's various groups.
- The persistent and complicated character of many social problems such as poverty and property crime.

Professional experts need to address such factors in trying to create policy that effectively intervenes in social problems.

Successful intervention in social problems typically includes the cooperation of large numbers of people—at least some of whom should occupy powerful positions within society. The federal government is a major player in social problem intervention since, presumably, it is proficient at combining the complicated sets of resources and actions necessary to implement public policy. When a negative condition is labeled "a social problem," groups that were not curious about the topic earlier may be drawn to participate in policy development and implementation.

In short, the complications of effective intervention in social problems require that remedies must always be compromised (and, thus, tainted) among the principal parties involved. Since each involved group has its own vested interest, it is also likely that each has its own preferred solution. There is no single correct solution to a specific social problem; each solution depends on what perspective one takes. These perspectives are ultimately subjective and require a value judgment.

Given these limitations to social policy, it is difficult to avoid solutions that mainly serve the interests of dominant groups or the federal government. Therefore, it is crucial to apply social ethics in attempting to address social issues. Social ethics proposes that distributive justice and fairness should be used as an advocate of the underdog: the poor, the sick, the homeless, children, oppressed social classes, and victims of institutional discrimination. Sociological insight combined with social ethics can be used to bolster alternative intervention to social problems.

Sociological understanding and social ethics can also sensitize society's gatekeepers—social, political, and religious leaders—and policy makers regarding the complexities of social problems and practical intervention. Sociological theories and research methodologies can be helpful in recommending and implementing intervention to social problems as well as evaluating the effectiveness of such intervention and alternative strategies. Although social problems negatively affect individuals, they are usually social in origin, definition, and solution. If we fail to understand the connection between how social factors result in obstacles for individuals, we cannot make policy choices that will effectively alleviate social problems.

SOCIAL MOVEMENTS AND ACTIVISM

Individual/group action is another way, besides social policy, to attack social problems. While social policy addresses social problems from top to bottom, social activism starts at the bottom—the grassroots level—and tries to build its way up. Social activism is based on individuals committing their time, resources, and efforts to a particular social issue. It is hoped that mass involvement will lead to social change.

Boycotts and socially responsible spending are two sides of the same coin that can be very effective in promoting a social cause. Individuals can and do make a difference by supporting companies that are socially responsible (e.g., environmentally conscious) and boycotting organizations that are irresponsible. Different motivations spark people to support groups that try to influence public policy or social change. Some people become active after they or a family member have become a victim of a particular social problem.

Voluntary collective change is present in many societies across the globe. At least some of those who are social activists should occupy positions of power or influence. Resources are usually needed to sway policy makers and influence others. Some socioeconomic groups tend to have better organization and clout than others because resources are unequally distributed among societal members. While the average person may attend a political rally or volunteer for a nonprofit organization, members of the higher classes attend fund-raising dinners or other political events that require a relatively large amount of money to attend.

Many people participate in social change by joining entrenched, national or international social movements such as the Green Party. Others prefer to operate at the grassroots level. These are perhaps the best ways for people to get involved with social change and be personally responsible for their own lives as well as touching the lives of others. Despite pervasive social inequality, social activism is one way for people to collectively take on social problems.

Social change is never permanent since social reality is being continuously negotiated among various competing parties. What is most important is the need to participate in attempts to develop effective intervention to social problems

SOCIAL ETHICS AND POLICY RECOMMENDATIONS

"Social intervention is any act, planned or unplanned, that alters the characteristics of another individual or the pattern of relationships between individuals" (Kelman & Warwick, 1978: 3). This includes such macro-level phenomena as public policy, national planning, military intervention in the affairs of other nations, and technical assistance. It also covers micro-level phenomena such as psychotherapy, neighborhood security watch programs, sensitivity training, and experiments done with human research participants.

There are four aspects of any social intervention that are likely to raise ethical issues: the choice of goals to which the change effort is directed, the definition of the point of the change, the choice of means used to implement the intervention, and the assessment of the results of the intervention. At each of these steps, the ethical issues that arise may involve conflicting ethical values, that is, questions about what values are to be maximized at the expense of what other values.

Ethical values in the human service professions in the United States (e.g., autonomy, privacy, fidelity, accountability) determine the choice of goals to which a change effort is aimed. Intervention is clearly designed to maximize a particular set of values and minimize the loss of specific other values. These "at-risk" values, consequently, serve as examples of acceptable costs in a given intervention.

For example, rapid demographic growth in ethnic minority populations, limited resources, and the sharply rising cost of health care has forced the government to set financial limits on various types of health-care delivery. Such public policy, ostensibly, benefits the common welfare. At the same time, policy makers should be concerned about the effects of this program on the ethical values of beneficence (maximum support and care by others in the maintenance or enhancement of one's well-being) and distributive justice (sharing material and/or human resources without regard to ethnicity, gender, social class, religion or other subcultural differences). These ethical values should be preserved because of their efficacy; it is necessary that they do not drop below some minimal level. Ethical values may affect the choice of goals not only in such explicit, conscious ways, but also in covert ways. This may occur when social policy commences with an unquestioned definition of a problem.

The definition of the target of change is often based on this type of implicit, unexamined conception of where the problem is. For example, public policy designed to improve health care for an economically disadvantaged subculturally diverse group may be designed to change institutional arrangements that have led to the systematic exclusion of this group from the economic mainstream of the society. Conversely, it may be designed to reduce the educational, environmental, or psychological "deficiencies" of the disadvantaged group itself. The choice between these two primary goals may well depend on one's worldview, life experiences, ideology, and ethical values: A focus on removing systematic barriers is more reflective of the values of the disadvantaged group itself, while a focus on removing deficiencies suggests the values of the more dominant segments of society.

Ethical values play a key role in an evaluation of the means chosen to implement a particular social policy. Questions about the methods of inducing change in individuals typically involve a conflict between the values of individual autonomy and social welfare. To what extent and under what conditions is a government justified in imposing limits or rationing medical procedures that are designed to eliminate or reduce life-threatening conditions?

Conflicting ethical values enter into a judgment of the consequences of social policy. One of the latent consequences of scientific medical treatment for disease in subculturally diverse patients may be a weakening of traditional subcultural ideology, authority structures, and family bonds. The extent to which we are willing to risk these consequences depends on whether we are more committed to traditional values or those values inherent in biomedical ethics. Clearly, there are important trade-offs to carefully consider. Our assessment of the consequences of a policy depends on what ethical values we are willing or unwilling to sacrifice in the interest of social change.

Health and health-care delivery are major problems for minority elderly of color. This is part of a larger ethical question. Disparity in health and effective access to health services cannot be considered separate from other dimensions of life, especially where public policy plays a massive role. There has been progress in some arenas; in other areas, social inequity still predominates. The elimination of blatant discrimination (e.g., involuntary racial segregation) through the legal system has not parlayed into active inclusion and full social participation for many minorities of color. This points us to another important context: stratification and ethnicity.

Ethnic background provides a unique historical calendar of life. Ethnic minorities face racial discrimination, prejudice, and prolonged poverty. Although whites face social problems, none are based on the color of their skin. There is a need to examine ethnic background and minority status in terms of social class, income level, access to quality health services, education, gender, age, living arrangements, and social support systems in the family and community.

IMPLICATIONS FOR SOCIAL JUSTICE

Overt barriers to health care for minorities of color (e.g., racially segregated health clinics and hospitals) have largely disappeared. However, institutional discrimination remains. This ranges from the sharp underrepresentation of ethnic minority physicians to informal norms, practices, and official policy. This effectively restricts access for minorities, the poor, and the uninsured. Racial discrimination barriers to health care are illegal. Nevertheless, barriers to equal access for minorities persist. There is rationing of health care, for example, for such procedures as renal dialysis, heart transplant, and a limit on the number of days for mental health services per year. There is also a preference for private-pay-insurance patients; physicians claim that they do not profit from government-supported health-care programs. Finally, there are restrictions on health care for the homeless and patients with a diagnosis of Alzheimer's disease or mental illness.

Folk illnesses and cures are frequently an element in an individual's particular ethnic identity (Chrisman & Kleinman, 1980). Ideas about health, illness, and healing are so closely tied to the values and behaviors of people's lives, knowledge about ethnicity may provide significant insight into the nature of the health ways of minority groups in the United States.

Ethnic cultures can provide the positive continuity of familiar and traditional roles (Holzberg, 1982). In the case of Mexican Americans, how does one argue against five hundred years of sustained influence in the United States? When we lose the right to be different, it costs us our liberty.

What will happen when poor people are unable to find work by the time their assistance expires? Are there enough jobs to go around? Are wages high enough to bring the poor out of poverty? Will job training be proficient and effective? What will happen to single working mothers who cannot afford child care on their own? What about the health-care needs of the working poor when their Medicaid ends?

Social policy should aim to reduce poverty through providing secure employment opportunities and decent health- and child-care benefits. Policy makers must stay clear of political considerations. Sometimes this means going against public opinion and, especially, the values and attitudes of one's constituency. For example, most people think that government spending on welfare should decrease rather than increase (Dowd, 1994). Less than one-third believe that welfare recipients really need help; more than two-thirds believe that welfare recipients are cheating the system ("Welfare Mistrust," 1996). Implicit in such attitudes is the assumption that welfare benefits are too high and recipients are crooked and wasteful.

It is economic inequality that underlies so much of the metaphorical walls that separate people. It is social ethics and distributive justice that can bridge these differences. By the middle of this century, the United States will no longer be a majority white country. The black–white paradigm—that fashioned the legacy of slavery, segregation, and discrimination—is not wide enough to cover the unique experiences and identities of the sharply increasing numbers of ethnic minority immigrants. The newly revamped federal agency dealing with immigrants should stress incorporating new immigrants into American society. Immigrants should be sheltered from employer retaliation when they assert their rights in the workplace. The link between ethnic background and economic inequality remains strong.

Decisions we make in the next few years will determine whether we will be building walls or bridges between people in the next fifty years. Building bridges, rather than walls, gives new hope to the promise of equality and the enduring, yet unfulfilled, ideal of liberty and social justice for all residents of the United States. In striving for distributive justice, I have focused on areas where dialogue and bridge building could bring about significant social progress. It is clear from the well-documented evidence of economic inequality that social justice is lacking in a country that insists on its commitment to freedom and democracy.

In terms of criminal justice, we need to stop the practice of trying juveniles as adults as well as stop the practice of placing juvenile and adult offenders in the same institutions. We should also end incarcerating nonviolent offenders with violent ones, particularly youth. We should cease our unsound War on Drugs and realize that education, prevention, and treatment must become the most important components in our efforts to fight the corrosive effects of drug abuse.

Our law must recognize that alcohol is a far more dangerous drug than marijuana. We should cease mandatory minimum sentencing and return to a policy of judicial discretion in sentencing. This would relieve the exponential growth of incarceration and prisons. We should abolish disparities in crack- versus powdered-cocaine offenses.

We must resist the pressures of discriminatory racial profiling in all its forms and manifestations. It reinforces negative stereotypes and further undermines the relationship between law enforcement and the community. We should provide competent and adequately compensated defense for indigents. We should renew an emphasis on rehabilitation. Clearly, an inmate cannot be rehabilitated without his/her consent. However, an inmate who chooses to be rehabilitated should have that opportunity. We should restore the voting rights of those who have paid their debt to society, encouraging their return as participating and contributing members of our democratic society.

We must recognize that quality public education is the key to tearing down walls between the haves and the have-nots. Education is the bridge to income equity. We should ensure that every child receives personal attention from competent, caring adults to enable him or her to reach full potential both academically and personally. We should restructure an educational system that is under attack, still ethnically segregated, and only marginally functional or conducive to learning.

We should develop, implement, evaluate, and continuously retune curricula that actively includes and celebrates multicultural contributions and traditionally suppressed voices. Such pedagogy would address both historical and current forms of institutional discrimination and foster critical reasoning in students. We should restructure public school financing by changing from the current property-tax-dominated system or voucher plan for public schools toward a more stable funding base that provides adequate resources for economically disadvantaged students.

We should begin to think of education in the broader context of community (or bridge) building by recognizing education as critical in creating an active, engaged, and socially responsible public. To accomplish this, we must develop a sense of community in schools so that students, parents, teachers, and administrators as well as civic and corporate leaders all converge to participate in a shared dialogue. We should explore innovative pedagogical techniques that develop social responsibility and youth leadership

Recognizing that corporate flight followed white flight to the suburbs, leaving the inner cities decaying from rampant unemployment and a rapidly disappearing tax base, policy makers in metropolitan regions must build metaphorical—if not actual—bridges to increase linkages between cities and suburbs. We need leaders who speak for all people and have the capacity to lead communities in developing a shared vision of social justice and implementing a plan of action. Such leaders should seek to build bridges within and across communities, rather than promoting walls of hatred, indifference, segregation, intolerance, and polarization. We should hold these leaders accountable for their words and actions.

CONCLUSION

There is no way to finish a social problems textbook.
Each attempt at a conclusion succeeds only in raising additional questions.

—Paul B. Horton and Gerald R. Leslie, *The Sociology of Social Problems*

Searching for solutions to social problems is an ongoing enterprise. Each conclusion leads to another step in the development of understanding. What is important is that social ethics be used to guide the search. Nevertheless, there is not likely to be a final answer.

At the beginning of this book, I expressed the hope that this text would guide students to acquire:

1. a sociological understanding of contemporary social problems and accurate information about them;
2. awareness of their social origins, collective definition, and how they might be effectively treated;
3. discernment on the importance of sociological theory, methods, and multilevel analyses;
4. a social ethics approach to public policy addressing social problems;
5. social activism—a commitment to positive change in society and in the larger global community.

Long after students have forgotten the scraps of statistics and detail presented in this book, I hope that you will retain and efficiently put to use a penetrating sociological imagination.

WHAT YOU CAN DO

- Donate your time, effort, and resources to combat poverty, homelessness, crime, mental and physical disease, illiteracy, racism, and domestic abuse.

- Boycott products and services that encourage prejudice or result in social inequality or institutional discrimination.
- Boycott companies whose policies or treatment of people is discriminatory or otherwise unfair.
- Honor the cultural diversity of others. This means a more open-minded attitude in relating with people who are unlike you.
- Heed the standards and rights that the law is intended to guard.
- Use social ethics to defy unfair laws and regulations.
- Oppose bigotry or stereotypes.
- Support educational and job-training programs.
- Develop your ability to critically evaluate mass media (film, television, advertising, radio, and newspaper, the Internet) to discern erroneous or corrupt ideas and media bias.
- There have been a number of creative ways of channeling the energy of disadvantaged young men into positive activities in the hopes of preventing criminal activity or preventing repeat criminal activity. In Los Angeles, an organization called "Jobs not Jail" has created six small businesses, such as the Homeboy Bakery, that employ and provide job skills for former gang members. In New York, another program teaches young boys a craft: boat making. The instructor and the boys build boats together and then enjoy the use of them. These types of programs are providing marketable skills, long-lasting friendships, and a sense of self-worth on the part of the participants. They also fly in the face of the tough-on-crime trend of building more prisons and incarcerating more people. Which perspective do you prefer and why? What can you do to get involved?
- One-third of all children in our society have no father (or, at least, one that is present). One-fourth of all children are poor. One-fifth of all children are on food stamps. Many others are abused or neglected at home. The numbers of frequently absent parents and latchkey children are on the rise. The rates of domestic violence are sharply increasing. School violence is an ever-present danger. Drug, alcohol, and tobacco abuse is a major problem for our children. All these phenomena suggest that children are in desperate need of help. What can you do to help? Be a tutor, coach, friend, or role model. Participate in programs such as Big Brother or Big Sister. Can you think of other ways to get involved and make a difference in at least one child's life?

APPENDIX: IMPLICATIONS FOR SOCIAL POLICY

- The most fundamental social problems in society are ultimately issues of power and justice.
- The key to addressing social problems is political pressure for social change. Such pressure should be based on principles of social ethics and distributive justice.
- The search for solutions to social problems starts with people intentionally working to change the social environment in which they live.
- Ethical social policy is community oriented—rediscovering strength in families; working for safety in our neighborhoods, schools, and churches; and supporting effective law enforcement and correctional strategies.
- Our social problems often carry over into the global community and are tied to crises in other societies, many of which are far less fortunate than our own.
- We can use evaluation research and social ethics to alleviate social inequality. We can use our resources to transform the environment to better meet the needs of each member of society.
- Given demographic trends soon placing ethnic minorities as the numeric majority in our nation, society should distribute resources that reflect such trends.
- Given the finite nature of resources, we must ethically justify the development of particular types of new policies at the expense of others or the acquisition of new knowledge in some areas while ignoring others.
- Resources used in medicine and biology are also needed to reduce gender and ethnic discrimination, urban decay, environmental pollution, and poverty and to improve the quality of education.
- Technologically induced dehumanization, the abuse of power, and the unjust distribution of scarce resources exemplify the need to develop and implement socially just laws and public policy.
- Social change is typically initiated by those who view that their needs and the needs of others like them are being unmet by existing institutions and policy.
- If our problems are shared by others and attributable to social conditions, we seek political or policy solutions.

- We have a responsibility to mobilize resources and attempt to convince policy makers and the public that we have legitimate claims and that our interests should be represented fairly.
- Social policy is supported, at least implicitly, by an explanation of the problem's cause and on a specific perspective of human nature.
- Social policy cannot increase one good without simultaneously decreasing another, or decrease one evil without strengthening one to which it is associated.
- While most Americans believe that government programs designed to help the poor have failed, many programs have demonstrably improved the lives of people trapped at the bottom of the economic ladder.
- Educational participation and academic achievement are critical for students as a foundation for occupational attainment and parity in political decision-making processes.
- It seems rather obvious that increasing class time should increase educational attainment.
- Educational intervention in disadvantaged families should include federal programs such as Head Start.
- Our schools should be funded by a fair formula that does not reward wealthy property holders with more elaborate schools and resources and penalizes poorer property holders.
- Poverty is essentially a work problem, not a welfare problem. Thus, we should use secure employment opportunities to base welfare reform.
- Current policies that reduce families on welfare do little to eliminate poverty; instead, they increase the number of families at risk.
- Widespread urban trends demonstrate changes in the labor and housing markets that have fostered income inequality and segregated the rich from the poor.
- It is important for policy makers to understand what it is like to be poor and live on welfare.
- Our laws, social policy, and culture value single mothers' cheap labor often at the expense of care for their children.
- If we are to significantly lessen poverty, we must invest in human capital potential, including remedial education for those members of our population who currently possess limited education and job skills.
- We should create secure and full employment for people who want jobs.
- Antipoverty policies should target the working poor as well as those on welfare.
- Despite its cost, investment in our decaying infrastructure and ineffective social services would significantly contribute to the betterment of society and enhance economic development.
- Since societal resources are finite, the question of distributive justice—the equitable distribution of resources among the various segments of our population—is crucial.
- We have come to depend on medicine to remedy an increasing array of contemporary social problems: drug addiction, genetic counseling, unwanted pregnancy, unwanted childlessness, suicide, sagging body parts, laziness, and crime, to cite just a few.
- Measurements of health in the United States confirm the failure of existing health care to recognize or respond effectively to the unmet needs and the barriers that exist.
- Health-care delivery in the United States has become excessively rationalized, increasingly fragmented, and too costly for those who need it the most: the poor, the elderly, children, women, and ethnic minorities. Although technically competent and highly esteemed, medical care is too expensive and unequally distributed.

- Given a pattern of gradual reduction in public spending, there is a move toward making people more responsible for their own welfare, health, and security.
- Ethnic minorities, despite the deleterious effects of institutional discrimination, have strong kinship bonds, the capacity for mutual help and self-help, adaptability of family roles, and strong religious tradition.
- Law has played a key role in the systematic servitude of racial and ethnic minorities as well as in the continuous process by which they have been used to lessen ethnic subjugation.
- There is evidence that white women have made economic gains through affirmative action at the expense of black men and vice versa.
- Psychological oppression is the most effective method of maintaining ethnic stratification.
- With recent immigration at a near-record high, ethnic minorities, particularly those in low-skill jobs, are losing out to immigrants in the American labor market. Because today's immigrants are largely non-European and nonwhite, their presence will intensify the competition for affordable housing and education opportunities among minority groups.
- Patterns of ethnic conflict and urban violence are associated with global migratory trends—both legal and undocumented immigration to the United States.
- Self-governance and the strong civil society that nurtures it are deeply threatened if citizens cannot count on a reasonable level of safety in their homes, churches, schools, neighborhoods, and communities.
- The War on Drugs has contributed to the early release of violent offenders.
- There is strong evidence that the viewing of violent, especially sexually violent, "entertainment" is associated with violent behavior.
- Legalizing marijuana would reduce crime.
- Current policy to attack predatory crime is misinformed.
- We should invest in basic research into the causes, prevention, and control of crime—and then use that knowledge ethically to create policy.
- Since health-care delivery resources are always finite, it is crucial that social ethics and distributive justice be implemented to ensure equitable distribution of health care.
- School-based health clinics are promising alternatives or complements to sex education.
- One solution to the unequal educational quality is to give parents the choice between sending their child to a neighborhood public school, a more effective public school not in the neighborhood or even in the same district, or (given financial assistance) a private school.
- I support alternatives to welfare, such as education, health care, job training, and work incentives that do not stigmatize participants.
- I propose raising the minimum wage high enough to provide an incentive to get off welfare.
- I propose a constitutional convention every twenty years.

REFERENCES

Abkiewicz, S. R., A. S. Ahmed, and M. A. Alli, 1987. "Conditions at Baragwanath Hospital." *South African Medical Journal* 72:361.

Abramovitz, M. 1996a. *Regulating the Lives of Women: Social Welfare Policy from Colonial Times to the Present*. Boston: South End Press.

———. 1996b. *Under Attack, Fighting Back: Women and Welfare in the United States*. New York: Monthly Review Press.

Adams, T., F. Duncan, and W. Rogers. 1988. *Persistent Urban Poverty: Prevalence, Correlates, and Trends*. Ann Arbor: University of Michigan Survey Research Center.

Agnelli, S. 1986. *Street Children: A Growing Urban Tragedy. A Report for the Independent Commission on International Humanitarian Issues*. London: Weidenfeld and Nicolson.

Ahmed, A. 1997. "Ethnic Cleansing: A Metaphor for Our Time." In *The Conceit of Innocence: Losing the Conscience of the West in the War Against Bosnia*, 35–65. Ed. S. G. Mestrovic. College Station: Texas A & M University Press.

Anderson, M. 1978. *The Political Economy of Welfare Reform in the United States*. Palo Alto, CA: Hoover Institution.

Anderson, M., and H. Taylor. 2002. *Sociology: Understanding a Diverse Society*. 2d ed. Belmont, CA: Wadsworth.

Associated Press. 1988. "Boston Set to Cut Ride on Buses to School." *Birmingham-Post Herald*, 27 December, C9.

Axin, J., and H. Levine. 1975. *Social Welfare: A History of the American Response to Need*. New York: Harper and Row.

Bachrach. L., ed. 1983. *Deinstitutionalization*. San Fransisco: Jossey-Bass.

Bandler, J. 1975. "Family Issues in Social Policy: An Analysis of Social Security." Ph.D. diss., Columbia University of Social Work, New York, New York.

Bane, M., and D. Ellwood. 1994. *Welfare Realities: From Rhetoric to Reform*. Cambridge: Harvard University Press.

Bane, M., and P. Jargowsky. 1988. *Urban Poverty Areas: Basic Questions Concerning Prevalence, Growth, and Dynamics.* Cambridge, MA: John F. Kennedy School of Government.

Baum, A., and D. Burnes. 1993. *A Nation in Denial: The Truth about Homelessness.* San Francisco: Westview.

Bauman, Z. 1998. *Globalization: The Human Consequences.* New York: Columbia University Press.

Beauchamp, T. L., and J. F. Childress. 1989. *Principles of Biomedical Ethics.* 3d ed. New York: Oxford University Press.

Belcher, J. R., and F. A. diBlasio. 1990. *Helping the Homeless: Where Do We Go From Here?* Lexington, MA: Lexington Books.

Belloc, N. B. 1973. "Relationship of Health Practices and Mortality." *Preventive Medicine* 2:67–81.

Belloc, N. B., and L. Breslow. 1972. "Relationship of Physical Health Status and Health Practices." *Preventive Medicine* 1:409–421.

Boston Foundation. 1989. *In the Midst of Plenty: A Profile of Boston and Its Poor.* Boston: Boston Foundation.

Bourgois, P. 2002. "In Search of Respect: Selling Crack in el Barrio." In *Mapping the Social Landscape: Readings in Sociology.* 3d ed., 244–255. Ed. S. Ferguson. New York: McGraw-Hill.

Bourne, B. E., M. R. Rip, and D. Woods. 1988. "Characteristics of Infant Mortality in the RSA, 1929–1983." *South African Medical Journal* 73:230–232.

Bowles, S., and H. Gintis. 1976. *Schooling in Capitalist America: Educational Reform and the Contradictions of Economic Life.* New York: Basic Books.

Braddock, J., R. Crain, and J. McPartland. 1984. "A Long-Term View of School Desegregation: Some Recent Studies of Graduates as Adults." *Phi Delta Kappa* 66:259–264.

Breslow, L. 1979. "A Positive Strategy for the Nation's Health." *Journal of the American Medical Association* 242:2093–2095.

Brody, J. 1991. "Problems of Children: A New Look at Divorce." *New York Times,* 7 June, B1.

Brooks, D. D., D. R. Smith, and R. J. Anderson. 1991. "Medical Apartheid: An American Perspective." *Journal of the American Medical Association* 266:2746–2749.

Burt, M. 1992. *Over the Edge: The Growth of Homelessness in the 1980s.* New York: Russell Sage Foundation.

Burt, M., and B. Cohen. 1989. *American's Homeless: Numbers, Characteristics, and the Programs That Serve Them.* Washington, DC: Urban Institute Press.

Butler, J. S. 1991. *Entrepeneurship and Self-Help among Black Americans.* Albany: State University of New York Press.

Butler, J. S., and K. I. Wilson. 1988. "Entrepreneurail Enclaves: An Exposition into the Afro-American Experience." *National Journal of Sociology* 2 (fall):127–166.

Byrd, R. 1991. "Sexual Activity Soars among Young Women." *Birmingham-Post Herald,* 5 January, 4A.

Cardenas, J. 1996. "Ending the Crisis in the K–12 System. In *Educating a New Majority: Transforming America's Educational System for Diversity*, 51–70. Ed. L. Rendon and R. Hope. San Francisco: Jossey-Bass.

Carroll, G. 1990. "Who Foots the Bill?" *Newsweek* (fall/winter):81–85.

Castells, M. 1991. *The Information City.* Oxford: Basil Blackwell.

Center for Law and Social Policy. 1997. "Welfare Changes Enacted." Available at http://www.igc.apc.org/handsnet2/welfare.reform/Articles/art.876261804.htm.

Centers for Disease Control. 1986. *Homicide Surveillance High Risk Racial and Ethnic Groups—Blacks and Hispanics, 1970–1983.* Washington, DC: U.S. Department of Health and Human Services, Public Health Service.

Chrisman, N. J., and A. Kleinman. 1980. "Health Beliefs and Practices among American Ethnic Groups." In *Harvard Encyclopedia of American Ethnic Groups*. Ed. S. Threnstrom. Cambridge: Harvard University Press.

Cohen, A. K. [1955] 1971. *Delinquent Boys: The Culture of the Gang.* New York: Free Press.

Children's Defense Fund. 1991. *The State of America's Children.* Washington, DC: Children's Defense Fund.

Coleman, J. 1988. "Social Capital in the Creation of Human Capital." *American Journal of Sociology* 94:95–120.

———. 1990. *Equality of Educational Opportunity.* Boulder, CO: Westview.

Coleman, J., E. Campbell, C. Hobson, J. McPartland, A. M. Mood, F. Weinfield, and R. York. 1966. *Equality of Educational Opportunity.* Washington, DC: U.S. Government Printing Office.

Coles, R., and G. Stokes. 1985. *Sex and the American Teenager.* New York: Harper Colophon Books.

College Board. 2000a. Table 2: "Average SAT Scores of Entering College Classes, 1967–2000." Available at http://www.collegeboard.org/press/senior00/table2.html.

———2000b. Table 4: "SAT Averages Rose for Most Racial and Ethnic Groups between 1990 and 2000." Available at http://www.collegeboard.org/press/senior00/table4.html.

Committee on Economic Security. 1985. *The Report of the Committee on Economic Security of 1935 and Other Basic Documents Related to the Social Welfare Act.* 50th Anniversary Issue. Washington, DC: National Conference on Social Welfare.

Conner, E., and F. Mullan, eds. 1983. *Community Oriented Primary Care: New Directions for Health Services Delivery.* Washington, DC: Institute of Medicine, National Academy Press.

Conrad, K. J., C. I. Hultmand, and J. S. Lyons, eds. 1993. *Treatment of the Chemically Dependent Homeless: Theory and Implementation in Fourteen American Projects.* New York: Haworth Press.

Cortese. A. 1980. "Ethnic Ethics: Subjective Choice and Inference in Chicano and Black Children." Ph. D. diss., University of Notre Dame.

———. 1982a. "Moral Development in Chicano and Anglo Children." *Hispanic Journal of Behavioral Sciences* 4:353–366.

———. 1982b. "A Comparative Analysis of Ethnicity and Moral Judgment." *Colorado Association for Chicano Research Revue* 1:72–101.

———. 1984a. "Standard Issue Scoring of Moral Reasoning: A Critique." *Merrill-Palmer Quarterly* 30:227–246.

———. 1984b. "Moral Judgment in Chicano, Black, and White Young Adults." *Sociological Focus* 17:189–199.

———. 1986a. "Habermas and Kohlberg: Morality, Justice, and Rationality." In *Current Perspectives in Social Theory*, 141–156. Ed. J. Wilson and S. McNall. Greenwich, CT: JAI Press.

———. 1986b. "The Inception, Evolution, and Current State of the Moral Development School of Lawrence Kohlberg." In *Structures of Knowing*, 327–346. Ed. R. Monk. Lanham, MD: University Press of America.

———. 1987. "The Internal Consistency of Moral Reasoning: A Multitrait-Multimethod Analysis." *Journal of Psychology* 121:373–386.

———. 1989a. "Structural Consistency in Moral Judgement." *British Journal of Social Psychology* 28:279–281.

———. 1989b. "The Interpersonal Approach to Morality: A Gender and Cultural Analysis." *Journal of Social Psychology* 129:429–442.

———. 1989c. "Beyond Justice and Legitimation: Interpersonal and Communicative Morality." *New Observations* 72:20–23.

———. 1990. *Ethnic Ethics: The Restructuring of Moral Theory.* Albany: State University of New York Press, 1990.

———. 1999. *Provocateur: Images of Women and Minorities in Advertising.* Boulder, CO: Rowman and Littlefield.

Cortese, A., and S. Mestrovic. 1990. "From Durkheim to Habermas: The Role of Language in Moral Theory," In *Current Perspectives in Social Theory,* 63–91. Ed. J. Wilson. Greenwich, CT: JAI.

Cottle, T. 1974. "What Tracking Did to Ollie Taylor." *Social Policy* 5(2):22–24.

Council on Ethical and Judicial Affairs, American Medical Association. 1989. "Black-White Disparities in Health Care." *Journal of the American Medical Association* 263:2344–2346.

Council on Scientific Affairs, American Medical Association. 1991. "Hispanic Health in the U.S." *Journal of the American Medical Association* 265:248–252.

Cross, M., ed. 1992. *Ethnic Minorities and Industrial Change in Europe and North America.* Cambridge: Cambridge University Press.

Cuomo, A. 1992. *The Way Home: A New Direction in Social Policy.* New York: New York City Commission on the Homeless.

Currie, E. 1993. "Toward a Policy on Drugs." *Dissent* 40(1):65–71.

———. 1998. *Crime and Punishment in America.* New York: Henry Holt.

———. 2000. "The Myth of Leniency." In *Crisis in American Institutions.* 11th ed., 389–398. Ed. J. Skolnick and E. Currie. Needham Heights, MA: Allyn and Bacon.

Daly, G. 1996: *Homeless: Policies, Strategies, and Lives on the Street.* London: Routledge.

Dana, M. R., J. M. Tielsch, C. Enger, E. Joyce, J. M. Santoli, and H. R. Taylor. 1990. "Visual Impairment in a Rural Appalachian Community." *Journal of the American Medical Association* 264:2400–2405.

Danziger, S., and P. Gottschalk. 1995. *America Unequal.* Cambridge: Harvard University Press.

Darley, J., and R. Fazio. 1980. "Expectancy Confirmation Processes Arising in the Social Interaction Sequence." *American Psychologist* 35:867–881.

Davis, M. 1992. *City of Quartz: Excavating the Future in Los Angeles.* London: Verso.

Deparle, J. 1997. "Half the States Unlikely to Meet Goals on Welfare." *New York Times* 1 October, 1.

DiIiulio, J. 2000. "Instant Replay: Three Strikes Was the Right Call." In *Crisis in American Institutions.* 11th ed., 408–416. Ed. J. Skolnick and E. Currie. Needham Heights, MA: Allyn and Bacon.

Dowd, M. 1994. "Americans Like G.O.P. Agenda, But Split on How to Reach Goals. *New York Times,* 15 December, A1.

Durkheim, É. [1897] 1951. *Suicide.* New York: Free Press.

———. [1903]. 1982. *The Rules of Sociological Method and Selected Texts on Sociology and Its Method.* Ed. S. Lukes. Trans. W. D. Halls. New York: Free Press.

———. [1912] 1965. *The Elementary Forms of Religious Life.* Trans. J. Swain. New York: Free Press.

———. [1925] 1961. *Moral Education.* Trans. E. K. Wilson and H. Schnurer. Glencoe, IL: Free Press.

Edelman, M. 1987. *Families in Peril: An Agenda for Social Change.* Cambridge: Harvard University Press.

Eggers, P. W., R. Connerton, and M. McMullan. 1984. "The Medicine Experience with End-Stage Renal Disease: Trends in Incidence, Prevalence, and Survival." *Health Care Financing Review* 5(3):69–88.

Ehrenreich, B. 1990. "Our Health-Care Disgrace." *Time,* 10 December, 112.

Ellwood, D. 1988. *Poor Support: Poverty in the American Family.* New York: Basic Books.

———. 1994. "Reducing Poverty by Replacing Welfare." In *Welfare Realities: From Rhetoric to Reform,* 143–162. Ed. M. Bane and D. Ellwood. Cambridge: Harvard University Press.

Enthoven, A. C. 1991. "Market Forces and Health Care Cost." *Journal of the American Medical Association* 266:2751–2752.

Eskey, K. 1990. "Americans Favor Choice of Schools." *Birmingham-Post Herald,* 24 August, A16.

———. 1991. "Adults Favor Longer School Year." *Birmingham-Post Herald,* 23 August, A1.

Farley, R. 1988. "Three Steps Forward and Two Back? Recent Changes in the Social and Economic Status of Blacks." In *Ethnicity and Race in the U.S.A.,* 4–28. Ed. R.D. Alba. New York: Routledge.

———. 2000. *Majority–Minority Relations.* 4th ed. Englewood Cliffs, NJ: Prentice-Hall.

Federal Bureau of Investigation. 2000. *Crime in the United States 1999.* Washington, DC: Federal Bureau of Investigation.

Felsman, K. 1984. "Abandoned Children: A Reconsideration." *Children Today* 13(4):13–18.

Fersh, R. 1991. *Community Childhood Hunger Identification Project.* Washington, DC: Food Research and Action Center.

Fiske, E. 1990. "Even at a Former Women's College, Male Students Are Taken More Seriously, a Researcher Finds." *New York Times,* 11 April, B8.

Forbert, S. 1979. "Wait" (audio recording) from the compact disc *Jackrabbit Slim.* New York: Sony Music.

Forster, M. F. 1994. *Measurement of Low Incomes and Poverty in a Perspective of International Comparisons.* Occasional Paper No. 14. Paris: OECD.

Freeman, R., and B. Hall. 1986. *Permanent Homelessness in America.* Cambridge, MA: National Bureau of Economic Research.

Furstenberg, F., S. Morgan, K. Moore, and J. Peterson. 1987. "Race Differences in the Timing of Adolescent Intercourse." *American Sociological Review* 52:511–518.

Gamoran, A. 1972. "The Variable Effects of High School Tracking." *American Sociological Review* 57:812–828.

———. 1993. "Alternative Uses of Ability Grouping in Secondary Schools: Can We Bring High-Quality Instruction of Low-Ability Classes?" *American Journal of Education* 102 (1):1–22.

Gardner, D. 1983. *A Nation at Risk*. Washington, DC: U.S. Government Printing Office.

Giamo, B., and J. Grunberg. 1992. *Beyond Homelessness: Frames of Reference.* Iowa City: University of Iowa Press.

Gilder, G. 1981. *Wealth and Poverty.* New York: Basic Books.

Gilligan, C. 1982. *In a Different Voice: Psychological Theory and Women's Development.* Cambridge: Harvard University Press.

Gilligan, J. 1997. *Violence: Reflections on a National Epidemic.* New York: Vintage Books.

Gold, C. H., C. Isaacson, and J. Levin. 1982. "The Pathological Basis of End-Stage Renal Disease in Blacks." *South African Medical Journal* 61:263–265.

Golden, S. 1992. *The Women Outside: Myths and Meanings of Homelessness.* Berkeley: University of California Press.

Gooderham, M. 1995. *Globe and Mail.* (Toronto) 11 October, A1.

Goodwin, D. W. 1994. *Alcoholism: The Facts.* Oxford: Oxford University Press.

Gordon, L. 1994. *Pitied but Not Entitled.* New York: Free Press.

Gordon, M. 1964. *Assimilation in American Life.* New York: Oxford University Press.

Graham, P. 1993. "Don't Let Judges Set Crooks Free." *New York Times*, 8 July.

Greenberg, J., and R. L. Cohen, eds. 1982. *Equity and Justice in Social Behavior.* New York: Academic Press.

Greve, J., with E. Currie. 1990. *Homelessness in Britain.* New York: Joseph Rowntree Trust.

Habermas, J. 1984. *The Theory of Communicative Action.* Vol. 1, *Reason and the Rationalization of Society.* Trans. T. McCarthy. Boston: Beacon Press.

Hadley, J., E. P. Steinberg, and J. Feder. 1991. "Comparison of Uninsured and Privately Insured Hospital Patients." *Journal of the American Medical Association* 265:374–379.

Hallinan, M. 1994. "Tracking: From Theory to Practice." *Sociology of Education* 67:79–84.

Handler, J. F., and Y. Hasenfeld. 1991. *The Moral Construction of Poverty: Welfare Reform in America.* Newbury Park, CA: Sage.

Harsanyi, J. C. 1982. "Morality and the Theory of Rational Behavior." In *Utilitarianism and Beyond*, 39–62. Ed. A. Sen and B. Williams. Cambridge: Cambridge University Press.

Havighurst, R. J. 1976. "The Relative Importance of Social Class and Ethnicity in Human Development." *Human Development* 19:56–65.

"Heart Disease Study Launched in Western Cape." 1990. *South African Medical Journal* 77:12.

Heilbroner, R. L. 1993. *Twenty-first Century Capitalism.* New York: Norton.

Henig, J. 1990. "Choice in Public Schools: An Analysis of Transfer Requests among Magnet Schools." *Social Science Quarterly* 71:69–82.

Henshel, R. 1990. *Thinking About Social Problems.* New York: Harcourt Brace Jovanovich.

Herskovits, M. J. 1972. *Cultural Relativism: Perspectives in Cultural Pluralism.* Ed. F. Herskovits. New York: Random House.

Holzberg, C. S. 1982. "Ethnicity and Aging: Anthropological Perspectives on More Than Just the Minority Elderly." *Gerontologist* 22, 249–257.

Horton, P. B., and G. R. Leslie. 1974. *The Sociology of Social Problems.* 5th ed. Englewood Cliffs, NJ: Prentice-Hall.

Institute of Medicine. 1988. *Homelessness, Health, and Human Needs.* Washington, DC: National Academy Press.

Jansson, B. 1988. *The Reluctant Welfare State: A History of American Social Welfare Policies.* Belmont, CA: Wadsworth.

Jencks, C. 1972. *Inequality: A Reassessment of the Effect of Family and Schooling in America.* New York: Basic Books.

———. 1994. *The Homeless.* Cambridge: Harvard University Press.

Kant, I. [1781] 1949. *Critique of Practical Reason and Other Writings in Moral Philosophy.* Trans. and ed. L.W. Beck. Chicago: University of Chicago Press.

———. [1788] 1950. *Critique of Pure Reason.* Trans. and ed. N. K. Smith. New York: Humanities Press.

———. 1963. *Lectures on Ethics.* Trans. L. Infield. Ed. L.W. Beck. Chicago: University of Chicago Press.

Kark, S. L. 1981. *The Practice of Community-Oriented Primary Health Care.* New York: Appleton-Century-Crofts.

Kass, L. R. 1985. *Toward a More Natural Science: Biology and Human Affairs.* New York: Free Press.

Katz, M. 1986. *In the Shadow of the Poorhouse: A Social History of Welfare in America.* New York: Basic Books.

———. 1989. *The Undeserving Poor: From the War on Poverty to the War on Welfare.* New York: Pantheon.

Kaufman, P., M. McMillen, and D. Sweet. 1996. *A Comparison of High School Dropout Rates in 1982 and 1992.* NCES 96-893. Washington, DC: U.S. Department of Education, National Center for Educational Statistics.

Kaus, M. 1992. *The End of Equality.* New York: Basic Books.

Kelly J. T. 1985 "Trauma: With the Example of San Francisco's Shelter Programs." In *Health Care of Homeless People*, 77–91. Ed. P. W. Brickner, L. K. Scharer, B. Conanan, A. Elvy, and M. Savarese. New York: Springer.

Kelman, H. C., and D. P. Warwick. 1978. *The Ethics of Social Intervention: Goals, Means, and Consequences.*

Kettles, A. N. 1987. "Difference in Trends of Measles Notifications by Age and Race in the Western Cape, 1982–1986." *South African Medical Journal* 72:317–320.

Klein, D. 1991. "Children at Risk." New York: Public Television, WNET. Aired on PBS, November 1.

Klopper, J. M. L., and L. Tibbit. 1988. "The Mamre Community Health Project." *South African Medical Journal* 74:319–320.

Knutzen, V., and D. Bourne. 1977. "The Reproductive Efficiency of the Xhosa." *South African Medical Journal* 51:392–394.

Koegel, P., and M. A. Burnam. 1988. *Alcoholism among Homeless Adults in the Inner City of Los Angeles*. Los Angeles: Planning Institute, University of Southern California.

Kohlberg, L. 1969. "Stage and Sequence: The Cognitive-Developmental Approach to Socialization." In *Handbook of Socialization Theory and Research*, 347–480. Ed. D. A. Goslin. Chicago: Rand McNally.

———. 1981. *Essays in Moral Development*. Vol. 1, *The Philosophy of Moral Development*. New York: Harper and Row.

———. 1984. *Essays in Moral Development*. Vol. 2, *The Psychology of Moral Development*. New York: Harper and Row.

Koretz, D. 1987. *Trends in Educational Achievement*. Washington, DC: U.S. Government Printing Office.

Kosterlitz, J. 1992. "A Sick System." *National Journal*, 15 February, 376–388.

Kozol, J. 1988. *Rachel and Her Children: Homeless Families in America*. New York: Crown.

Larner, J. 1991. "Fighting the 'War on Drugs.'" *Dissent* 38 (2):241–244. (Special Section: Social Breakdown; interview).

Lement, C. 1999. *Social Things: An Introduction to the Sociological Life*. Lanham, MD: Rowman and Littlefield.

Liebow, E. 1993. *Tell Them Who I Am: The Lives of Homeless Women*. New York: Free Press.

Lifton, R. J. 1992. "Victims and Survivors." In *Beyond Homelessness: Frames of Reference*, 129–156. Ed. B. Giamo and J. Grunberg. Iowa City: University of Iowa Press.

Link, B., E. Susser, A. Stueve, J. Phelan, R. E. Moore, and E. Struening. 1994. "Lifetime and Five-Year Prevalence of Homelessness in the United States." *American Journal of Public Health* 84(12):1907–1912.

Livingston, J. 1994. *Rogue Primate*. Toronto: Key Porter.

Logan, J., P. Taylor-Gooby, and M. Reuter. 1992. "Poverty and Income Inequality." In *Divided Cities: New York and London in the Contemporary World*, 129–150. Ed. S. Fainsein, I. Gordon, and M. Harloe. Oxford: Blackwell.

Logan, J. C., R. D. Alba, and T. I. McNulty. 1994. "Ethnic Economies in Metropolitan Regions: Miami and Beyond." *Social Forces* 72 (March):691–724.

Lusane, C., and D. Desmond. 1991. *Pipe Dream Blues: Racism and the War on Drugs.* Boston: South End Press.

Maciones, J. 2002. *Social Problems.* Upper Saddle River, NJ: Prentice-Hall.

Mannheim, K. [1936] 1971. *Ideology and Utopia.* Trans. L. Worth and E. Shils. New York: Harcourt, Brace, and World.

Massing, M. 1991. "Can We Cope with Drugs?" *Dissent* 38(2):236–240. (Special Section: Social Breakdown).

Mauer, M., and T. Huling. 2000. "Young Black Americans and the Criminal Justice System." In *Crisis in American Institutions* 11th ed., 417–424. Ed. J. Skolnick and E. Currie. Needham Heights, MA: Allyn and Bacon.

Mayhew, H. 1967. *London Labor and the London Poor, a Cyclopaedia of the Condition and Earnings of Those That Will Work,* New York: A. M. Kelly.

McCay, B., and J. Acheson, eds. 1987. *The Question of the Commons: The Culture and Ecology of Communal Resources.* Tucson: University of Arizona Press.

McCord, C., and H. P. Freeman. 1990. "Excess Mortality in Harlem." *New England Journal of Medicine* 322:173–177.

McCoy, A., and A. Block. 1992. *War on Drugs: Studies in the Failure of U.S. Narcotics Policy.* Boulder, CO: Westview.

McKey, R., L. Condelli, H. Ganson, B. Barrett, C. McConkey, and M. Plantz. 1985. *The Impact of Head Start on Children, Families, and Communities.* Washington, DC: U.S. Government Printing Office.

McLemore, S., H. Romo, and S. Gonzalez Baker. 2001. *Racial and Ethnic Relations in America.* 6th ed. Boston: Allyn and Bacon.

McQuiston, J. 1991. "Food for Poor Is Said to Cost More." *New York Times,* 15 April, B5.

Mead, L. 1986. *Beyond Entitlement: The Social Obligations of Citizenship.* New York: Free Press.

Messina, R., P. Mazzuia, D. Vidoni, and M. Impagnatiello. 1992. "Networking Consumers' Participation in a Community Mental Health Service: Mutual Support Groups, 'Citizenship' and Coping Strategies." *International Journal of Social Psychiatry* 38:68–73.

Meyers, B. 1984. "Minority Group: An Ideological Formulation." *Social Problems* 32:1–15.

Mills, C. W. 1959. *The Sociological Imagination.* New York: Oxford University Press.

Mink, G. 1995. *The Wages of Motherhood: Inequality in the Welfare State, 1917–1942.* Ithaca, NY: Cornell University Press.

Mji, D., and K. N. Vallabhjee. 1990. "Health in Post-apartheid South Africa." *South African Medical Journal* 78:122–123.

Molteno, C. D., and M. A. Kibel. 1989. "Post Neonatal Mortality in the Matroosberg Divisional Council Area of the Cape Western Health Regions." *South African Medical Journal* 75:575–578.

Momeni, J. A. 1989. *Homelessness in the United States.* Vol. 1, *State Surveys.* New York: Greenwood.

———. 1990. *Homelessness in the United States.* Vol. 2, *Data and Issues.* New York: Greenwood.

Mooney, C. 1989. "Professors Are Upbeat about Profession but Uneasy about Students, Standards." *Chronicle of Higher Education* 36:1.

Morgan, H. 1995. *Historical Perspectives on the Education of Black Children.* Westport, CT: Praeger.

Morse, J. 1999. "Cracking Down on the Homeless." *Time,* 20 December, 69–70.

Murray, C. 1984. *Losing Ground: American Social Policy, 1950–1980.* New York: Basic Books.

———. 1988. *In Pursuit of Happiness and Good Government.* New York: Simon and Schuster.

Nadelmann, E. 1992. "America's Drug Problem: A Case for Decriminalization." *Dissent* 39(2):205–212.

National Coalition for Homeless Veterans. 2000. "Policy Issues." Available at http://www/nida.nih.gov/Infofax/tobacco.htm.

National Electrical Manufacturers Association. 2002. "MRI Sets U.S. Record in Revenue, Unit Sales in 2001." Available at http://www/nema.org/indexnema.cfm/1437/2E7ECFA1-857E-4BF2-A73FEC2A2212CDA6#modality.

Nieves, E. 2000. "Homeless on $50,000 a Year in Luxuriant Silicon Valley." *New York Times,* 20 February, 1A, 16A.

Nightingale, E. O., J. Geiger, M. A. Hannibal, L. Hartmann, R. Lawrence, and J. Spurlock. 1990. "Apartheid Medicine: Health and Human Rights in South Africa." *Journal of the American Medical Association* 264:2097–2107.

Niner, P. 1989. *Homelessness in Nine Local Authorities: Case Studies of Policy and Practice.* London: HMSO.

Nussbaum, B. 1988. "Needed: Human Capital." *Newsweek,* 19 September, 100–101.

Nutting, P. A., M. Wood, and E. M. Connor. 1985. "Community-Oriented Primary Care in the United States." *Journal of the American Medical Association* 253:1763–1766.

O'Brien, D. 1991. *Civil Rights and Civil Liberties, Volume Two.* New York: Norton.

Organization for Economic Cooperation and Development (OECD). 2000. *Education at a Glance 2000.* Paris: Organization for Economic Cooperation and Development.

Otten, M. W., S. M. Teutsch, D. F. Williamson, and J. S. Marks. 1990. "The Effect of Known Risk Factors on the Excess Mortality of Black Adults in the United States." *Journal of the American Medical Association* 263:845–850.

Persell, C. 1990. *Understanding Society: An Introduction to Sociology.* New York: Harper and Row.

Peterson, I. 1999. "After Decades of Dismissal, the Suburbs Win Coverts." *New York Times,* 5 December, A1.

Piaget, J. [1932] 1965. *The Moral Judgment of the Child.* 2d ed. New York: Free Press.

"Policy Statement on Discrimination in Medical Practice." 1989. *South African Medical Journal* 75:560.

Portes, A. 1981. "Modes of Structural Incorporation and Present Theories of Immigration." In *Global Trends in Migration*, 279–297. Ed. M. M. Krita, C. B. Keely, and S. M. Tomasi. Staten Island, NY: CMS Press, 1981.

———. 1996. *The New Second Generation.* New York: Russell Sage Foundation.

Portes, A., and R. L. Bach. 1985. *Latin Journey.* Berkeley: University of California Press.

Public Broadcasting Service. 1999. *The Snitch.* Video. Frontline Public Affairs Series. FROL-971.

Quadagno, J. 1988. *The Transformation of Old Age Security: Class and Politics in the American Welfare State.* Chicago: University of Chicago Press.

———. 1994. *The Color of Welfare: How Racism Undermines the War on Poverty.* New York: Oxford University Press.

Ratnesar, R. 1999. "Not Gone, but Forgotten?" *Time,* 8 February, 30–31.

Rawls, J. 1971. *A Theory of Justice.* Cambridge: Harvard University Press.

Regan, E. 1994. *Infrastructure Investment for Tomorrow.* Public Policy Brief 141. New York: Jerome Levy Economics Institute, Bard College..

Rendon, L., and R. Hope, eds. 1996. *Education a New Majority: Transforming America's Educational System for Diversity.* San Francisco: Jossey-Bass.

Resources for Youth. 1997. *California Survey: February/March.* San Francisco: Fairbank, Maslin, Maulin, and Associates.

Reyes, L. M., and L. D. Waxman. 1989. *A Status Report on Hunger and Homelessness in American Cities: 1989.* Washington, DC: U.S. Conference of Mayors.

Rice, J., and A. Hemmings. 1988. "Women's Colleges and Women's Achievement: An Update." *Signs* (spring):546–559.

Riordan, C. 1990. *Girls and Boys in Schools.* New York: Teachers College Press.

Rip, M. R., and D. E. Bourne. 1988. "The Spatial Distribution of Infant Mortality Rates in South Africa." *South African Medical Journal* 73:224–226.

Robinson, J. C. 1991. "HMO Market Penetration and Hospital Cost Inflation in California." *Journal of the American Medical Association* 266:2719–2723.

Ropers, R. 1991. *Persistent Poverty: The American Dream Turned Nightmare.* New York: Insight Books/Plenum.

Rosenheck, R., and A. Fontana. 1994. "A Causal Model of Homelessness among Male Veterans of the Vietnam Generation." *American Journal of Psychiatry* 151:421–427.

Rosenthal, R., and L. Jacobson. 1968. *Pygmalion in the Classroom: Teacher Expectation and Intellectual Development.* New York: Holt, Rinehart, and Winston.

Ross, D. P., E. R. Shillington, and C. Lochhead. 1994. *The Canadian Fact Book on Poverty—1994.* Ottawa: Canadian Council on Social Development.

Rossi, P. H. 1989. *Down and Out in America: The Origins of Homelessness.* Chicago: University of Chicago Press.

Rossi, P. H., J. D. Wright, G. A. Fisher, and G. Willis. 1997. "The Urban Homeless: Estimating Composition and Size." *Science* 235:1336–1341.

Rostand, S. G., K. A. Kirk, E. A. Rutsky, and B. A. Pate. 1982. "Racial Differences in the Incidence of Treatment for End-Stage Renal Disease." *New England Journal of Medicine* 306:1276–1279.

Sarlo, C. 1992. *Poverty in Canada.* Vancouver, BC: Fraser Institute.

Scholosser, E. 2000. "More Reefer Madness." In *Deviant Behavior,* 117–124. Ed. L. Salinger. Guilford, CT: Dushkin/McGraw-Hill.

Schutt, R. K. 1992. *Responding to the Homeless: Policy and Practice.* New York: Plenum.

Schwartz, E., V. Y. Kofie, M. Rivo, and R. V. Tuckson. 1990. "Black/White Comparisons of Deaths Preventable by Medical Intervention: U.S. and the District of Columbia, 1980–1986." *International Journal of Epidemiology* 19:591–598.

Schwarz, J. 1992. "Everybody Loves a Drunk." *American Demographics,* March, 13.

Secombe, K. 1999. *So You Think I Drive a Cadillac? Welfare Recipients' Perspectives on the System and Its Reform.* Needham Heights, MA: Allyn and Bacon.

Seedat, Y. K., S. Naicker, R. Rawat, and I. Parsoo. 1984. "Racial Differences in the Causes of End-Stage Renal Failure in Natal." *South African Medical Journal* 65:956–958.

Sherman, D. 1992. "The Neglected Health Care Needs of Street Youth." *Public Health Report* 107(4): 433–440.

Simpson, E. L. 1974. "Moral Development Research: A Case Study of Cultural Bias." *Human Development* 17:81–106.

Singer, S. J. 1991. "Problems in Gaining Access to Hospital Information." *Health Affairs* 10(2):148–151.

Skolnick, J. 2000. "'Three Strikes, You're Out' and Other Bad Calls on Crime." In *Crisis in American Institutions.* 11th ed., 399–407. Ed. J. Skolnick and E. Currie. Needham Heights, MA: Allyn and Bacon.

Slavin, R. 1990. *Achievement Effects of Ability Grouping in Secondary Schools: A Best Evidence Analysis.* Madison: National Center on Effective Secondary Schools, Wisconsin Center for Education Research.

Slessarev, H. 1988. "Racial Tensions and Institutional Support: Programs during a Period of Retrenchment." In *The Politics of Social Policy in the United States,* 357–379. Ed. M. Weir, A. S. Orloff, and T. Skopcol. Princeton, NJ: Princeton University Press.

Sraffa, P., ed. 1951. *Works and Correspondence of David Ricardo.* Cambridge: Cambridge University Press.

Staed, J. 1990. "Suit Seeks New School-Funding Plan." *Birmingham-Post Herald,* 4 May, A1.

Stodghill, R. 1998. "Where'd You Learn That?" *Time,* 15 June, 52–60.

Subcommittee on Health of the Committee on Ways and Means, U.S. House of Representatives. 1990. *Private Health Insurance: Options for Reform.* Washington, DC: U.S. Government Printing Office.

Tepperman, and Blain. 1999. *Think Twice: Sociology Looks at Current Social Issues.* Upper Saddle River, NJ: Prentice-Hall.

Texas Hospital Association. 1991. *Women and Children First: A Plan for Improving Texas' Maternal and Child Health Outcomes in the 1990's.* Austin: Texas Hospital Association.

Thomas, S. 1995. "Exchanging Welfare Checks for Wedding Rings: Welfare Reform in New Jersey and Wisconsin." *Affilia* 10:120–137.

Trattner, W. 1989. *From Poor Law to Welfare State.* 4th ed. New York: Free Press.

Trevino, F M., M. E. Moyer, R. B. Valdez, and A. S. StroupBenham. 1991. "Health Insurance Coverage and Utilization of Health Services by Mexican Americans, Mainland Puerto Ricans, and Cuban Americans." *Journal of the American Medical Association* 265:233–237.

Urdry, J., and J. Billy. 1987. "Initiation of Coitus in Early Adolescence." *American Sociological Review* 52:841–855.

U.S. Bureau of Justice Statistics. 1993. *National Crime Victimization Survey, 1992.* Washington, DC: Department of Justice.

———. 1995. *Sourcebook of Criminal Justice Statistics, 1994.* Washington, DC: U.S. Government Printing Office.

———. 1997. *Prisoners in 1996.* Washington, DC: U.S. Department of Justice.

———. 1998. In *Crisis in American Institutions.* 11th ed. Eds. J. Skolnick and E. Currie. Needham Heights, MA: Allyn and Bacon.

———. 2002. Criminal Victimization 2001: Changes 2000–2001 with Trends, 1993–2001. Washington, DC: U.S. Department of Justice.

U.S. Census Bureau. 1990. *Current Population Reports.* Series P-60. Washington, DC: U.S. Government Printing Office.

———. 1999. *School Enrollment—Social and Economic Characteristics of Students: October 1998 (Update).* Current Population Report P20-521. Washington, DC: U.S. Government Printing Office.

———. 2000a. *Educational Attainment in the United States—March 2000 (Update).* Current Population Reports P20-536. Washington, DC: U.S. Government Printing Office.

———. 2000b. "Type of Family (All Races) by Median and Mean Income: 1947 to 1999." Table F-7: Available at http://www.census.gov/hhes/income/histinc/F07.html.

———. 2000c. *Poverty in the United States, 1999*. Current Population Report P60-210. Washington, DC: U.S. Government Printing Office.

———. 2001. *Resident Population Estimates of the United States by Sex, Race, and Hispanic Origin: April 1, 1999, to July 1, 1999, with Short-Term Projections to November 4, 2000*. Available at http://www.census.gov//population/estimates/nation/intile3-1.txt.

U.S. Congress. 1983. "House Committee on Banking, Finance, and Urban Affairs." *Homelessness in America*. Washington, DC: U.S. Government Printing Office.

U.S. Department of Education. 1994. *The Condition of Education: 1993*. Washington, DC: National Center for Education Statistics.

U.S. Department of Health and Human Services. 2000. "Administration for Children and Families. Temporary Assistance for Needy Families (TANF) Program." *Third Annual Report to Congress, August*. Washington, DC: Administration.

U.S. Department of Housing and Urban Development (HUD). 1984. *A Report to the Secretary on the Homeless and Emergency Shelters*. Washington, DC: Office of Policy Development and Research.

———. 1989. *A Report on the 1988 National Survey of Shelters for the Homeless*. Washington, DC: Office of Policy Development and Research, Division of Policy Studies.

———. 1995. *Review of Stewart B. McKinney Homeless Programs Administered by HUD: Report to Congress*. Washington, DC: Office of Policy Development and Research.

———. 1999. *Homeless in America*. Press Release 99-258, 8 December. Available at http://www.hud.gov/pressrel/pr99-258.html.

U.S. Department of Labor. 1994. *Employment and Earnings*. Vol. 30, no. 4. Washington, DC: U.S. Department of Labor.

U.S. House of Representatives, Committee on Ways and Means, 1996. *1996 Green Book*. Washington, DC: U.S. Government Printing Office.

U.S. National Center for Education Statistics. 1999. *Dropout Rates in the United States: 1997*. Washington, DC: U.S. National Center for Education Statistics.

U.S. National Commission on Excellence in Education. 1983. *A Nation at Risk: The Imperative for Educational Reform: A Report to the Nation and the Secretary of Education*, United States Department of Education/by the National Commission on Excellence in Education. Washington, DC: The Commission: [Supt. of Docs., U.S G.P.O. distributor].

U.S. Social Security Board. 1940. *Social Security Yearbook 1939: Annual Supplement to the Social Security Bulletin*. Washigton, DC: U.S. Government Printing Office.

Vogel, E. 1979. *Japan as Number One*. New York: Colophon Books.

Watson, S., and H. Austerberry. 1986. *Housing and Homelessness: A Feminist Perspective*. London: Routledge and Kegan Paul.

"Welfare Mistrust." 1996. *USA Today*, 2 July, A1.

Wickham, D. 2000. "Homeless Receive Little Attention from Candidates." *USA Today*, 24 October, 17A. Available at http://www.USAToday.com/usatonline.

Wilson, W. 1996. *When Work Disappears: The World of the New Urban Poor.* New York: Knopf.

Wilson, K. L., and W. A. Martin. 1982. "Ethnic Enclaves: A Comparison of the Cuban and Black Economies in Miami." *American Journal of Sociology* 88 (July):135–160.

Winfrey, John C. 1998. *Social Issues: The Ethics and Economics of Taxes and Public Programs.* Oxford: Oxford University Press.

Wright, J. D. 1989. "Address Unknown: Homelessness in Contemporary America." *Society*, 26(6):45–53.

Wright, J. D., and E. Weber. 1987. *Homelessness and Health.* Washington, DC: McGraw-Hill

Wyndham, C. H. 1986. "Mortality Rates of Black Infants in Soweto Compared with Other Regions of South Africa." *South African Medical Journal* 70:281–282.

Yach, D. 1988. "Infant Mortality Rates in Urban Areas of South Africa, 1981–1985." *South African Medical Journal* 73:232–234.

Zernike, K. 2000. "A Gap in Test Scores Becomes a Talking Point." *New York Times*, 13 August, A3.

Index